HISTORIC BUTE:
Land and People

HISTORIC BUTE:

Land and People

Anna Ritchie

Editor

The Scottish Society for Northern Studies

2012

Published in Scotland by
The Scottish Society for Northern Studies
c/o Celtic and Scottish Studies, School of Literatures,
Languages and Cultures, University of Edinburgh,
27 George Square, Edinburgh EH8 9LD

ISBN 0-9535226-4-4

Front cover: Land and seascape in southern Bute (© John Baldwin);
back cover: The Bute Mazer (© National Museums of Scotland)

Printed by Shetland Litho,
Gremista, Lerwick, Shetland ZE1 0PX

Contents

Foreword

WITH a pivotal position in the Firth of Clyde, Bute commands sea-routes into and out of much of inland Argyll, west-central Scotland and beyond. It displays quite distinct landforms and habitats that are more characteristically rough and boggy north of the Highland boundary fault (Rothesay to Scalpsie Bay), and generally more gentle and fertile to the south. Not unlike Arran, albeit less rugged, it is a fine mix of Highland and Lowland, and embodies so much of what can be found more widely across Scotland.

The name, too, has created much discussion. Rothesay reflects Viking activity: most probably ON *Ruðri* + *ey*, Ruairidh's island, with *Rothersay* (1321) a scotticised alternative for *Baile Bhòid*, the township of Bute. If not pre-Celtic, Bute (Gael. *Bòd*, ON *Bót*) may originate in OIr *bót*, fire, hence a possible **Inis Bòit*, the island of fire, with reference to 'watch' or signal fires once used as a means of communication. Or may it be related to Welsh *bod* and Irish *both*, a dwelling, a term that could also apply to a church or chapel? Simon Taylor and Gilbert Márkus have noted that the distribution of *both* in Scotland suggests a link with onetime British- or Pictish-speaking areas, in which case the word may originally be P-Celtic rather than Q-Celtic and the island called after an early ecclesiastical site, most likely Kingarth. Looking outward, Gaelic links *Bòd is Ìle is Aràinn* (Bute and Islay and Arran), which W J Watson and others have suggested may indicate an ancient island grouping corresponding to Ptolomy's *Eboudai*. And in the fourteenth and fifteenth centuries, agriculturally-productive Stewart lands were grouped as Bute, Arran and the Cumbraes (along with Cowal and Knapdale).

For much of the nineteenth and twentieth centuries, Bute was best known for agriculture and tourism. Creameries and holiday-hordes from Scotland's industrial heartlands are now gone, but the island is regaining a reputation for its natural and cultural heritage, and its diverse and accessible landscapes. Farming remains a mainstay of the economy; and small-scale industry includes a mix of old and new: boat-building, boat-repairing, quarrying and fishing alongside speciality foods, fashion fabrics, printed circuit boards, a call centre, visitor attractions and community-focussed initiatives.

These essays were presented at the Scottish Society for Northern Studies' conference on Bute in 2010, and happily complement *The Archaeological Landscape of Bute* (Edinburgh: RCAHMS 2010). They focus on varying aspects of Bute's eventful past: Viking raiders and settlers; sagas; the interaction of Norseman, Celt and Scot; early Christianity, saints and cults; agricultural fertility and Stewart ownership; the Bute or Bannatyne Mazer; seventeenth-century witch-hunts; pre-improvement settlement and landholding; and radical eighteenth-century changes in agriculture and farm buildings that quite changed the face of the land. For today's rural landscape would be as unrecognisable to seventeenth-century Brandanes as any prehistoric landscape.

It gives great pleasure to thank all involved in helping to organise the conference, not least the Buteshire Natural History Society, the Discover Bute Landscape Partnership Scheme and fellow committee members, in particular Bridget Paterson, Paul Duffy, Angus Hannah, Anne Speirs, Isabell Mcarthur, Craig Borland, Linda Riddell and Molly Rorke. The Scottish Society for Northern Studies is volunteer-run, and no conference or publication appears without the commitment and dedication of many. We owe a huge debt not only to contributors who so freely share their research and to those who have helped to fund publication, but also to Anna Ritchie for her painstaking approach to editing the essays. We are grateful to all, and very much hope that *Historic Bute: Land and People* will not just please, but stimulate further investigation both on Bute and further afield.

John Baldwin
President
Scottish Society for Northern Studies

Edinburgh
March 2012

Acknowledgements

WE ARE very grateful to Professor Stephen Driscoll and Alex Hale for their kindness in acting as referees for the volume, to Dr Christopher Lowe and Headland Archaeology Ltd for allowing us to use the 'hostage stone' from Inchmarnock as fig 3.2, to Ian G Scott for allowing us to use his drawing of the rune-inscribed cross from Inchmarnock as fig 4.2, to George Geddes for his help with photographs, and to John Baldwin for allowing us to use his photographs as the cover image and fig 1.4, and Kevin Macleod for kindly scanning fig 3.4. We are also grateful to Sarah Thomas for fig 3.3, to David Caldwell for fig 3.5 and to Matthew Molony for fig 11.1. The editor would like to thank Shetland Litho for their patience and expertise.

The publication of this volume has been made possible by the grants very generously provided by Sir Gerald Elliot, the Robert Kiln Charitable Trust, the Discover Bute Landscape Partnership Scheme, the Royal Commission on the Ancient and Historical Monuments of Scotland, the Strathmartine Trust, the Marc Fitch Fund, the Dr J N Marshall (Island of Bute) Memorial Trust and the Hunter Trust. We are most grateful for this essential assistance.

Chapter 1

From *Goill* to *Gall-Ghàidheil*: place-names and Scandinavian settlement in Bute

Gilbert Márkus
University of Glasgow

AT THE end of the eighth century the shores of Britain and Ireland experienced a new threat to the life and prosperity of native communities when the first wave of Viking attacks took place. In some areas the violence was so severe in its character, and so sustained, that native society, whether Pictish or Gaelic, seems to have disappeared. The complete lack of any pre-Norse place-names in Orkney, for example (apart from the name Orkney itself), suggests an effective ethnic cleansing of the area.

But Viking raiders did not have a uniform impact in all the areas which they assailed. It may be that in some places the violence was never anything more than occasional raiding, while in other places the initial assault and taking of spoil was followed eventually by expropriation of land and resources, and by permanent settlement by Scandinavians (*goill* 'foreigners' in Gaelic, as in the title of this article). We should not assume that where such settlement took place it always followed the same lines of establishment and development, whether social, cultural or political.

The problem for the historian seeking to give an account of this process of settlement – how it took place, when, and in what form – is that there is so little documentary evidence from that period. What evidence there is is generally either fragmentary or late and unreliable, or both. This means that the study of place-names in the areas of Scandinavian raiding and settlement becomes all the more important. But a particular set of place-name data is capable of more than one interpretation and can lead to diametrically opposed conclusions. In the following pages I will identify one such set of data which has been interpreted in two very different ways. I will argue in support of one of those interpretations, and I will examine the place-names of Bute and show how Scandinavian place-names in the island tend to confirm that interpretation.

Place-names: topographical and habitative

The set of data which I am going to discuss was clearly outlined by Nicolaisen in 1976. He noticed what seemed to to be a significant difference between two distribution maps of Scottish place-names coined in Old Norse (hereafter ON): one map (fig 1.1) showed names which might be called 'topographical', containing ON *dalr* 'valley'. The other distribution map shows settlement-names containing 'habitative' elements such as *bólstaðr*, *staðir* and *setr* (fig 1.2), all of which are words referring to farming settlements, to places where people actually lived. The two maps below (derived from Nicolaisen 1976, 93 and 95) show a striking difference between the distributions of these two types of name. In the western isles and in areas all along the western coast north of the Clyde, *dalr* is fairly common, but there are no

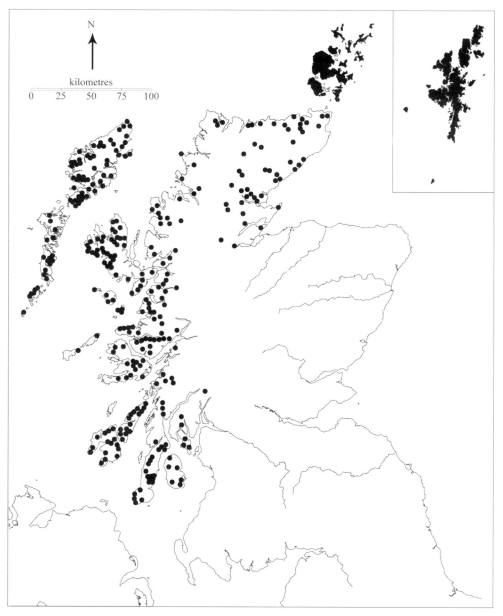

Fig 1.1 Place-names in ON *dalr* (after Nicolaisen 1976).

bólstaðr names at all in Kintyre or Knapdale, nor in Bute and Arran, and there are very few on considerable tracts of the western sea-board. How do we explain the fact that there are areas of Scotland where ON *dalr* is common but ON *bólstaðr* is absent?

Nicolaisen explained the difference between the two maps by arguing that place-names containing *dalr* were not indicators of Scandinavian settlement. While place-names containing

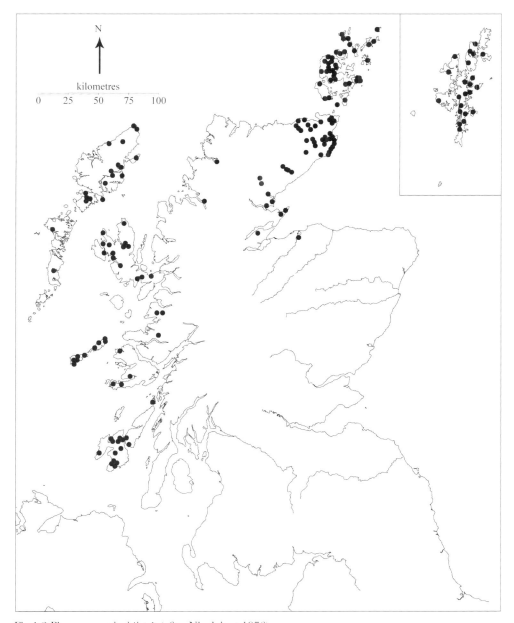

Fig 1.2 Place-names in *bólstaðr* (after Nicolaisen 1976).

habitative elements such as *bólstaðr* clearly denote actual Scandinavian settlement (and the distribution of place-names in *staðir* and *setr* is very similar to that of *bólstaðr*), place-names containing *dalr* (and *vík* 'bay', *nes* 'headland') should not be understood to denote settlement at all. He writes:

> ... names in *dalr* – apart from being found wherever *staðir*, *setr* and *bólstaðr* are at home – occur in large numbers in other areas, especially on the mainland, which ... cannot be said to be part of the Norse settlement area proper. In this respect it must be remembered that *dalr* refers to natural features, although the name of a valley was quite often, at a later date, transferred to a settlement situated in it. A distribution map of *dalr*-names is therefore not a map of permanent Norse settlement but rather of the sphere of Norse influence. It includes those areas adjacent to permanent settlements in which seasonal exploits such as hunting and fishing and summer grazing were carried out, and probably the odd military raid or friendly visit (1976: 94–5).

Thus the distribution of ON place-names containing topographical names does not, for Nicolaisen, indicate the extent of Norse settlement in Scotland. In a later article, discussing the lack of ON habitative elements in the place-names of Arran, where there are nevertheless several place-names containing the 'topographical' *dalr*, he employs an effective and attractive image for these names. He calls them 'onomastic graffiti' (1992: 8), the gift to the island of occasional visitors who left their mark on a landscape in which they never actually settled. This view has had some influence among later toponymists such as Ian Fraser (1999: 59).

Alternative explanations

Neverthelesss, we can imagine various other ways of explaining the data described above. For example one might propose in some areas where *dalr* thrives but *bólstaðr* is now absent that there had once been names containing *bólstaðr*, but that before they were entered into any of our surviving records these names were replaced by a new layer of Gaelic settlement-toponymy. This is very unlikely, for Gaelic clearly revived perfectly well in the islands too, but *bólstaðr* has survived there in significant numbers. The replacement of original *bólstaðr*-names by later Gaelic place-names is not convincing as a general explanation of the pattern.

But there are serious problems with Nicolaisen's explanation of the data. First of all it is hard to believe that a *dalr*-name given by visiting Norse-speakers to a valley in Gaelic-speaking Bute would displace the original Gaelic name of the valley among the native population living in and around that valley. Why would people in a local Gaelic-speaking community accept and perpetuate a name for a significant feature in their own landscape which had been coined in a language other than their own by people who only visited their island occasionally?

Another problem with Nicolaisen's explanation is his assumption that '*dalr* refers to natural features'. Certainly as a lexical item the word *dalr* means 'valley', a natural feature. But *dalr* in place-names functions in a different way from *dalr* in ordinary speech. Nicolaisen's remark that 'the name of a valley was quite often, at a later date, transferred to a settlement situated in it' merely assumes that place-names containing *dalr* were originally the names of valleys. But this is not necessarily true. Of settlement-names coined in ON, many of the earliest, and many of the most important, are coined in topographical elements such as *dalr* and *vík*. It does not follow from the existence of a settlement on Arran called Brodick (from *breið-vík* 'broad bay') that the name was first attached to the bay and was then 'at a later date transferred to the settlement'. It is just as likely that the settlement was the first referent of the name, distinguished from other settlements by being the one by the broad bay. The bay may never have been referred to as a *breið-vík* except as a descriptor of the location of the settlement. It might be illuminating to consider a parallel in a Pictish context: Aberdour in Fife is a Pictish name, containing **aber* 'outflow, burn-mouth, river-mouth' and **duvr* 'water, burn, river'. Now according to Nicolaisen's principle, we should regard this as a topographical name later applied to the settlement (the town and parish). But this would be a problematic name for a topographical feature. The function of a name is to distinguish a particular object from a number of others to which a speaker might be referring. But how would the name 'Aberdour' serve to distinguish this burn-mouth from any of the other burn-mouths on this stretch of coastline? As a settlement-name, however, it would work perfectly well: this settlement is distinguished from others in the vicinity as the one beside the mouth of the burn (in this case the mouth of the Dour Burn). The name is surely not a topographical one later transferred to a settlement, but a name originally coined as a settlement name, describing that settlement in terms of its significant topographical feature.

We cannot say that this has been the pattern in all cases. There may be settlement-names with topographical elements which were originally coined as the names of hills, valleys, bays and so on, and later transferred to settlements, but the pattern of naming settlements directly with topographical elements is well established. It also seems that many Scandinavian primary settlements (the earliest and most important) have names coined in topographical elements (Crawford 1987: 111), while secondary settlements created by subdivision of those original lands, or by bringing peripheral lands into cultivation or other use, are more likely to have names coined in habitative elements. This means that we cannot treat the distribution map of *dalr* 'valley' as if it were a map of merely topographical names for valleys. It might be a map of settlement-names which were created by their ON-speaking occupants by *reference* to local topographical features (as opposed to being existing names transferred from local topographical features).

Primary and secondary: Norse and Gaelic

Andrew Jennings and Arne Kruse have argued in various contexts that in an 'outer zone' where ON place-names use both topographical elements like *dalr* and habitative elements like *bólstaðr*, this is the result of early Scandinavian settlement which continued as occupation by ON-speakers during the ninth century and later, throughout the period when secondary settlements were being established. The word *bólstaðr* seems to have been productive of place-names from around the end of the ninth century (Gammeltoft 2001), about a hundred years after the first arrival of Viking raiders. For Jennings and Kruse the 'inner zone', where we find *dalr*-names but no *bólstaðr*-names, lacks these *bólstaðr*-names not because it lacked secondary settlements, but because by the time these secondary settlements were being established and given names the people creating them were speaking Gaelic (Jennings 2004; Kruse 2005; Jennings & Kruse 2009a; 2009b). Far from indicating a lack of Norse settlement in the 'inner zone', the *dalr* place-names indicate settlement at an early stage, while the lack of *bólstaðr* place-names (and those containing other habitative elements) indicates that the original Norse settlers had settled so thoroughly that they had become incorporated into a regional Gaelic-speaking community. The explanation of the difference between the inner and outer zones is therefore not one of different degrees of Norse settlement, but one involving the different political circumstances in which that settlement took place. In the inner zone, the Norse settlers became Gaelicised early because they were incorporated fairly rapidly into the native structures of Gaelic lordship and its concomitants – fiscal, cultural and probably religious too.

Jennings and Kruse have argued that this scenario is supported by the place-name evidence in the 'inner zone', such as that of the Carradale area of Kintyre. In this area all the major settlements have names containing as their generic element ON *dalr*, while smaller secondary settlements contain no ON habitative elements, but are coined in Gaelic elements such as *achadh* 'field, small farm', *peighinn* 'pennyland', *lethpheighinn* 'half-penny land' (Jennings 2004; Jennings & Kruse 2009a: 95–6).

We may now turn to Bute, an island in the same part of the 'inner zone' as eastern Kintyre. Borrowing the methodology of Jennings and Kruse we will examine the place-names of this island to see if a similar pattern might be apparent. Much of what I say about Bute place-names in the following pages represents data and analysis drawn from my forthcoming monograph, *The Place-Names of Bute*, very much abbreviated for the purposes of this article.

Before looking for the above-mentioned pattern of ON primary settlement-names and Gaelic secondary settlement-names, we should note that there are several place-names in Bute that point towards a Scandinavian presence on the island but which are not immediately relevant for illustrating this pattern. One, albeit one coined in Gaelic, is Dunagoil near Kingarth at the south end of Bute. The name appears to represent *dùn nan gall* 'fort of the foreigners', or perhaps *dùn a'ghoill* 'fort of the foreigner' (singular), and it should be noted that Gaelic *gall* 'foreigner' very commonly applies to Scandinavians in medieval sources. Though this interpretation of the name cannot be regarded as certain, it is corroborated by aspects of the archaeology of the site such as the remains of two buildings nearby which have been interpreted as Viking type long-houses, while a bronze weight of Scandinavian character (c AD 900) has been found there too (RCAHMS NS05SE 30; Geddes & Hale 2010: 30).

Other place-names appear to be coined in ON. Here are a few of them, identified by their grid references, with selected early forms and very brief discussion. In what follows, for the sake of brevity, I will not provide the references to the sources of early forms given, nor discuss the contexts in which they appear. For these, and fuller details and discussion, see Márkus forthcoming.

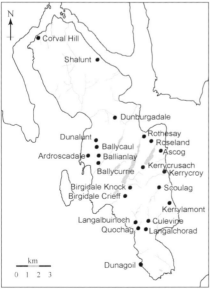

Fig 1.3 Bute with place-names discussed in this chapter.

SHALUNT NS048711

> *Schowlunt* 1440,
> *Scheulont* 1449
> *Schowlunt* 1450
> *Schalowont* 1496
> *Scha<u>land* 1506
> *Schauland* 1507
> *Schawland* 1527
> *Schaluint* 1617
> *Shallunt* 1681
> *Shalunt* 1705

The name seems to contain ON *sjár* and ON *lund* and means 'sea wood'. It is on the shore in the forested northern part of Bute.

ROTHESAY NS086637

> *Rothyrsay* 1283 x 1286
> *Rothir'* 1295
> *Rothersay* 1321
> *Rothisay* 1370s
> *Rothysay* 1370s
> *Roth<er>say* 1376
> *Roth<er>isay* 1380
> *Rothissay* 1391
> *Rosay* 1390 x 1406
> *Rothesay* 1408
> *Rothyrsay* 1409
> *Rothirsay* 1409
> *Rothyrsay* 1445
> *Rothissay* 1489

I would suggest that the name contains ON *ey* 'island' and the personal name *Ruðri*, a Norse name subsequently adopted by Gaelic-speakers as *Ruairidh*. The name is now that of the main urban settlement of Bute, but it was probably originally the name of the island itself.

ROSELAND NS094641

> *Roisland* 1588
> *Rosland* 1591
> *Rosland* 1610 x 1615
> *Rosland* 1654
> *Rossland* 1655
> *Rosland* 1662
> *Rosland* 1670
> *Rossland* 1689
> *Rossland* 1759
> *Rosslin* 1759

ON *hrossa* 'horse' + *land* 'land, farm'. The place is now a caravan site in the burgh of Rothesay, but in the medieval period it was a small farm on the hill above the town. When Rothesay was occupied by ON-speakers, this was presumably where horses were kept for the use of the occupants of the settlement below, on the site of the later medieval castle whose visible remains now do not pre-date the thirteenth century.

If my interpretation of the name is correct, this name should be regarded as an ON settlement-name, not a topographical one. It is hard to imagine circumstances where 'horse-land' could be applied to any feature other than a farm where horses were kept or bred (see Rixson 2010: 136–7, for the suggestion that ON *land* should be seen as a 'habitative' element).

DUMBURGADALE NS062660
>   *Dunburgadale* 1864
>   *Dumburgadale* 1869

The name (now obsolete) is Gaelic as it now stands, *dùn* 'fort' and the existing name *Borgadale. But that existing name itself is clearly an ON one and must refer to the broad

valley lying north of Dumburgadale itself. It contains *borg* 'fort, dome-shaped hill' and *dalr* 'valley'. In the vicinity are two potential referents for the *borg*: the first is the hill-top fort at Dumburgadale itself, overlooking the presumed valley of *Borgadale, while the second is the dramatic mound in the middle of the valley now called Cnoc an Rath (a name which means 'hillock of the fort') which is still something of a puzzle to archaeologists. It may be a fort, a moot-hill, or something else entirely.

Fig 1.4 Cnoc-an-Rath
(© John Baldwin)

CORVAL HILL NR996729

>*Corval Hill* 1780 x 1782
>*Corval Hill* 1869

The name as it now stands was coined in Scots or Scottish Standard English, but it contains the existing name Corval, which was probably the name of the same hill. It seems to contain ON *fjall* 'hill, mountain'. What the Cor- part of the name represents I cannot say, but it may represent a personal name, or perhaps ON *korf* 'basket' with reference to the shape of the hill.

The place-names of Bute discussed above are not the names of large primary farms which might have been subject to subdivision in some secondary development, and they cannot be used to test the thesis of Jennings and Kruse about ON primary and Gaelic secondary settlement-names. They do nevertheless suggest a convincing degree of Norse settlement on the island. The following names also point towards Norse settlement of Bute, but are grouped together here because they all appear to be ON names of primary settlements, large farms, which were subsequently divided and whose divisions were given Gaelic names.

ASCOG NS104630

>*Ascok* 1427
>*Ascok* 1459
>*Ascok* 1503 x 1504
>*Ascok* 1510
>*Eskek* 1545 x 1546
>*Askok* 1546
>*Askok* 1554
>*Ascoks* 1564
>*Eskoks* 1576
>*Ovir Askoke* 1578
>*Nadir Askoke* 1578
>*Askogis* 1585
>*Askokis* 1585
>*Myde Askok* 1588

The name probably represents ON *askr* + ON *vík* 'ash-tree bay'. For the realisation of *vík* in the Clyde with final *-ok* compare for example Sannox on Arran (from ON *sand-vík* 'sandy bay'), a plural form of the name which appears in singular form as *Sennock* 1654, and in plural form as *Sannokes* 1548, *Sannocks* 1685, and *Sannox* 1661 (Fraser 1999: 92).

Ascog had a value of £3 or 4½ merks in Old Extent. When it was subdivided it formed various smaller units: Kerrycroy and Kerrycrusach, both containing Gaelic *ceathreamh* 'quarter', and also *Over Ascog, *Nether Ascog and *Mid Ascog, employing Scots affixes. Scots appears in the place-names of Bute rather earlier than might be expected of an island in this position, and this is probably explained in part by the fact that centuries of royal, shrieval and burgal administration were centred at Rothesay and brought a strong influence of Scots to bear in what was otherwise a Gaelic-speaking environment.

In any case, Ascog corresponds to the 'Kintyre pattern': primary settlement named in ON with a name formed from a topographical element *vík*, subsequent secondary settlements named in Gaelic and Scots.

BIRGIDALE NS07 59

> *Brethadale* 1440
> *Brigadile* 1449
> *Byrgadill* 1450
> *Brigadill* 1506
> *Brigadilknok* 1506
> *Bargadill Knok* 1507
> *Brigadell* 1512
> *Brigadell* 1512
> *Birgadulknok* 1517
> *Brigadull* 1540 x 1542
> *Brigydulcrok* 1547
> *Briggadilknok* 1552 x 1553
> *Birgadaleknok* 1557
> *Birgadilchrif* 1563
> *Brigadouleknok* 1588
> *Birgadillcraif* 1632
> *Birgadilknok* 1637

The second element, the generic, is ON *dalr*. The 1440 form suggests that the specific element might be ON *breiðr* 'broad', but later forms point to another word: perhaps *bryggja* 'pier, bridge'; or *berg* 'rock, boulder, precipice'; or *byrgi* 'enclosure, fence'. It is impossible to be certain which of these words forms the specific, largely because the spelling of the first element in the forms until the sixteenth century varies so often between the *birg-* and *brig-* forms.

The lands of Birgidale were valued at £5 in Old Extent, and they were already divided into two parts when it first appears in the record in 1440. These two divisions of Birgidale were eventually called Birgidale Crieff (Gaelic *craobh* 'tree') and Birgidale Knock (Gaelic *cnoc* 'hill, hillock'). This is therefore a substantial primary settlement with a Norse name whose subdivisions were named in Gaelic, albeit in this case with names containing the existing ON name Birgidale. It is not clear when the divisions acquired their names in *craobh* and *cnoc*. It may have been long before their first appearance in the surviving record as described here.

LANGAL NS 08 56

> *Langil* 1440
> *Langill* 1449
> *Langil* 1450
> *Langilculcathla* 1506
> *Langilculcreich* 1506
> *Langilwenach* 1506
> *Langilculcathla* 1507

Langwilculcreich 1507
Languilbenach 1507
Langulchulchoich 1540
Langull 1540 x 1542
Langulbunnag 1546 x 1552
Langilbunnage 1555
Langillculquhi 1595 x 1601
Mid Langill vocat. *Langill-culchoy* 1610 x 1615
Langill-culchoy 1610 x 1615
Langil-cuilchlachlane 1632 ['alias *Langil-cord*']
Langrewinnag 1654
Langrechoulchych 1654
Langre choul na cachaly 1654
Lagreineclachland 1655 ['otherwise *Lagil<c>ord*']
Lagil<c>cord 1655

This name probably contains ON *langr* 'long' and ON *völlr* 'field'. ON *gil* 'ravine, gully' would be formally possible, especially given the early forms in final -*gil*, but there is no obvious 'long ravine' in the area for this to refer to.

If we are to understand ON *völlr* in the narrow sense of 'field', it should really be regarded as a 'habitative' element, reflecting Scandinavian settlement, since 'a field suggests permanence' (Rixson 2010: 135). But ON *völlr* might simply mean 'level ground' in some contexts, without necessarily reflecting enclosure or farming of the ground, and it may be unwise to make too large a claim on the basis of this name.

Langal as a whole was valued at £8 in Old Extent, but was already divided into four equal parts when it first appears in the record (1440), each worth 40 shillings. By 1507 one of the four parts of Langal had been renamed as Culevine (*Couleyng*) which name it still possesses. The other three parts were renamed with affixes, –*culcathla* (now Langalchorad), –*culcreich* (later *Langalchechag*; now simply Quochag) and –*benach* (now Langalbuinoch). The word-order and orthography of early forms of these affixes strongly suggests a Gaelic origin; however the spellings of the names of these subdivisions undergo such severe mangling that it is hard to say what Gaelic elements they represent. If it can be accepted that they are Gaelic in origin, however, we can say that Langal also exemplifies the pattern observed by Jennings and Kruse in Kintyre.

*ROSCADALE NS03 63

Ardrossigille 1319 x 1321
Ardrossigille 1475
Ardrossigille 1475
Ardrossigelle 1475
Ardroskedellis 1573
Ardroskedillis 1577
Nethir Ardroskedillis 1577
Ovir Ardroskedillis 1577
Ardrosgedill 1592

> *Ardroskitillis* 1623
> *Arolroskedel* 1654
> *Ardroskidull Uachterach* 1661
> *Ardroscidell* 1662
> *Ardroskadill* 1662
> 2 *Ardros-Kittallis* 1670
> *Uper Ardroskitall* 1672
> *Nether Ardroskitall* 1672
> *Laigh Ardroskadale c.*1753
> *Upper Ardroskadale c.*1753
> *N<ether> Ardrosadale* 1797
> *Upper Ardrosadale* 1797

This name survives only as incorporated into the Gaelic name Ardroscadale, which is composed of *àird* 'height, promontory' (or perhaps *àrd* 'high') and the existing name *Roscadale. Between 1475 and 1573 a significant change appears in the spelling of the name, which makes it difficult to be sure of what the original meaning of *Roscadale was. The fourteenth- and fifteenth-century forms point towards ON *hrossagil* 'ravine of the horses', but forms from the sixteenth century onwards look more as if they represent a name containing ON *dalr*. If *Roscadale does contain *dalr* 'valley' as its second element, the name must have referred to the valley which lies immediately east of Ardroscadale, since Ardroscadale itself is a ridge of high ground forming a promontory. That valley is on record from 1440 as a farm with the Gaelic name Dunalunt, and that farm was itself subsequently subdivided into four farms: Dunalunt, Ballycurrie, Ballicaul and Ballianlay. The most likely sequence of events then would be that there was a settlement called *Roscadale whose centre was in the valley. That farm was subsequently divided into *Roscadale and Ardroscadale (each of these farms having a value of 12 merks or £8 in Old Extent), and *Roscadale subsequently renamed in Gaelic as Dunalunt, which in turn was subdivided into four farms of 3 merks or £2 each, all with names in Gaelic.

If Ardroscadale is understood to contain *dalr* it will fit the pattern we are looking for: primary settlement of a large farm with a name in ON and secondary settlements by subdivision created with Gaelic names.

A third possible interpretation of this name is possible, however. It might be understood as being a Gaelic name incorporating *àird* and the ON personal name Hrossketil: 'Hrossketil's promontory'. This personal name, attested elsewhere in the insular Norse world, would make sense both of the sixteenth-century and later forms, and also the earlier ones since the *ketill* element of the name was regularly reduced by the eleventh or twelfth century to *Hroskell*. The main difficulty with this suggestion lies in explaining why the earliest forms of Ardroscadale show what would be the later (reduced) form of Hrossketill, while the later forms of the place-names show the earlier (unreduced) form of the personal name. The vagaries of the recording and survival of written and oral versions of place-names may sufficiently explain this anomaly, however, and thus we might have here not an example of a Norse primary settlement being subdivided into Gaelic secondary settlements, but rather a farm named in Gaelic (*àird*) after a Scandinavian owner, Hrossketill.

SCOULAG NS101599

> *Sculogmor* 1440
> *Scoullogmore* 1444
> *Scowlogmore* 1449
> *Skologmore* 1450
> *Skulogmore* 1453
> *Scologmore* 1456
> *Scologmore* 1457
> *Skowloch* 1505
> *Mydskowlok* 1528
> *Nederskowlok* 1528
> *Scolok* 1537 x 1539
> *Scowlokis* 1590 x 1601
> *Scoulock* 1654
> *Scoulock Meanack* 1654
> *Scoulak* 1667
> *Upper Scoulack c.*1753

The origin of the name is obscure, but the most likely generic element here is ON *vík* 'bay'. The first element may be *skjól* 'shelter, cover, protection', a word which appears to have been loaned into Gaelic as *sgùl* (MacLennan 1925, s.v. *sgùl*). It is possible, however, that the name was coined in Gaelic *sgùl* with *–ag* suffix, hence 'shelter-place'.

The estate of Scoulag first appears in 1440 already divided into parts, with the largest part designated by Gaelic *mòr* 'large', being valued at 5 merks. This division was later re-named Kerrylamont (Gaelic *ceathram* 'quarter' + personal name Lamont). The remainder of Scoulag was subdivided into four other parts, *Nether Scoulag, *Middle Scoulag, *Kerrymoran and *Kerryniven, each of them valued at 4 merks, the first two named in Scots, the last two named in Gaelic *ceathramh* 'quarter'.

If the ON explanation of Scoulag given above as 'shelter-bay' is accepted, we have another instance here of a large estate (£14 or 21 merks in Old Extent) with an ON name later subdivided into five parts with names coined in Gaelic and Scots.

The Gall-Ghàidheil of Bute

The place-names of Bute seem not only to show clear evidence of Scandinavian settlement, but also to conform in several cases to the pattern observed by Jennings and Kruse in the Carradale area of Kintyre: large primary settlements with names coined in ON, smaller secondary settlements with names coined in Gaelic (or in some cases Scots). There are no farm-names in Bute coined in ON *bólstaðr*, *setr* or *staðir*, which suggests that by around AD 900, when place-names with those elements were being coined elsewhere, the descendants of Scandinavian settlers had ceased to speak ON and were now speaking Gaelic. An alternative explanation is conceivable, namely that the Scandinavian settlers had been removed from the island by Gaels before they got a chance to create or name their secondary settlements. But the fact that Bute (like Arran) was part of the diocese of Sodor makes any notion of the ejection of the Scandinavian settlers implausible: Sodor was merely the ecclesiastical expression of the secular territory of the Isles around AD 1100 whose rulers, at least in theory, owed obedience and tax to Norwegian overkings.

Around the middle of the ninth century a new ethnic or political group comes into view in the Irish annals, the *Gall-Ghàidheil*, literally 'the foreign Gaels'. They are Gaels, but they are regarded as 'foreign' in some respects, as Scandinavians (Clancy 2008; Jennings & Kruse 2009b). They first appear in the annals with a leader called Ketill, a Scandinavian name, although it is noteworthy that Ketill has the Gaelic by-name *Find* 'fair, white'. The earliest evidence we have for a possible location for this newly emerging group is, remarkably enough, on Bute itself. As discussed recently by Thomas Clancy, the feast of St Blane is mentioned in the Martyrology of Tallaght as celebrated on 10 August, and his entry there proclaims *Blaani episcopi Cind Garad i nGallgaedelaib*, '(feast of) Blane bishop of Kingarth among the Gall-Ghàidheil', in a text which probably dates to the mid- or late ninth century (Martyr Tallaght 62; Clancy 2008: 30). Kingarth in Bute is 'among the Gall-Ghàidheil' then, as far as the writer was concerned. The evidence of place-names on Bute and Kintyre, and perhaps in other areas of the 'inner zone' discussed above, is that Scandinavians settled here during the ninth century in sufficient numbers and with sufficient strength to be able to form important farming and/or fishing settlements which they named in their own language, but that during the course of the ninth century these settlers were assimilated into a Gaelic-speaking culture (Clancy 2008; Jennings & Kruse 2009b). This can surely be seen as the kind of linguistic context that might give rise to the expression Gall-Ghàidheil as the name of a new political entity in the mid-ninth century.

There is an enormous gap in the documentary record between the Scandinavian settlement and the earliest surviving written records of Bute place-names. Apart from the church of Kingarth and the name Bute itself, no place-name on this island is recorded before the thirteenth century. Among those Gaelic place-names cited above which I have argued were named by Gaels as sub-divisions of older larger farms with ON names, many of them first appear in the record even later than that. The first recorded dates for the appearance of those names are as follows:

Kerrycroy	1440
Kerrycrusach	1440
Birgidale Crieff	1507
Birgidale Knock	1506
Langal Culcathla	1506
Langal Culcreich	1506
Langalbenach	1507
Culevine	1506
Dunalunt	1440
Ballycaul	1507
Ballycurrie	1506
Ballianlay	1662

The gap between the proposed initial Scandinavian settlements and the earliest recorded occurrences of the Gaelic names of the sub-divisions of those settlements is therefore one of some four or five centuries. This means that we cannot offer any certainty as to the date of the coining of those Gaelic names, nor therefore of the creation of the subdivision of the original estates which had ON names. In some cases, such as those names containing Gaelic *baile*, we can be fairly certain that they were *not* the names of very early Gaelic subdivisions of the larger estates, simply because *baile* does not appear in any place-name in Scotland prior to the late eleventh century. Balchrystie, Newburn parish, Fife is the earliest, appearing in a record of a grant made in 1070 x 1093 (*St A. Lib.* 115; Taylor & Márkus 2008: 477–8). It is inconceivable, therefore, that Ballycurrie, Ballycaul and Ballianlay were the original names of very early secondary settlements. In the case of such a *baile*-name we might imagine that the secondary settlement was created early but had a different name before it was re-named using *baile*, in which case we have no idea what its original name was, nor even what language it was coined in. It might perhaps have contained ON *bólstaðr*, *staðir* or *setr*, before being replaced with a Gaelic name, though I think that is unlikely, and it would raise the question as to why such names survived in the outer zone but not in Bute. Or it might have been a name using some Gaelic element other than *baile*, such as *ceathramh* 'quarter' (like Kerrycrusach, Kerrycroy, Kerryniven, Kerrymoran etc mentioned above), or perhaps an element referring to the value of the land such as *peighinn* 'penny-land' or *leth-pheighinn* 'halfpenny-land' (such as appears in two names in North Bute, Lenihall and Lenihuline), or perhaps an element referring to some feature of the landscape such as *dùn* 'fort, hill' (as appears in Dunburgadale and Dunalunt).

In the case of the names of secondary settlements containing Gaelic *ceathramh* 'quarter' or *mòr* 'big', it is more difficult to ascertain a likely time-frame for their coining. It seems possible that these were the original Gaelic names of ninth- or tenth-century settlements carved out of, or added to, estates named in ON. The same might be said for Gaelic *craobh* 'tree' and *cnoc* 'hill', which also form names of secondary settlements, though they appear quite late in the Bute record.

Overall it seems that the pattern observed by Jennings and Kruse in Kintyre is broadly replicated in Bute, though there are difficulties implicit in the lack of early records and consequently in our ability to assign dates to the formation of Gaelic names of secondary settlements. But the pattern we can observe in the distribution of various place-name elements in Bute and in western Scotland more generally, when taken together with the appearance of the Gall-Ghàidheil in the mid-ninth century and their association with Bute in the more-or-less contemporary Martyrology of Tallaght, and with the likely dating horizons for the formation of names in *bólstaðr*, is suggestive of the early transformation of a Scandinavian settler population in Bute into a settled Gaelic-speaking community, integrated into the structures of the wider Gaelic-speaking region, but with continuing Scandinavian associations, as implied by the name Gall-Ghàidheil.

If Ardroscadale on Bute does not contain an existing *dalr*-name, but is rather *àird-Hrossketill* 'Hrossketill's promontory' as suggested as a possibility above, it would provide a nice glimpse of this process of the Gaelicisation of Scandinavian settlers: the *gall* or 'foreigner' Hrossketill (or his family or neighbours) gave his farm a Gaelic name. If so we might imagine that we had discovered the name of one of the original Gall-Ghàidheil at home in the heart of his own people's territory.

Note

This chapter represents a distillation of parts of the work done by the author as a toponymic contribution to a wider research project on the history and archaeology of Bute under the auspices of the *Discover Bute Landscape Partnership* <www.discoverbute.com>.

References

Clancy, T O 2008 'The Gall-Ghàidheil and Galloway', *J Scottish Name Studies* 2, 19–50.

Crawford, B E 1987 *Scandinavian Scotland*. Leicester: Leicester University Press.

Fraser, I A 1999 *The Place-Names of Arran*. Glasgow: The Arran Society of Glasgow.

Gammeltoft, P 2001 *The Place-name Element 'bólstaðr' in the North Atlantic Area*. Copenhagen: Rietzel.

Geddes, G & Hale, A 2010 *The Archaeological Landscape of Bute*. Edinburgh: RCAHMS.

Jennings, A 2004 'The Norse place-names of Kintyre', in Adams, J & Holman, K (eds) *Scandinavia and Europe 800–1350: contact, conflict and coexistence*, 109–19. Turnhout: Brepols.

Jennings, A & Kruse, A 2009a 'One coast – three peoples: names and ethnicity in the Scottish west during the early Viking period', in Woolf, A (ed) *Scandinavian Scotland – twenty years after*, 75–102. St Andrews: St John's House Papers 12.

Jennings, A & Kruse, A 2009b 'From Dál Riata to the *Gall-Ghàidheil*', *Viking and Medieval Scandinavia* 5, 123–49.

Kruse, A 2005 'Explorers, Raiders and Settlers. The Norse impact upon Hebridean place-names', in Gammeltoft, P, Hough, C & and Waugh, D (eds) *Cultural Contacts in the North Atlantic Region: the evidence of Names*, 141–54. Lerwick: NORNA, Scottish Place-Name Society, Society for Name Studies in Britain and Ireland.

Maclennan, M 1925 *A Pronouncing and Etymological Dictionary of the Gaelic Language*. Edinburgh (reprinted Aberdeen, 1979): Acair & Aberdeen University Press.

Márkus, G forthcoming *The Place-Names of Bute*. Donington: Shaun Tyas.

Martyr Tallaght *The Martyrology of Tallaght*, ed R I Best & H J Lawlor, 1931. London: Henry Bradshaw Society.

Nicolaisen, W F H 1976 *Scottish Place-Names*. London: Batsford.

Nicolaisen, W F H 1992 'Arran Place-Names: a Fresh Look', *Northern Studies* 28, 1–13.

RCAHMS Royal Commission on the Ancient and Historical Monuments of Scotland Archive <http://www.rcahms.gov.uk?>.

Rixson, D 2010 'The Shadow of Onomastic Graffiti', *J Scottish Name Studies* 4, 131–58.

Taylor, S with Márkus, G 2008 *The Place-Names of Fife, volume 2: Central Fife between the Rivers Leven and Eden*. Donington: Shaun Tyas.

St Andrews Lib *Liber Cartarum Prioratus Sancti Andree in Scotia*, Bannatyne Club, 1841.

Chapter 2

Scandinavians in Strathclyde: multiculturalism, material culture and manufactured identities in the Viking Age

Courtney Helen Buchanan
University of Glasgow

THE British kingdom of Strathclyde appeared in written records in the late ninth century following a Viking siege of Alt Clut (Dumbarton Rock), the stronghold of Strathclyde's early medieval predecessor, the kingdom of Dumbarton. Not much is known about Scandinavian activity in Strathclyde after this attack, although the hogback monuments at Govan have been seen as a sign of continued Scandinavian presence in this region (eg Crawford 2005). With the discovery of several recent Treasure Trove finds and the excavation of a Viking Age cemetery at Midross, it is possible to explore Scandinavian involvement in Strathclyde beyond the Govan hogbacks, and determine the various contexts of contact and interaction in which those hogbacks, and other items, were created, used, and understood.

Background

The evidence for Scandinavians in Strathclyde is limited in both the established written and archaeological sources. Although there are a few historical references in the chronicles, there has been very little work done on the place-name evidence here. The archaeological studies have focused primarily on the Govan hogbacks, although some attention has been given to the burial at Boiden and the Port Glasgow hoard. The sources are now available to begin to contextualise these finds with others in the region, and in turn Scandinavians within Strathclyde.

Theoretical underpinnings

Understanding the Scandinavians in Strathclyde during the Viking Age requires an approach based on postcolonial theoretical concepts. It must be understood that contact and interaction between peoples of different cultural backgrounds will lead to fundamental changes in both groups. In order to interact meaningfully, an arena in which both groups can understand the other must be created, called the Third Space (Bhabha 2004). The contexts of contact and interaction are crucial to understanding the Third Space created, because different contexts of interaction will create different Third Spaces. Within the Third

Space, social, political, religious, gender, age and ethnic identities will be deconstructed and reconstructed to enable individuals to negotiate and succeed in the Third Space. Thus the Third Space becomes an arena that is neither one nor the other, but something new altogether, and from this new arena, new forms of material culture emerge.

Written sources

The first explicit mention to this region is found in the Annals of Ulster (AU) in 870 when Óláfr (Old Irish: Amlaíb) and Ívarr (Old Irish: Ímar) from Dublin sacked Dumbarton Rock (Ail Cluaithe): 'Amlaíb and Ímar, two kings of the Norsemen, laid siege to [Ail Cluaithe] and at the end of four months they destroyed and plundered it' (AU 870.6). After they successfully sacked and plundered Alt Clut, and probably the surrounding regions, Óláfr and Ívarr returned to Dublin the following year 'with two hundred ships, bringing away with them in captivity to Ireland a great prey of Angles and Britons and Picts' (AU 871.2). Interestingly, and perhaps very significantly, it was only after Alt Clut was sacked by Óláfr and Ívarr that the term Strathclyde appeared in the records. It was still a British kingdom and still held much of the same territory, but there must have been a reason for the name change. It has been proposed that this might have been the result of a change in location for the stronghold of the kingdom, perhaps moving farther up the Clyde towards the ecclesiastical site at Govan (Broun 2004: 111–12; Dalglish & Driscoll 2009: 29–30). A move eastward up the river could have made the British kingdom more accessible to the interior of Scotland rather than the isles, and indeed two years after Artgal, king of the Britons of Strathclyde, was killed (AU 872.5), Halfdan, based on the River Tyne in Northumbria, is recorded to have often raided amongst Strathclyde Britons (*A-S Chron* 874). Using the waterways from the east coast to the Clyde would have been much more effective than moving overland from the Tyne valley to the Clyde valley.

This turbulent decade for the British kingdom in Strathclyde is followed by almost complete silence in the histories, broken in the tenth century by only two passing references. The first possible textual mention is an unnamed king of the Cumbrians who formed part of the northern alliance against Æthelstan of Wessex at the battle of Brunanburh in 937. In 937, the Anglo-Saxon Chronicle and the Chronicle of the Kings of Alba both record the Battle of Brunanburh, which pitted a 'northern alliance' against Æthelstan of Wessex (*A-S Chron* 937; *Chron Alba*, p157). In both sources, the northern alliance included Constantine, king of Alba, Óláfr Guthfrithson, the Viking king of Dublin, and an unnamed king of the Cumbrians. This is the only reference to a possible king of the Cumbrians, and it is most likely that this king was the same king of Strathclyde, whose territory in the tenth century encompassed the area south-western Scotland and north-western England down to the River Eamont (Clarkson 2010: 172). The last reference is to the raid in 945 upon Cumbria (in *A-S Chron*) or Strathclyde (in *Annal Camb*) by Edmund of Wessex, who then ceded the territory to Mael Coluim, king of Scots (*A-S Chron* 945; *Annal Camb* 946).

Place-names likewise do not offer much insight into the contacts and interactions of Scandinavians with the locals of Strathclyde. Little work has been done on Old Norse place-names in this area, and what work has been done recently has focused on the two clusters of –byr names, one in Ayrshire and the other along the Clyde (Grant 2005; Taylor 2004). However, earlier work has brought up interesting possibilities of Old Norse place-names in

Strathclyde, but there has been no modern follow-up. Some of the place-names in the Clyde region include Gorbals, thought to be from the Old Norse gorr-balkr, 'built-walls' (Bremner 1904: 377), and Eaglesham, the earliest form of which is recorded to be Egil's ham in 1158 (Bremner 1904: 377). Thus, there is not much written evidence for peaceful interaction except for two clusters of –byr place-names which might indicate a tenth-century settlement by Old Norse speakers. However, the fact that Óláfr and Ívarr spent four months engaged in a siege upon Alt Clut would suggest that there was more interest in this region than just taking loot and slaves. It is probable that a force of Scandinavians or Hiberno-Scandinavians would have been left at Alt Clut to ensure it remained in Scandinavian control. Another clue that Scandinavians may have had a more permanent presence in Strathclyde after the sack of Alt Clut is the northern alliance of 937 (*Chron Alba*, p157; *A-S Chron* 937). The successors of the men engaged in resistance during the siege were now allied with each other and Alba, which is an indication that channels of communication and interaction between the Scandinavians and Strathclyde Britons were not completely hostile. Finally, Strathclyde only has two meaningful geographical concentrations of place-names and a few possible random names. This indicates that any settlement in the landscape by Old Norse speakers was not dominant, and probably much more integrated with local settlements and estates.

Archaeological sources

Like the written sources, there is not much archaeological evidence that could attest to permanent settlement and interaction by Scandinavians in this region, except for the tantalising concentration of five hogback stones at Govan. Other than these, there was a hoard found at Port Glasgow, Inverclyde, in the seventeenth century which included two silver arm-rings, one made of three silver rods twisted together and the other a lozenge-sectioned type often called 'ring money', and a number of (now lost) coins. Another antiquarian find, and more apt to indicate permanent presence, was the burial found at Boiden, Argyll and Bute, in the nineteenth century. In the top part of a mound were a sword, a spearhead, and a shield boss (Stewart 1854: 144). Supposedly, there was a cairn on the top of the mound, but it appears to have no longer been there when the discovery was made. The final artefacts come from the excavation of Dumbarton Rock in the 1970s where a sword pommel and two lead weights, one plain and one decorated with a glass bangle fragment, were found (Alcock & Alcock 1990: 113–15). They interpreted these as evidence of the siege, and certainly the pommel fits nicely into that scenario. The two lead weights may, however, attest to a different kind of activity occurring on the site, that of trade between a Scandinavian merchant and others. It would seem likely, then, that this probable trade occurred after the siege.

In addition to the five hogbacks at Govan, there are two others in this region that also appear in churchyards: one at Luss, Argyll and Bute, which is in close proximity to the burial at Boiden, and one up the Clyde at Dalserf, South Lanarkshire (Lang 1975: 224, 229). The hogbacks at Govan are amongst the earliest hogbacks found in Scotland, dating to the tenth century (Lang 1975: 212; Ritchie 2004: 17). Significantly, they represent the largest concentration found on a single site outside of York itself, and are the largest hogbacks found in Scotland (Lang 1975: 1994; Ritchie 2004: 1; Daglish & Driscoll 2009: 31). As in other parts of southern Scotland and northern England, hogbacks are tied to the presence of a Scandinavian population that had access to enough resources to commission such massive stone monuments. The most common explanation for their appearance at Govan goes back to the entries regarding Óláfr and Ívarr: these hogbacks could signify a refuge for the 'grandsons of Ívarr' who were active in the kingdoms of Dublin and York throughout the later ninth and tenth centuries (eg Crawford 2005: 20). However, in light of new archaeological evidence within Strathclyde, a new explanation may be needed for the presence of these hogbacks.

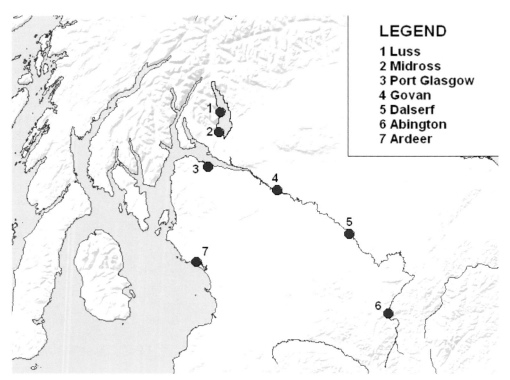

LEGEND

1 Luss
2 Midross
3 Port Glasgow
4 Govan
5 Dalserf
6 Abington
7 Ardeer

Fig 2.1 Map of the study area (© Esri 2009 with amendments by the author).

Isolated finds and new archaeological evidence

There are only a handful of Treasure Trove and isolated finds from this region. They include the Hunterston brooch, an antiquarian find from the Hunterston Estate in Ayrshire. It is a fine piece of Insular metalwork that made its way into the hands of a Norse speaker, who carved runes on the back that claim the brooch as Melbrigda's (O'Floinn 1989: 91; for further discussion on this brooch and the runes, see Grieg 1940, Olsen 1954, and Stevenson 1974). There was an axe-head and a possible wooden club found in Loch Doon, Ayrshire, and another axe-head found near Loch Long, Argyll and Bute. Also in Ayrshire, a ringed-pin was discovered in the nineteenth century during the excavation of Lochlee Crannog (Munro et al 1879: 232), and an Arabic dirhem was found through metal-detection at Stevenston Sands, Ayrshire. Finally, a sword pommel was found at Abington, Biggar, South Lanarkshire.

The most significant new evidence for understanding Scandinavian activities, and their subsequent interactions with the locals of Strathclyde, comes from Midross, Argyll and Bute. The Viking-Age cemetery at Midross that was recently excavated by GUARD (Glasgow University Archaeological Research Division) sheds new light on this region. Near the cemetery is the burial at Boiden, mentioned above. Batey (in Becket et al forthcoming) puts forward the possibility that the Boiden burial is not an isolated grave, but rather part of the burial complex from Midross. The cemetery contains 15 burials radiocarbon dated to the late ninth and tenth centuries; six of these contained grave goods (Batey in Becket et al forthcoming). Two of the graves held multiple finds, with the remaining four containing only one grave good. Grave 051190 contained a whetstone, a slotted tool, a knife blade, an iron fitting or rod, and an Anglo-Saxon coin fragment attached to the iron fitting or rod. The knife blade is most likely a kitchen blade as opposed to a weapon, and fits with the domestic nature of these finds. The whetstone is made of Eidsborg schist from the Telemark region of Norway, which demonstrates a material link between Scandinavia and this community in the ninth or tenth centuries. The other grave with multiple grave goods, grave 0510248, contained a shale arm-ring and finger-ring, a copper-alloy bracelet, and a blue glass bead. These items are all adornment and decorative items, and it is tempting to see the occupant's gender as female based on these finds; however it cannot be stated with certainty. The other four graves contained one grave good each; grave 0510270 contained a child-sized shale arm-ring; grave 0510214 contained a knife blade; grave 0511801 contained a pierced Anglo-Saxon penny; and grave 0511803 contained a knife blade. One final find from the site, although not found in a grave but probably indicating another furnished male grave, is a shield boss that was found in the ditch circling the cemetery. It is possible this item has been displaced by ploughing (Batey pers comm). Contemporary with these six furnished graves are nine unfurnished graves, which could indicate a population drawing upon Scandinavian and local traditions in their burial rites. While these graves may not indicate a biologically Scandinavian population (Batey in Becket et al forthcoming), the Scandinavian element in their burial rites is clear, and would imply such an element in their daily routines as well.

Contextualising Strathclyde

The finds by themselves do not amount to a very widespread distribution within Strathclyde, and even when mapped with the known place-names and sculptures, only a few concentrations are evident (fig 2.2 – overleaf). However, the overlaps of each strand of evidence are intriguing and more significant than may be initially evident.

The first important observation is that all of the finds are on or very near waterways. Second, almost all of the stray finds overlap with another piece of non-portable or contextualised evidence. The Arabic dirhem from Stevenston Sands is located near the cluster of six –byr place-names in Ayrshire, while in the same vicinity are the ringed-pin from Lochlee crannog and the axe-head and club from Loch Doon. At the mouth of the Clyde, the axe-head from Loch Long is near to the hoard from Port Glasgow. Further up the Clyde, the pommel from Abington is near two of the Lanarkshire –byr place-names and in the vicinity of the hogback at Dalserf. Thus, it appears the Clyde and its tributaries were at the heart of the Scandinavian activities in Strathclyde.

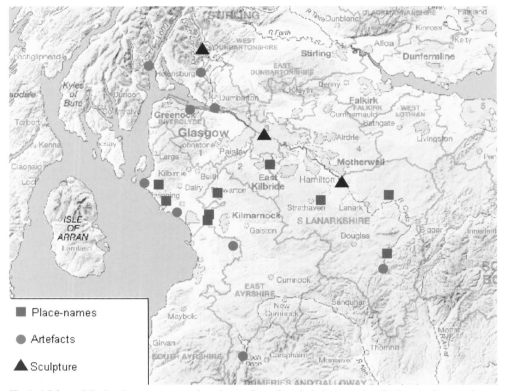

Fig 2. 2 Map of finds, place-names, and sculpture from Strathclyde (contains Ordnance Survey data © Crown Copyright and database right 2011).

The River Clyde: gateway to Scotland and the east coast

The importance of the Clyde in navigating between the west and east coasts of Scotland has been cited often, almost entirely in relation to the probable portage between the Clyde and the Forth (Smyth 1984; Crawford 1987; 2005) (see fig 2.3). However, there are many other options for travel into the interior of Scotland (and even northern England) by way of the Clyde, and the distribution of the material discussed above has highlighted a few alternative routes.

The northern route

The first, and more famous, route from the Clyde to the interior of Scotland and the east coast is the northern route. From the mouth of the Clyde, one could navigate north via a short overland portage across theisthmus and over to the River Forth. The most likely overland portage along this route would be from Rutherglen along the Clyde to Blackness and Bo'ness on the Forth (fig 2.3), as later medieval Glasgow merchants were thought to use this route (Dennison 2007: 50, 53). It has been postulated that this route was mainly used for transport between Dublin and York, primarily as one route utilised by merchants between the two Viking towns. Evidence along this route includes the Port Glasgow hoard at the mouth of the Clyde, the finds from Dumbarton Rock, the hogbacks at Govan and possibly the evidence from Boiden, Midross, and Luss. This route justifies the need to control Dumbarton Rock as a primary gateway into the Clyde, and thus the four-month-long siege of the stronghold is easily explained. Even the seemingly isolated burial at Boiden could be explained by intermittent warring activity on the Clyde and its tributaries. However, the hogbacks at Govan and Luss is more difficult to explain with this transient military and mercantile presence. Even harder to explain by this hypothesis is the cemetery at Midross. As discussed above, this cemetery is significant because it demonstrates a settled population which buried its dead following a Scandinavian tradition of inhumation with grave goods. However, it is also significant because the cemetery contains contemporary unfurnished graves and is very near the 'pagan' burial at Boiden. As Batey has suggested (in Becket et al forthcoming), Boiden and Midross are likely to be part of the same cemetery. Within this one burial complex, there is evidence of the older, overtly pagan tradition and of newer, hybridised burial rites among Scandinavian populations in Britain. This would indicate that although Scandinavians were present here, they were not alone but settled amongst Britons with whom they would have had frequent interaction.

Clearly, this northern route is more than just a trade highway used by Scandinavian merchants as the shortest water route between Dublin and York. The Clyde, its northern tributaries, and Loch Lomond were more significant than this, and settlements along the route were probably more frequent than the evidence currently suggests. Another unsatisfactory element of the old trade highway explanation is that this model does not explain the finds farther eastward along the Clyde.

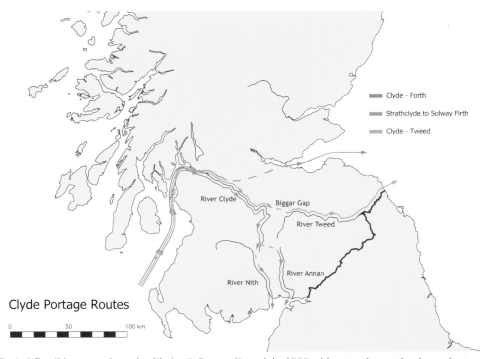

Fig 2. 3 Possible routes from the Clyde (© Crown Copyright 1999 with amendments by the author).

The southern route

Travelling farther inland up the Clyde, several opportunities for portages to other waterways, and thus other destinations, become available. The first option is another route to the east coast, but instead of connecting to the Forth, a portage at the Biggar Gap would lead to the Tweed and a route to the east coast. Along this route, the hogbacks at Govan and the hogback at Dalserf all serve as indicators of Scandinavian presence, and the sword pommel from Abington is conveniently located along the portage point at the Biggar Gap. There is also evidence along the Tweed of Scandinavian communities established there, which would no doubt make the trip from Dublin to York easier and more fruitful for merchants looking to sell their items. Included in that category are the hogbacks from Stobo, Ancrum, Bedrule (2), Nisbet (2), and Lepitlaw (Ritchie 2004: 17–9; Crawford 2005: 16). Several Treasure Trove and Portable Antiquities Scheme finds have also been recovered along the Tweed route, including a strap-end from Cornhill-on-Tweed, Northumberland; a strap-end, lead weight, and silver ingot from Maxton, Scottish Borders; a silver ingot from Sprouston, Scottish Borders; and a stone mould from Newstead, Scottish Borders. The ingot from Sprouston fits into the ingot mould from Newstead perfectly, while on another face is a mould for what is likely to be a Thor's hammer (fig 2.4). There are also the two hoards from this region which further attest to Scandinavian presence along the Tweed. The hoard from Gordon contained a gold finger-ring, a silver arm-ring, two silver ingots, and a silver pin (Graham-Campbell 1995: 102), and the hoard from Jedburgh contained a silver ring and about 100 silver coins (Graham-Campbell 1995: 100).

The final piece of artefactual evidence for Scandinavians along the Tweed is the five coin finds from Jedburgh (Graham-Campbell 1995: 86). The concentration of the hogbacks and artefacts is remarkable in their proximity to the Tweed (fig 2.5). Given all this data, and the

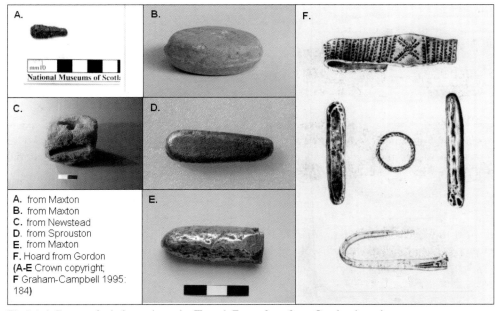

Fig 2.4 A-E: stray finds from along the Tweed; F: artefacts from Gordon hoard.

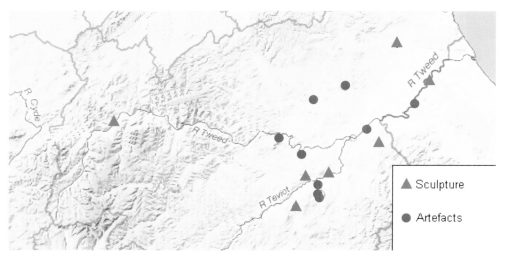

Fig 2.5 Map of artefacts and hogbacks along the Tweed.

attested route via the Biggar Gap from prehistory onwards, the Clyde-Tweed route should be seen as a major, if not primary, river route from west to east coasts in southern Scotland, which would have easily been exploited by sea-faring Scandinavians travelling between the two coasts.

A second possible southern route from the Clyde would take one into the Solway Firth region via the rivers Nith and Annan. This route would incorporate the hogbacks at Govan and Dalserf, as well as a hogback at Annan, and place-names along the Clyde and in Dumfriesshire. This would be a possible inland route to the Solway from the Clyde, but it would seem likely that this route would have been utilised to travel to Cumbria once Strathclyde incorporated it in the tenth century. There is also the sculptural link between the (non-Viking) crosses at Govan, Galloway, and Cumbria (Driscoll et al 2005: 145), which further suggests this waterway provided a means of easy transport between regions.

The Firth of Clyde: meeting place of the mainland and the Isles

Given the demonstrated importance of waterways and the relatively sparse evidence, artefactual and otherwise, from the mainland coast of the Firth of Clyde, it is necessary to look to the isles of the Clyde to understand these finds. In order to contextualise the material from the mouth of the Clyde and Ayrshire coast, it will be analysed in conjunction with the known evidence from Bute, Arran, and the Cumbraes.

From the mouth of the Clyde comes the Port Glasgow hoard, containing two silver arm-rings and silver coins, and the axe from Loch Long. On the Ayrshire coast, there is the Arabic dirhem from Stevenston Sands, the Hunterston brooch, and the ringed-pin from Lochlee crannog. The other known archaeological evidence from the Firth of Clyde consists of two burials from Arran, two isolated finds from Bute, a stone sculpture from Great Cumbrae with Anglo-Scandinavian carvings, a possible hogback from Bute, and several finds from the recent excavation at Inchmarnock. The two burials from Arran were found around Lamlash Bay, one at Millhill and the other at King's Cross Point. The burial from Millhill contained a single-edged sword and a shield boss of Irish Sea type A (convex) (Harrison 2000: 65–8). The burial at King's Cross Point contained a whalebone plaque, a copper styca of Archbishop Wigmund of York (837–54), and a probable wooden chest (Greig 1940: 26–7; Graham-Campbell & Batey 1998: 96). The burial at Millhill has been interpreted as a male burial (Harrison 2000, 65), while the one at King's Cross Point has been interpreted as female (Graham-Campbell & Batey 1998: 96). The two isolated finds from Bute are a sword hilt from Drumachloy Farm (Graham-Campbell & Batey 1998: 97) and a decorated lead weight from Little Dunagoil, topped with a boss from a Scandinavian oval brooch (Graham-Campbell & Batey 1998: 98). The two pieces of stone sculpture include a possible hogback from St Blanes, Kingarth in Bute (Ritchie 2004: 16), and a possible lintel stone from Millport, Great Cumbrae, with Anglo-Scandinavian aspects in its carvings (Batey 1994: 67–9).

The finds from the Inchmarnock excavation (Lowe 2008a) include a rune-inscribed cross slab (Fisher 2008: 100–3); a collection of hnefatafl boards, including three complete ones, two almost-complete ones, and at least seven fragmentary ones (Ritchie 2008: 117–19); an inscribed slate depicting four figures, three of which are mail-clad warriors and one that is not (fig 3.2) (Lowe 2008b: 151–6); a broken polyhedral-headed ringed-pin, missing its ring (Franklin 2008a: 178–9); an arrowhead and spearhead that are 'in keeping with Norse' types (Franklin 2008a: 181–3); a comb with parallels in late-Norse Scottish contexts and thirteenth-century Scandinavian contexts (Franklin 2008b: 186–8); and a rim-sherd of a steatite bowl (Franklin 2008c: 246).

These finds, when combined with those from the study area, give evidence of a small Scandinavian population active in the Firth of Clyde. The two burials found on Arran seem to represent both genders from their grave goods, which indicates that these activities were more than just militaristic. Further, there is evidence of a diverse monastic town at Inchmarnock that may be similar to Whithorn in its 'international' make-up, with a small population of Scandinavians residing in the monastic town. What is particularly striking is the steatite bowl rim-sherd from Inchmarnock, for the only other one like this known from the Irish Sea region is from Whithorn (Nicholson 1997: 464). Another possible similarity to Whithorn would be the proximity to a beach market: in the Firth of Clyde there is the one at Stevenston Sands, represented by the Arabic dirhem, and for Whithorn, there is the beach market at Luce Sands. Further evidence for trade activities in the Firth of Clyde comes from the silver hoard at Port Glasgow, as well as the decorated lead weight from Bute. Finally, the permanence of the Scandinavian population here may be evident in the possible hogback from St Blanes, Bute, and the lintel stone with Anglo-Scandinavian aspects from Millport, Great Cumbrae. This sculptural tradition is in keeping with the idea that there were links between the Firth of Clyde and the Solway Firth region.

Discussion

When combined, the evidence of artefacts, sculpture, place-names, and the histories helps contextualise the Scandinavians' activities in Strathclyde. However, it is clear that the situation in Strathclyde is different from those in other areas of Scandinavian settlement in Scotland. Whereas the Northern and Western Isles were removed from known power centres of early medieval Scotland, Strathclyde (or more properly, the Kingdom of Dumbarton) was the heart of the northern British kingdom. The Scandinavians who were active in Strathclyde left a different mark upon it than those who were active elsewhere. Before discussing the interactions and identities of the inhabitants of Strathclyde during the Viking Age, it is first crucial to understand the Scandinavians' place within the British kingdom.

The Scandinavian element to the Kingdom of Strathclyde

The cemetery at Midross is of great significance when discussing the Scandinavians within Strathclyde. Here, finally, is evidence of a settled population that has chosen to bury their dead in a way reminiscent of Viking traditions. The close proximity to the burial at Boiden further strengthens this connection, as do the pierced Anglo-Saxon coin and the whetstone made of Norwegian schist. This settled population of Scandinavians also helps explain the finds in the region, from the hoard at Port Glasgow to the dress items and weapons found throughout Strathclyde, and it is clear that Scandinavians were active throughout this region and not isolated to one locale. More importantly, there is more evidence supporting local Scandinavian populations throughout Strathclyde, and explanations for the hogback stones no longer have to rely upon the historical references to the grandsons of Ívarr.

In regards to the importance of the five hogbacks at Govan, most explanations have sought to demonstrate an elite settlement or takeover of the British kingdom by the Dublin Norse (eg Crawford 2005). There is, however, an alternative, minimalist explanation to these hogbacks: Clarkson (2010: 164) argues that the hogbacks at Govan need not represent anything more than an artist's awareness and incorporation of Viking and Scandinavian styles and motifs into his catalogue of artistic influences, possibly with the arrival of 'friendly Hebridean Vikings'. However, this explanation is problematic as the 'Hebridean Vikings', 'Dublin Norse', and 'York Scandinavians' were not interchangeable, while hogbacks do not occur in the Hebrides and only one is known in Ireland at Castledermot, Co. Kildare (Abrams 2010: 3). They have been repeatedly demonstrated to originate in the York area. Thus, the best explanation for the hogbacks in Strathclyde is not an artistic adoption from Hebridean Vikings, but the result of a local population of Scandinavians who were familiar with, and perhaps brought with them, the carving traditions in York and northern England.

Although there are definite connections between the hogbacks of Strathclyde and those in northern England, the traditions are different. In England, as can be seen at various ecclesiastical sites in Cumbria and Lancashire, hogbacks occur alongside other monuments that sometimes display some aspect of Viking or Scandinavian culture, either through artistic styles or scenes from Old Norse religious tales. In Strathclyde, these monuments are not accompanied by other Viking-style sculptures. Indeed, although there is a great amount of contemporary sculpture from Govan, none of the pieces displays any aspect of Scandinavian influence (Driscoll et al 2005: 145). Therefore, there must be a specific reason and meaning behind these hogbacks in Strathclyde, a meaning that has been forged in a different context than that of northern England. Looking at the three sites at which the hogbacks are found, Govan, Luss, and Dalserf, each site has an apparent early dedication to a local saint. At Govan, it is dedicated to St Constantine, at Luss, to St Kessog, and at Dalserf, to St Serf. Could these hogbacks be one way in which the Scandinavian community chose to demonstrate their acknowledgement of the religion and customs of their new lands?

There is no evidence of an elite Scandinavian group supplanting local elites in this region. The –byr place-names of the Strathclyde region indicate probable Scandinavian settlement within the region at certain farms, but this settlement was probably sanctioned by a local lord and not in place of him (Taylor 2004: 135). However, it is probable that these names indicate settlement during the late ninth and tenth centuries (Fellows-Jensen 1990: 55; Taylor 2004: 138), about the same time as Scandinavian settlement occurred in areas of northern England. This aligns well with the historical record, as settlement before the sack of Alt Clut would be highly unlikely. It is probable that the military campaign opened up Strathclyde to the possibility of settlement by Scandinavians.

The siege of Alt Clut, attested historically and demonstrated by the pommel found in the ramparts, was the major military interaction of the ninth century. It established the Dublin Norse as the enemies of the Britons, and the subsequent destroyers of Alt Clut. However, this was not the only type of military interaction between Scandinavians and Britons in Strathclyde. In the tenth century, the northern alliance against Æthelstan at the battle of Brunanburh saw a united fighting force of Scandinavians and Britons (as well as Albans). This would have been a significant interaction between these two peoples, and, although there may be little material evidence for the interactions, surely the mindset between the two groups was significantly altered. The new role of Scandinavians as ally instead of foe could have been the instigator that allowed peaceful settlement of Scandinavians in Strathclyde and the beginnings of integrations between Scandinavians and locals that are demonstrated by the placements of the hogbacks at local ecclesiastical sites. This peaceful interaction can also be seen at the tenth-century cemetery at Midross, where people were buried alongside each other by two different burial customs.

It is likely that the most frequent interaction between Scandinavians and locals in Strathclyde was through trade. The importance and significance of the waterways for trade routes between the Western Isles, the Irish Sea, and the east coast are clearly the primary reason for Scandinavian activity within Strathclyde. Local trading at certain places along the routes probably occurred, especially if there were settled Scandinavian populations there. This can be seen in the weights from Alt Clut, the coins from the Port Glasgow hoard, and the Arabic dirhem from Stevenston Sands. At the other end of the trade route, in the Tweed valley, more items of trade, such as the ingots from Sprouston and Maxton, and the lead weight from Maxton, demonstrate the trading activities on that end of the route as well.

The evidence for Scandinavian settlement within Strathclyde is demonstrated by the cemetery at Midross and the hogback sculptures. Both point to a colonisation of sorts, but rather than dominating the locals, in Strathclyde the settlers were most likely subjects to a local overlord. Clearly there was a section of the Scandinavian settlers who held enough wealth and influence to commission the hogback monuments at the important ecclesiastical and royal site at Govan, but the lack of any other Viking or Scandinavian elements to the carvings there indicates that they were only one part of the elite patrons of Govan. The multiple types of burial practices at Midross demonstrate the Scandinavians' integration with the local communities, rather than remaining separate from them. This would imply that there was not the same volume of Viking settlers in Strathclyde as in other parts of Britain, and to survive and live, they needed to integrate with the local British communities. Finally, the place-names give no indication of an elite take-over as do those in the Northern or Western Isles, but rather, they again point to small pockets of Scandinavian speakers within a mainly local, British-speaking landscape. The lack of topographical names in Strathclyde also indicates that this settlement probably occurred later than the settlements in the Northern or Western Isles, which again would support the prospect of a tenth-century date for Scandinavian settlement within Strathclyde.

Manufactured identities

Within these three contexts of contact and interaction, identity formation would have constantly occurred among both the Britons and Scandinavians. In the case of military encounters, there are two very different instances of contact and interaction that would have led to very different identities being formed. In the first instance, the siege of Alt Clut, the interactions were aggressive and non-peaceful; neither group had incentive to understand or communicate to significant degrees with the other group. Therefore, identities formed during this siege were likely to reinforce the ethnic distinctions between the two groups: Britons would have displayed a more British identity, and the Scandinavians would have displayed a more Scandinavian or Viking identity, rather than incorporating any aspects of the other group. In the second instance, the battle of Brunanburh, the Britons allied themselves with the Scandinavians against a common enemy of Æthelstan of Wessex. In this context, the two groups may not have had the incentive to differentiate themselves from each other as much as from the army of Æthelstan. Any identity formation in this campaign would probably emphasise the non-Englishness of the warriors, rather than overt attempts to reconcile the differences between Briton and Scandinavian. However, as allies, it is probable that practices and perhaps material culture would have been witnessed and exchanged on a daily basis, and, although a conscious reconstruction of identity to accommodate new practices and materials would not have ensued, an unconscious reworking of one's identity likely would have occurred. A better understanding of each others' culture and practices would have laid the foundations for more peaceful means of interaction between Scandinavians and Britons, such as trade and settlement.

During interactions of trade, identities that allowed the participants to engage advantageously were likely to have been constructed. This may have been displayed by certain items of dress a Scandinavian trader would have worn on his or her person to identify him- or herself as friendly trader and not aggressor. For instance, the ringed-pin found at Lochlee crannog could be seen as such an item, signalling the trader's origins in Viking Dublin and carrying similar items to exchange. Within local populations, identities may not have been so overtly constructed, but by choosing to trade with a Scandinavian, a Briton would have reconstructed his identity to acknowledge the Scandinavian as an ally rather than a threat. This identity formation would have been subtle, and perhaps not even displayed visibly; however, the new identity would have enabled the Briton to be more welcoming of Scandinavians as settlers.

In the settlement situations is where most evidence is found of a Third Space being created by Scandinavians and the Britons they settled amongst. The hybridisation of practice that resulted from such Third Space creation can be seen in two pieces of evidence from this case study: the runic inscription on the Hunterston brooch, and the cemetery at Midross. On the Hunterston brooch, the hybridisation of practice in one or two individuals is evident, for an Irish name is inscribed in Norse runes. Whether it was Melbrigda who inscribed the runes or a Norse speaker who presented the brooch to Melbrigda, the incorporation of two different language practices is seen in this one piece. The identity of Melbrigda would have been shaped by connections, possibly familial, with both Irish/Gaelic and Norse speaking communities, in which not only words but presumably materials, practices, and ideas were also exchanged. This identity would no longer have been Irish/Gaelic or Norse, but a hybridisation of the two, created in the Third Space in order to negotiate it.

Hybridisation of practice is seen more clearly in the cemetery at Midross. Here, there is a mixture of burial practices evident in a contemporary period of time: there is the overtly Viking warrior burial from Boiden, the six furnished graves with items that identify their owners as Scandinavians, and the remaining nine unfurnished contemporary graves. It is probable that the unfurnished graves, given their orientation, represent Christian burial rites, and the Boiden burial represents the pagan burial rite. However, the six furnished graves that are placed in and amongst the nine unfurnished ones represent this Third Space formed from the two traditions meeting each other. While it cannot be established whether the inhabitants of the furnished graves, or those who buried them, were pagan or Christian, this is clear evidence that the community was aware of both burial traditions and purposely chose a new burial rite to commemorate the dead here. The creation of a new burial rite signals the creation of a new identity, based not solely on one aspect, such as ethnicity or religion, but one that incorporates aspects, practices, and beliefs important to both ethnicities and religions. Therefore, this community at Midross was no longer 'Scandinavian' and 'Briton', but a new community with roots in each tradition which saw itself as a unified group.

Conclusions

It is clear that Strathclyde was crucial to Scandinavian activities throughout the British Isles. Although it may never have been under control of the Scandinavians, there was clearly enough Scandinavian presence in this region to allow merchants to travel through and settlers to establish themselves here. The 'cultural highway' that the Clyde became during the Viking Age was of course not limited solely to Scandinavian traffic, for it would have enabled travel of Britons, Northumbrians, Scots, and Albans to other parts of northern Britain. It was a highway that enabled contact and interaction between peoples of different ethnic backgrounds, languages, religions, and daily practices, which in turn resulted in new identities formed by these people. It is during this period of multicultural interaction that the histories switch from narrating the stories of ethnically-determined political units to geographically-determined political units, and it is likely that these new identities were a large part of that process.

Acknowledgements

My thanks to Dr Colleen Batey, who read and commented on early drafts of this article, and to the delegates at the 2010 meeting of the Scottish Society for Northern Studies, whose comments and questions helped the ideas contained in this article take solid form. Thank you also to Stuart Campbell at Treasure Trove Scotland who provided information and images for several of the items discussed here, and to Gavin MacGregor and Colleen Batey, who allowed me access to early versions of the forthcoming report on the Midross Cemetery. This paper was written before the new work on the place-names of Bute became available (Gilbert Márkus, Chapter 1 above).

References

Abrams, L 2010 'Conversion and the Church in Viking-Age Ireland', in Sheehan, J & O Corrain, D (eds) 2010 *The Viking Age: Ireland and the West. Papers from the Proceedings of the Fifteenth Viking Congress, Cork, 18-27 August 2005*, 1-10. Dublin: Four Courts Press.

Alcock, L & Alcock, E A 1990 'Reconnaissance excavations on Early Historic fortifications and other royal sites in Scotland, 1974-84: 4, Excavations at Alt Clut, Clyde Rock, Strathclyde, 1974–75', *Proc Soc Antiq Scot* 120, 95–149.

A-S Chron Anglo-Saxon Chronicle, ed and transl by M Swanton, 2000. London: Phoenix.

Annal Camb Annales Cambriae A.D. 682–954: texts A–C in Parallel, ed & trans D N Dumville, 2002. Cambridge: University of Cambridge, Department of Anglo-Saxon, Norse and Celtic.

Annals of Ulster (to AD 1131), ed by S MacAirt & G MacNiocall, 1983. Dublin: Dublin Institute for Advance Studies.

Batey, C E 1994 'The sculptured stones in Glasgow Museums', in Ritchie (ed), 63–72.

Becket, A, MacGregor, G, Maguire, D & Sneddon, D forthcoming *Life and death on the Bonnie Banks: Ten thousand years at the Carrick Midross, Loch Lomond*. Edinburgh: Society of Antiquaries of Scotland.

Bhabha, H 2004 *The location of culture*. London: Routledge.

Bremner, R L 1904 'Some notes on the Norsemen in Argyllshire and on the Clyde', *Saga-Book* III, 338–80.

Broun, D 2004 'The Welsh identity of the kingdom of Strathclyde, ca.900 – ca.1200', *Innes Review* 55, 111–80.

Clarkson, T 2010 *The men of the north: the Britons of southern Scotland*. Edinburgh: John Donald.

Crawford, B E 1987 *Scandinavian Scotland*. Leicester: Leicester University Press.

Crawford, B E 2005 *The Govan hogbacks and the multi-cultural society of tenth-century Scotland*. Glasgow: Friends of Govan Old.

Chron Camb Annales Cambriae.

Chron Alba Chronicle of the Kings of Alba. Ed and transl by B Hudson, in Hudson, B T 1998 'The Scottish Chronicle', *The Scottish Historical Review* 77, 129–61.

Daglish, C & Driscoll, S T 2009 *Historic Govan: archaeology and development*. Edinburgh: Historic Scotland.

Dennison, E P 2007 'A Tale of Two Towns', in Baxter, N (ed) *A Tale of Two Towns: A History of Medieval Glasgow*, 46-55. Glasgow: Neil Baxter Associates, on behalf of Glasgow City Council.

Driscoll, S T, Forsyth, K & O'Grady, O 2005 'The Govan School revisited: Searching for meaning in the early medieval sculpture of Strathclyde', in Foster, S & Cross, M (eds), *Able minds and practiced hands*, 135–58. Dublin: Four Courts Press.

Fellows-Jensen, G 1990 'Scandinavians in Southern Scotland?', Nomina 4, 41–59.

Fisher, I 2008 'Early medieval sculpture', in Lowe, 101–14.

Franklin, J 2008a 'Metalwork', in Lowe 2008a, 178–5.

Franklin, J 2008b 'Bone and antler', in Lowe 2008a, 187–9.

Franklin, J 2008c 'The artefacts from site 8', in Lowe 2008a, 246–8.

Graham-Campbell, J 1995 *The Viking-Age gold and silver of Scotland (AD 850-1100)*. Edinburgh: National Museums of Scotland.

Graham-Campbell, J & Batey, C E 1998 *Vikings in Scotland: An archaeological survey*. Edinburgh: Edinburgh University Press.

Grant, A 2005 'The origin of the Ayrshire -by names', in Gammeltoft, P, Hough, C & Waugh, D (eds) 2005 *Cultural contacts in the North Atlantic region: The evidence of names*, 127–40. Lerwick: NORNA.

Grieg, S 1940 *Viking antiquities in Scotland. Viking Antiquities II*. Oslo: Aschehoug.

Harrison, S H 2000 'The Millhill Burial in Context: Artifact, culture, and chronology in the "Viking West"', *Acta Archaeologica* 71, 65–78.

Lang, J T 1975 'Hogback monuments in Scotland', *Proc Soc Antiq Scot* 105, 206–35.

Lang, J T 1994 'The hogback monuments: a re-appraisal', in Ritchie (ed), 123–33.

Lowe, C E 2008a *Inchmarnock: an early historic island monastery and its archaeological landscape*. Edinburgh: Society of Antiquaries of Scotland.

Lowe, C E 2008b 'Non-text inscribed slates', in Lowe 2008a, 151–78.

Munro, R, Rolleston, G, Balfour, I B & Borland, J 1879 'Notice of the excavation of a crannog at Lochlee, Tarbolton, Ayrshire', *Proc Soc Antiq Scot* 13, 177–241.

Nicholson, A 1997 'The stone artefacts', in Hill, P H (ed) 1997 *Whithorn and St Ninian: The excavation of a monastic town*, 447–64. Stroud: Sutton.

O Floinn, R 1989 'Secular metalwork in the eighth and ninth centuries', in Youngs, S (ed) *The Work of Angels': Masterpieces of Celtic Metalwork 6th-9th centuries AD*, 72–124. London: British Museum Publications.

Olsen, M 1954 'Runic inscriptions in Great Britain, Ireland and the Isle of Man', in Shetelig, H (ed) *Viking Antiquities in Great Britain and Ireland VI: Civilization of the Viking settlers in relation to their old and new countries*, 151–234. Oslo: Aschehoug.

Ritchie, A 2004 *Hogback gravestones at Govan and beyond*. Glasgow: Friends of Govan Old.

Ritchie, A 2008 'Gaming boards', in Lowe 2008a, 116–28.

Ritchie, A (ed) 1994 *Govan and its Early Medieval sculpture*. Stroud: Alan Sutton Publishing Ltd.

Smyth, A P 1984 *Warlords and holy men: Scotland AD 80-1000*. London: Edward Arnold.

Stevenson, R B K 1974 'The Hunterston Brooch and its significance', *Medieval Archaeology* 18, 16–42.

Stewart, H J 1854 'Notice of the discovery of some ancient arms and armour, near Glenfruin, on the estate of Sir James Colquhoun of Luss, Baronet', *Proc Soc Antiq Scot* 1, 142–5.

Taylor, S 2004 'Scandinavians in Central Scotland: bý- placenames and their context', in Williams, G & Bibire, P (eds) 2004 *Sagas, Saints, and Settlements*, 125–45. Leiden: Brill.

Chapter 3

The Norse in the west with particular reference to Bute

Barbara Crawford

University of St Andrews

THIS broad-based study will cover the period when the islands off Scotland's west coast came under Norse control, after the settlement of Vikings in the Hebrides in the ninth century and up to the fading of Norwegian power which ended with the Treaty of Perth in 1266.[1] The southern Hebrides were ruled from the Isle of Man for some of this time, and the islanders also lay under the remoter authority of the kings of Norway (from the end of the eleventh century) and the archbishops of Trondheim (from 1152/3).[2] I want to stress the importance of the wider political and cultural networks as far as the Norse impact is concerned, which can help to give a context for the cultural and linguistic influence.

First of all we start off with the sea route by which the invaders from Scandinavia arrived off the coasts of north Britain. This was a sea route of immense significance in the history of the Viking raiding and trading world; from Norway to Shetland and Orkney, and then down the west coast of Scotland to the Irish Sea and Dublin. Later it extended north-west to Faeroe and Iceland.

The Hebridean world was a very important part of this sea route. After these islands had been settled and over-run in the late eighth and ninth centuries, a Norse-Gaelic network was established which stretched from Lewis, to Iona, Islay and Kintyre (and Bute). Indeed this area has been designated part of the 'Insular Viking zone' comprising primarily Ireland, Wales and the Isle of Man, but also including the Scottish Western Isles (Etchingham 2001: 145). Bute, along with the other Clyde islands, is not directly on this sea route but is part of another maritime zone more closely associated with the inner coastal waters of the Clyde estuary. Indeed those who controlled Bute commanded the Clyde and thus the western gateway to the heart of the Scottish kingdom (MacDonald 1997: 111) and to the Clyde-Forth route (which was an important means of crossing from the west coast to eastern Scotland, see Crawford 1987: 26, 51).

This 'insular Viking zone' was a complex maritime world where the Norsemen met Celtic culture and became absorbed in political and military struggles for supremacy, adding their own North Sea and Scandinavian element to this ethnic hotch-potch. The name for this mixed breed used in contemporary Irish sources is 'Gall-Gaedhil', the 'foreign Gael' (foreign that is to the Irish). The recent enlightening and important study by Thomas Clancy (2008) argues that Bute was the Gall-Gaedhil heartland.

The historical evidence for what was happening is fragmentary with generalised statements like that by Prudentius of Troyes who wrote under the year 847 'the [Irish] Scots, after being attacked by the Northmen for very many years, were rendered tributary; and [the Northmen] took possession, without resistance, of the islands that lie all around, and dwelt there' (Anderson 1922, I: 277). The Irish, Welsh and Icelandic sources are difficult to interpret and even more difficult to reconcile. The Hebridean element is the sparsest, for there is little or no documentary evidence actually emanating from the Hebrides until the Chronicle of Man starts to record the doings of the kings of Man in the late eleventh century. Until then our knowledge of the situation in the islands is drawn from the sagas about the earls of Orkney, and the Irish or Welsh annals about the Celto-Norse dynasties which dominated Ireland, most importantly Dublin, and the Isles. These sources tell us about the deeds of the earls and the rulers of the Irish kingdoms, as well as church events. And it is an entry about St Blane in the Martyrology of Tallaght, calling him 'bishop of Kingarth in Gall-Gaedhil' which has been one of the foundation stones on which Thomas Clancy has built his argument that Bute was central to the Gall-Gaedhil area.

In some ways this insular world had a maritime unity, which despite the great distance from north Lewis to the southern tip of Kintyre was quickly accessible to people with effective shipping. But in other respects it was easily divided between widely-differing zones of influence, so that the north Hebrides had more in common with north Scotland and the Northern Isles, while the south Hebrides were, and historically had been, a part of Argyll and the kingdom of Dál Riada, and very open to influence from Ireland. The impact of the Vikings throughout this maritime zone must have been severe, and is now more fully recognised as being a very important phase of the history of the area. The impact was severe because the area was vulnerable to attack by mobile crews of warriors who were also very efficient sailors of ships. The few historical records we have provide enough evidence to show that the attack was directed against the monastic communities which lived in these islands, and which were totally defenceless against those who wished to exploit them for their own enrichment (Dumville 1997). The images of slave-raiding, both early medieval and modern, may not be far from the truth of the matter (figs 3.1 & 3.2). For the Vikings these coasts, peninsulas and islands were ideal pirate lairs, and individual leaders of boatloads of Norwegian raiders would have found a familiar maritime landscape which they could take over and exploit and which provided them with security and status.

In the absence of historical evidence place-names are a very important source of information about the scale, scope, and depth of impact of Norse settlement all over the British Isles. The Norse place-names in the islands and coasts of the Clyde estuary probably resulted from settlement which took place after the fall of Dumbarton Rock to the 'two kings of the Northmen', Olaf and Ivarr, in AD 870. The Annals of Ulster also record that 'a very great spoil of people – of English, and Britons and Picts' was brought in two hundred ships to Ireland in captivity (Anderson 1922, I: 301, 302–3). This important victory gave control of this waterway and the lower reaches of the Clyde, as well as access into the heart of Scotland, to the Viking rulers of Dublin. As regards the importance of the scatter of Norwegian place-names in the islands and peninsulas of the outer waters of the Clyde we now have some recognition that these names are highly significant thanks to the pioneering work of Andrew Jennings and Arne Kruse (Jennings 1996; 2004; Kruse 2004)

Fig 3.1 An evocation of a Viking raid on the monastery of Tavistock in Devon by Lorenz Frølich (©
The Museum of National History, Frederiksborg Castle, Denmark)

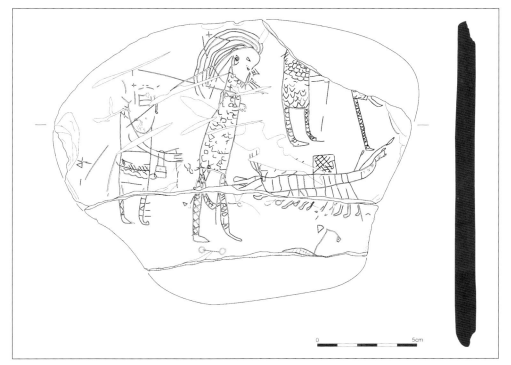

Fig 3.2 A contemporary image of a possible hostage-taking on a slate from the monastic site of
Inchmarnock (© Christopher Lowe and Headland Archaeology Ltd).

Because these names were mostly topographical (relating to landscape features) and not habitative (identifying farm settlements) they were therefore spurned as evidence of permanent settlement. I argued otherwise long ago (Crawford 1987: 111; 1995: 6–13) and the detailed study of the geographical circumstances of such names which has now been undertaken, particularly those ending in 'dale' (*dalr*) in the inner Hebrides (Jennings 2004; Kruse 2004), is beginning to show how important the Viking settlement was in areas like Bute, although not creating settlements as permanently Norse as further north.[3]

Langal at the south end near Kingarth is the same as Langal/Langwell names elsewhere in north Scotland (Crawford 2004; Crawford & Taylor 2003). It derives from ON *lang-völlr* = 'long field or level plain' (which appears to describe the area very well). Langal in Bute was originally a large estate of 12 merks (Markus forthcoming), and subsequently divided, as the two Langal farms today have Gaelic suffixes. This is what might be called a topographical name because it is only telling us that a field was the main feature of the Norse settlement, which is not usually considered to be a habitative name (that is a farm-name). But it is being used as a farm-name in this area where the *bolstaðr*, *-staðr* and *-setr* names appear not to have been coined (just as Langwell names are found in parts of north Scotland where habitative names are sparse). For some reason this *völlr* element replaced the normal habitative place-names. Thus Langal, and other *völlr* names, tell us of permanent Norse settlement.

The proper ON habitative names were never given or never remained permanently imprinted in the toponymic landscape because the spread of Gaelic meant that the giving of Norse names was cut short, and thus the full possible range never developed. The Gaelic language survived more fully or was revived earlier in the southern Hebrides than in the Western Isles, which probably explains the arrested nature of Norse habitative names (Macniven 2008, 31–2). The strong Scottish influences following on from political changes after 1266 are probably responsible for the disappearance of many Norse names. But there is a still-surviving stratum of Old Norse topographical names in Bute which can be used to provide evidence of the establishment of Norse speakers and land-owners.

Turning now to archaeological evidence, which is material evidence for the actual presence of Vikings, we have even sparser sources of information, particularly noticeable in the absence of pagan graves. Some of the Norse graves in the Hebrides provide evidence of a rich warrior elite, and from islands close to Bute, as for example from Arran. The graves on the islands of the southern Hebrides, like Colonsay and Oronsay, Islay and Eigg, supply material evidence of the final resting-places of Norse settlers, men and women, who had taken possession of these islands: islands which are strategically located for control of the sea routes between the north Hebrides and the Irish Sea, and which provided them with ideal settlement locations for their lifestyles in the early Viking age.

No recognised pagan grave survives from Bute, but the Drumachloy sword-hilt is probably from a Norse grave.[4] It is unusual for a sword hilt of that quality to be found in a context other than in association with a pagan grave.[5]

There is the problem of the excavated site of Little Dunagoil. It is not possible to say that the 'long-houses' on that site are anything earlier than medieval, although the bronze-capped lead weight which was found relates to other known sets of Viking lead weights such as those preserved from the famous Kiloran Bay burial in Colonsay. Its ornamental mount is said to consist of an openwork boss of a Scandinavian oval brooch of late ninth or early tenth century date (Graham-Campbell & Batey 1998: 98) and is therefore undoubtedly Viking. Had this object simply survived and been re-used at a later date?

Although not from Bute itself the rune-stone from nearby Inchmarnock is a very remarkable Norse artefact (Fisher 2001: 79) (fig 4.2). It is one of only three from western Scotland (there are far more from the Northern Isles). All three in west Scotland are Christian memorials, and two of them use the word *kross* rather than *stein* (as is more usual in the north). It is probably testimony to stronger Celtic Christian influence.

Saga evidence is very definitely not material evidence and in fact is very uncertain historical evidence. Most sagas are literary sources written down in Iceland in the thirteenth/ fourteenth centuries and record what had been handed down as tradition about the Viking Age and the heroic deeds of their forebears. This had happened many centuries earlier, and in transmission there is no doubt that a lot of erroneous and fabulous information had accreted around the stories. However these stories tell us that places were remembered where events had taken place much earlier throughout the Viking world. One of the more fabulous sagas, *Grettir's Saga*, tells of an incident when one band of Norsemen got into a fight with some Vikings 'who lay up in winter in the Barra Isles' and the sea battle took place in narrow straits off Bute (Anderson 1922, I: 326).

> Two Vikings-Vigbiod and Vestmar were raiding in the Hebrides and plundering in Scotland's firths.
>
> Thrond and Onund went to oppose them and learned that they had sailed in to the island which is called Bute. They took five ships and Onund put them between two cliffs; there was a great channel there which was deep, and ships could sail one way only, and not more than five at a time. Onund made the five ships go forward into the strait in such a manner that they could immediately let themselves drift, with hanging oars, when they wished, because there was much sea-room behind them. There was also a certain island on one side, under it he made one ship lie and they carried many stones to the edge of the cliff, where they could not be seen from the ships.
>
> (*Grettir's Saga* chap 4. Adapted from Anderson 1922, I: 326).

Now this must be recording some memory of the narrow sea passage through the Kyles (fig 4.1). Why would Bute be mentioned unless it were a familiar name to the Icelandic saga tellers? That is not to say that they would know where it was but the topographical circumstances of ships being constrained by the tide in narrow straits must be telling us that Bute was known to be a part of the Norsemen's world and the maritime circumstances of this fight were remembered. Or the situation was considered to be a good place to locate your story of a sea battle.

This evidence may be thin and scattered and unimpressive on its own but when all is added up – the archaeology, the place-names, the runestone and the saga reference – it suggests that Bute was very much part of the Viking world, even if that world became rapidly Gaelicised in the tenth century. It had its place, and an important place, in the inner Hebrides insular society of mixed Gaelic-Norse ethnicity and cultural identity.

The tenth century

The tenth century started with the expulsion of the Norse from Dublin (in 902), an event thought to be particularly important for the strengthening of Hiberno-Norse settlement in north-west England where many of the expelled probably fled to and also to the Clyde islands. We then move from a period when individuals and their followings seized and dominated islands in what must have been an initial inchoate phase, to the growth of larger dynastic groupings with leaders who bear the title of 'lord' or 'king' of the Isles. The first individual given the title *rí Innse Gall* ('king of the Isles of Foreigners' i.e. the Hebrides) appears in the Irish and Welsh sources in the late tenth century. Godfrey/Gothfrith Haraldsson (Gofraid Mac Arallt) 'whose sphere of influence seems to have encompassed Man and the Isles' (McDonald 1997: 31) is recorded as ravaging Anglesey and Dyfed in the 970s and 980s. He probably shared power over the Hebrides with his brother Maccus, who is called 'king of many islands' when he joined with other rulers from the north to meet with the Anglo-Saxon King Edgar at Chester in 972 (*A-S Chron* 'E'). Who these Haraldssons where and where they came from does not concern us especially, but their evident links with Ireland are possibly significant (Hudson 2005). In 974 one of them raided Scattery Island in the Shannon and carried off into captivity Ivarr, king of Limerick (Etchingham 2001: 172 and refs there cited), which suggests that the Haraldssons may have had connections with Limerick and that their father may have been the Haraldr, king of Limerick who died in 940, apparently a son of Sigtrygg, grandson of Ívarr who had restored Viking control of Dublin in 917. These are all scions of the *Uí Ímair* (sons of Ivarr) dynasty which had founded Dublin in the mid-ninth century and ruled the whole of the Irish Sea region and Argyll, dominating the sea lanes through the Hebrides (Downham 2007). Individual members of this dynasty sometimes had complete authority throughout the area, which in the tenth century included northern England and the city of York; but more usually the different insular parts would be ruled by a 'brood' of 'cousinly princes' who squabbled among themselves for the overkingship, with a 'natural tendency to fission' (Woolf 2004: 96). If Godfrey and Maccus Haraldsson were indeed as intimately bound in with the most powerful Norse dynasties in Ireland as this theory suggests (making them nephews of Olaf Cuaran, king of Dublin), then their period of dominance as kings of the Isles would have drawn the Hebrides into the Irish Sea world.

If we turn to the material evidence of silver hoards from this period found throughout the Northern and Western Isles this reveals the sort of wealth that could be amassed at this time by the Norse settler communities (silver hoards of brooches, coins and hacksilver are indisputably associated with the economic activity of Norse raiders and traders). The Inner Hebrides and Orkney have the greatest number of hoards but all pale into insignificance compared with the remarkable number of hoards from the Isle of Man. In the Clyde estuary the hoard found in Port Glasgow dates to about 975 (Graham-Campbell 1976: 125). There is also the Plan Farm hoard from Bute which is a very interesting hoard indeed even although it is not strictly a Viking hoard.[6] The reason why it is not included as a Viking hoard is because of the coins of David 1 which are included in it and which tell us therefore that it was deposited about AD 1150. So it seems not to have much to do with the Viking Age but to stem from a later time when coined silver was the main means of exchange. However, it included gold finger rings (fig 3.3) and a silver ingot, which are of tenth- or eleventh-century date and which are more 'Viking' in character. Thus it is a very unusual deposition

Fig 3.3 Gold finger rings from St Blane's
Bute (from Graham-Campbell 1995, pl 73).

of twelfth-century date which included some older items dating probably from the late tenth or eleventh centuries. What were these items doing still circulating in a later, non-Norse and medieval world? Clearly they still had value.

Hogback stones are a sculptural form of grave monument which occurs in parts of Scandinavian Scotland, and which is recognised as a result of some form of Scandinavian influence (Crawford 1987; 1994; 2005; Ritchie 2004). They are considered to be evidence of a style of burial monument developed by settlers of Scandinavian origin in northern England and in southern and eastern Scotland in the late tenth and eleventh centuries (Lang 1974). Distribution maps of hogback stones do not include examples from Bute but there are two possible examples of a variant form of the hogback stone. That at Ardnahoe is now built into a wall at the farm as part of the wall coping. It is difficult to tell exactly what this remarkable triangular-shaped stone may once have been. It is 4 to 5 feet long of rough ?sandstone without any surviving carving or tegulation. One end is rough and appears to be broken. The other end has a slight swelling which may have once been some carved feature but this needs expert investigation. There is no evidence of any curving on the ridge. It may well have been a grave cover, and the triangular shape suggests that it could be identified as an example of the 'kindred coped monument'. Similarly we have the very fine coped stone at Kingarth (Ritchie 1994: 16 n5, ill 9). These are not true hogback stone grave covers but monuments which hint at some distant descent from those earlier remarkable house-shaped graves of the dead.

Orcadian domination

The Iona silver hoard dated to around 986 coincides with the report of an attack on the monastic community at Christmas time in the Irish Annals, and there is further evidence of much disruption in the Irish Sea zone in the later tenth century. It is likely that there was a challenge to the Haraldssons and that their control in the islands became insecure, perhaps due to the extension of the earl of Orkney's influence in the area (Etchingham 2001: 179). Godfrey Haraldsson was killed in Dál Riata in 989 (Annals of Ulster) and, although the evidence is circumstantial, it is generally thought that Earl Sigurd Hlodversson of Orkney, one of the most powerful of the northern earls, appears to have expanded his authority southwards over the Hebrides and filled the vacuum (Crawford 1987: 66–7; Hudson 2005: 75).

The territorial assessment units called ouncelands/pennylands were imposed on the Hebrides while they lay under the authority of the Earls of Orkney, probably in the late tenth century under Sigurd the Stout. Bute is included in the area where pennylands are known, because there is place-name evidence from the farm-name peinn leighinn (contracted to 'Leni' in Lenihal and Lenihuline) meaning half pennyland. There were 18 pennylands in the Hebridean ounceland, and it is likely that Bute was valued at 2 ouncelands (Denis Rixson pers comm).

Orkney overlordship extended over the Hebrides until the aftermath of the death of Earl Thorfinn in the mid-1060s. Then we are told that in the places he had conquered 'people broke away and looked for protection from those who held the lands by birthright' (*Orkneyinga Saga*, chap 32). The effects of such change in lordship are however not easy to estimate. There is no doubting that there was a pull between the Celtic and the Norse worlds and that the Hebrides were on a cusp between these two worlds. In the hierarchy of settlement and power, we move between the individual farmers settled on the land, local chieftains such as jarl Gilli, the more powerful overlords to whom such local chieftains had to submit (like the kings of Man and the Isles or the earls of Orkney), and at the top of the pile the national rulers, seeking to extend a kingdom's authority out to its natural frontiers, territorial or maritime. In this category we have primarily the Norwegian rulers to consider, for the Irish kingdoms were too fragmented to extend power to the islands, even though the rulers of Dublin were eager to exercise their authority over Man and the Isles (McDonald 1997: 32). The Scottish kings were not yet powerful enough within their heartlands to think, or care, about the maritime world in the west.

The eleventh century: Danish and Norwegian ambitions

The kings of Norway were able and willing to consider the settlements in the west as integral parts of their kingdom when they were strong enough to leave their own territory and embark on expeditions west to enforce their authority and demand submission. This happened once they had unified the disparate parts of the *norðr weg* (Norway) and eastern provinces under their authority in the late tenth and early eleventh centuries. The next phase of Norwegian royal ambition to have an effect, and a powerful one, on the Hebrides was at the very end of the eleventh century. In 1098 King Magnus Olafsson *berfœttr* ('Barelegs') launched two expeditions aiming to reassert Norwegian authority over the Northern and the Western Isles, and to use the Isle of Man as a base for controlling the lands around the Irish Sea (Power 1986: 107–32). The king's skald, Bjorn Cripplehand, left graphic descriptions of the destruction then wrought throughout the Hebrides, including Kintyre, which is incorporated into King Magnus' own saga, as written by Snorri Sturlason (*Heimskringla*, *The saga of Magnus Barefoot*, chap 9, 10). Bute is not mentioned in these verses and probably escaped attack for Magnus was intent on controlling the Irish Sea world, including north Wales and Northern Ireland.

Magnus was also interested in forcing the issue over the exact boundary between his overlordship and that of the Scots king. When he returned to Scotland from Anglesey his saga says that men went between him and the Scots king 'and a peace was made between them'. According to *Orkneyinga Saga* (chap 41) it was King Malcolm (*recte* Edgar) who sent messengers to offer a settlement. It must have been agreed that Norwegian authority thereafter would be restricted to the islands off-shore and it is said that 'Magnus was all the winter in the southern isles', during which period his men went all over the fjords rowing within and around all islands to claim them for the king (*Heimskringla*, chap 11). He also had himself dragged in a skiff over the isthmus at Tarbert in order to claim the peninsula of Kintyre as an island belonging to Norway. This meant that Bute and the other Clyde islands remained, however nominally, part of the kingdom of Norway for another one and a half centuries.

This was ambitious and threatening intervention from Scandinavia in the whole Insular Viking zone, and it is not easy to know how the situation might have developed if Magnus had not got himself killed in Ulster on his second expedition of 1102. He had returned because of Muirchertach's interference in the Kingdom of the Isles (Woolf 2004: 101). In the aftermath of his death there was uncertainty about the succession in the kingdom of Norway, his son Sigurd returned to Norway to claim his father's power in a disputed inheritance situation, and the Hebrides were once more drawn into the Irish Sea world.

The twelfth century: ecclesiastical links

One important twelfth-century development which must have strengthened the Norwegian connection was the establishment of the archdiocese of Nidaros (Trondheim) in 1152–3, in which the diocese of the Hebrides (*Suðreyar*) was included (Beuermann 2002: 62–8). The history of the bishopric before this date points to its subjection to first Canterbury and then York and there was the possibility that it might have come under the new archbishopric of Dublin, founded in 1151/2. Indeed it has been argued that Godred Olafsson's rather surprising visit to Norway in 1152 (the first evidence of any contact between Norway and the kingdom of Man since 1103), when the Manx Chronicler says that he did homage to King Inge, (*Chron Mann*, f.36r) may have been prompted by his desire to take his kingdom under the Norwegian ecclesiastical cloak rather than be subjected to Dublin (Beuermann 2002: 68). It certainly indicates that King Godred was looking for a counter-balance to Irish influence within his kingdom.

The complex history of the bishopric in the next century does not suggest that the Norwegian church played a very active role in the choice of bishops (Woolf 2003: 174–7). Nor can we imagine that the bishops with their see based at Peel in the Isle of Man played a very active role in the outermost corners of their diocese, apart from making occasional visitations. As has been suggested recently different regions in the diocese with their own distinctive cultural traditions probably had their own head churches (Woolf 2003: 180), where the bishops would call in from time to time. These were Snizort in Skye and Rodil in Harris in the north Hebrides, Iona as the most important spiritual centre of the Hebridean world, and Kingarth in Bute in the Clyde estuary (fig 3.4).

Fig 3.4 Map of the bishopric of the Sudreys (drawn by Dr Sarah Thomas).

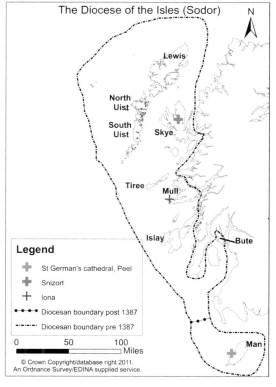

The Diocese of the Isles (Sodor)   N

Lewis

North Uist

South Uist   Skye

Tiree   Mull

Islay   Bute

Legend

✚ St German's cathedral, Peel

✚ Snizort

✚ Iona

•—•—• Diocesan boundary post 1387

------- Diocesan boundary pre 1387

0   50   100
                    Miles

Man

© Crown Copyright/database right 2011.
An Ordnance Survey/EDINA supplied service.

The creation of the archbishopric of Trondheim in 1152–3 and the incorporation of the diocese of the Hebrides (Sodor/*Suðreyar*) within it was doubtless a means of strengthening Norwegian authority in the area, but recent assessment makes it clear that Magnus *berfæt*'s successors had in general other political priorities (like civil war) to occupy them and were in no position to exert pressure on the kings of Man (Beuermann 2002: 81–2). The visit of Godred Olafsson, son of King Godred of Man, to Norway in 1152–3 was probably prompted by pressures within the Irish Sea zone, or within the kingdom itself caused by the rise of Somerled.

Thus, the twelfth century was a time when external influences in the Hebrides became less important, and political change was engendered from within the islands. First of all there was the growth of the political structures in Man itself. The dynasty of Godred Crovan was 'a mixed breed of Norse-Celtic adventurers' whose experience of political authority had been gained in Ireland, Scotland and sometimes England. The language of the court and culture included both Norse and Irish elements, although the exact mix of the two has been a cause of much dispute among historians. Then there was an Anglo-Norman element, which Olaf son of Godred would have experienced when he was resident at the court of Henry I of England, and it was probably his experience there which influenced Olaf into later regularising the bishopric in his kingdom and fostering monastic communities in Man itself (McDonald 1997: 207–18).

We can guess that there may have been mechanisms for collecting taxes or renders on the kings' behalf, and we know from later evidence that the Hebridean Islands were grouped into four for judicial representation at the annual legal assembly at Tynwald in the Isle of Man (Megaw 1956: 167). There must have been more local judicial assemblies at which economic and military obligations would have been assessed, but only the Council of the Isles, held at Finlaggan, Islay, is recorded (Crawford 1987: 289).[7] Perhaps the only suggestion one can make with some confidence is that the cultural situation in the Outer Hebrides is likely to have been more conservative than anywhere else in the Manx kingdom. The Norse element was possibly more lasting there than anywhere else, and the Norse language possibly survived there longer. The place-name evidence certainly tells plainly of the more lasting nature of the Norse linguistic strain in the Outer Isles than in the Inner Hebrides (Oftedal 1955; Jennings 1996; Stahl 2000). However the research undertaken into the toponymy of Bute by Gilbert Markus has shown that a substantial number of topographical place-names have survived in Bute, some of which were important estates in the medieval period (forthcoming).

This putative distinction between the Outer and Inner Hebrides was however not maintained with the rise of Somerled macGillebrigte (his forename is ON *sumarliði* = 'summer warrior') and the dominance of his family in the last century of the Norwegian period (fig 3.5). Somerled has traditionally been seen as the great Gaelic lord leading a Celtic revival (McDonald 1997: 57), but it would be very difficult to say what his priorities were in ethnic terms, although his deadly rivalry with the King of Man is the dominant feature of his rise and fall. After the battle of the Epiphany in 1156 between Godred and Somerled the Kingdom of the Isles was divided between them which the Manx chronicler sees as the cause of the ruination, or break-up of the kingdom (*Chron Mann*, f.37v). It certainly resulted in the difficult situation whereby some of the Outer Isles were retained by the kings of Man but separated from their central power bases by treacherous waters, while the chieftaincy of

Somerled and his sons controlled all the southern Hebrides south of Ardnamurchan (possibly including Arran and Bute; McDonald 1997: 56).

Following the death of Somerled in 1164 Godred re-established himself in the Outer Hebrides but then the Uists, Benbecula and Barra appear to have become part of the territory

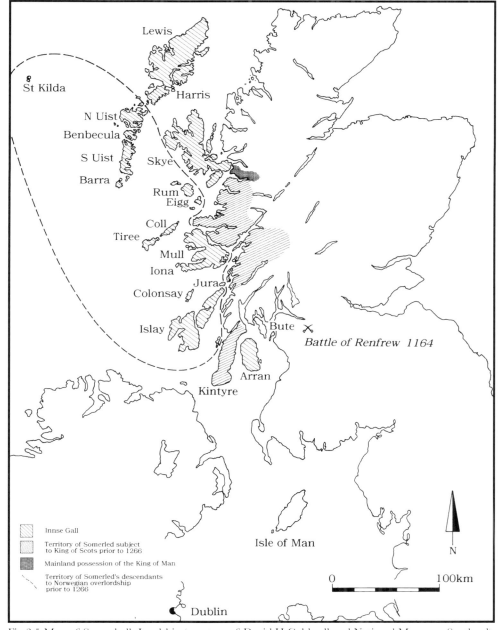

Fig 3.5 Map of Somerled's Lordship (courtesy of David H Caldwell and National Museums Scotland).

of Angus, third son of Somerled, and on his death in 1210 the Lordship of Garmoran passed to his nephew Ruari, second son of Ranald, from whom the Lords of Garmoran descended (McDonald 1997: 70, 80). The Uists, Benbecula and Barra were therefore drawn into the Inner Hebridean world and linked as a maritime lordship with Rum, Eigg, and the mainland territories of Knoydart and Moidart. The consequences of this would seem inevitably to have been a 'gaelicisation' of the remoter communities on the western fringe. The southern third was eventually held by the MacDonalds which possibly included Arran and Bute (McDonald 1997: 70). The uncertainty over Bute's importance in the developments of this period is revealed by the uncertain phrases which Andrew McDonald uses when discussing these events. But there seems little doubt that despite the lack of evidence Bute's strategic position meant that the power strategies would have revolved around its possession, and this is demonstrated by the developments in the following century, and in particular the building of Rothesay castle. Alexander II's campaign of 1222 was 'possibly aimed at royal control of Arran and Bute' (McDonald 1997: 84), and in 1230 a Scottish garrison held Rothesay castle. The Stewart family's attempted extension of power over the Clyde from Renfrewshire to the island of Bute is demonstrated in Alan fitz Walter's grant of Kingarth with its lands and chapels to the family's monastic foundation, Paisley Abbey, at the beginning of the thirteenth century (pre 1204).[8]

There are therefore many uncertainties about Bute's position in this period. It was a frontier island and political control over it was being disputed between the Gaelic-Norse rulers and the Scottish family of Stewart in particular, with the evident involvement of the Scottish kings in the following century.

The thirteenth century

Once the civil wars in Norway had ceased there was a serious attempt to increase authority over the kings of Man, and a plundering raid in the west by Norwegian 'pirates' in 1209 compelled King Ragnvald and his son Godred to go to Norway to renew their oaths of allegiance and pay the overdue tribute (Anderson 1922, II: 381; McDonald 2007: 134–5; Crawford forthcoming, where the reconciliation is compared with the terms imposed on the Orkney earls).

The growth of a strong Norwegian kingship under Hakon Hakonsson saw a repeat of the earlier royal ambitions; a king who was well established at home wished to seek glory overseas and reassert authority in his colonial dominions, or 'skattlands' as they were called (Imsen 2010, passim). In Hakon's case this was in direct response to the expanding power of the Scottish kings, who by this date desired to have the islands off the west coast of Scotland within their control, as a symbol of their imperial authority. The story is a complex one, concerning the relationship of the Norwegian king with the kings of Man and members of the Somerled dynasty in the Hebrides.[9] We have a remarkably full account of the events leading up to the royal expedition of 1263 and of King Hakon's war cruise to the Hebrides in his own saga, written almost contemporaneously (*Hacon's Saga*, chaps 318–27).

In that account Bute features quite notably and was evidently at the centre of claims between the Northmen and the Scots. When King Hakon was lying with his fleet at Gigha (ON *Guðey*), he sent some ships to Bute 'to meet those who had been sent thither'. Then there is the account of a 'ship-captain whose name was Rudri' who was with the Northmen (*þar var ok við Norðmönnum einn skipstjórnar-maðr, er Ruðri hét*: chap 321), who thought he had a claim by birth to Bute.[10] Because he had failed to 'get the island from the Scots' he, along with his two brothers, came to King Hakon and they swore oaths and became his men. There appears to have been a skirmish over 'the castle' (presumably in Rothesay), and Rudri killed nine men, after which the island came under King Hakon, and this reconquest is recorded in the verses of Sturla Thordarson:

> Ferð vannfrið-skerðis
> Fræg ok óvægin
> Bót af baug-njótum
> Breiða guð-leiðum
> (*The dauntless henchmen of the king, the man of war so worshipful, broad Bute conquered for their lord from the God-detested race*) (*Hacon's Saga*, p338)

Bute was then a base for the Norwegians who, led by Rudri, harried the settlements of the nearby coast of Scotland. Negotiations were initiated by the Scots and the Norwegians reciprocated by sending an embassy to King Alexander in Ayr. But the peace negotiations foundered on King Hakon's claim to all the isles, which the king of Scots specifically refused with regard to the Clyde islands of Bute, Arran and the Cumbraes (*Bot ok Herrey ok Kumreyjar*). He would not give them up, and neither would Hakon relinquish them, so these islands were the crucial factor over which negotiations broke down.

One wonders why Hakon was so determined to retain Bute, Arran and the Cumbraes. He took his fleet into the Clyde and sailed in under the Cumbraes evidently in defiance of any authority which King Alexander might have exercised in the locality. This situation ended up with the rout at Largs on October 3rd. Hakon would have been far better to stay outside the Clyde zone, but he clearly thought that he could control this area with sea power. Why did he want to do so? What was so important about these islands? They are very strategic and control access in and around the Clyde estuary. Bute had a particularly strategic importance in controlling the route to the portage at Tarbert, and during the stay in the Cumbraes Hakon sent sixty ships up Loch Long to the portage at Tarbert and 'they drew them up there over the land to a great lake which is called Loch Lomond' (chap 323). This raiding party was led by King Magnus of Man, king Dougal and his brother Alan, and they harried in the district around the lake 'and wrought there great damage'. But this did not do any good as regards the situation of the Norwegian party in the Clyde which was partly destroyed by great storms before the skirmishes on land.

After the inconclusive encounter at Largs the Norwegian fleet sailed back north round Cape Wrath, reaching Orkney on 29 October. The decision was taken to overwinter there before sailing back to Norway. Whatever Hakon had intended might be his next move in the assertion of his authority in the west, his death over the winter spelled the end of Norwegian political hegemony in the Hebrides.

The Treaty of Perth 1266

The political negotiations which led to the Treaty of Perth were conducted in a statesmanlike spirit between the envoys of Hakon's peaceable successor, Magnus Hakonsson 'the Lawmender', and members of the Scottish government. The treaty itself is formulated as if the Western Isles were 'sold' to Scotland, with a clause that 100 marks a year were to be paid 'in perpetuity'. One of the conditions included was that supporters of King Hakon were not to be punished 'for the misdeeds or injuries or damage which they have committed hitherto', and they could choose to leave or to stay, and if they chose to leave 'they may do so, with their goods, lawfully, freely, and in full peace', that is, without any reprisals (Donaldson 1970: 35) Presumably these conditions would be publicised in the islands, but we have little evidence of what the results of the political change were in islands like Bute. It must always have been an area of hybrid settlement and culture, and that is reflected in its place in Gall-Gaedhil territory. From the ninth to the thirteenth centuries Bute, Arran and the Cumbraes were strategically-located islands in a maritime world of mixed ethnic identity. They were frontier islands where Norse and Scottish culture met and where national political ambitions clashed.

Notes

1   I use the term 'Norse' as a more general Scandinavian cultural term than 'Viking', which is not applicable for most of the period.
2   Thomas Clancy's seminal assessment of the main territorial/insular base of the Gall-Gaedheil, and with the important excavations at Inchmarnock now published, which has a most informative historical introduction by Richard Oram and Paula Martin. All of these authors have in recent years helped to put Bute into a better-understood wider cultural framework.
3   The work undertaken by Gilbert Markus on the nomenclature of Bute as part of the Bute Landscape Project will revolutionise our understanding of the importance of the Norse place-names of the island.
4   Graham-Campbell and Batey (1997: 97) do not commit themselves to postulating that it was so.
5   Wainwright commented on the absence of stray weapon finds 'warriors do not leave their swords casually in barns or byres, nor do they throw them on middens' (1955: 152).
6   This hoard was not included in my map of Viking hoards (1987) nor by Graham-Campbell and Batey (1998).
7   The site of Cnoc an Rath ('Atingerar') lies at a strategic position between Ettrick and Kaimes (interest in which was aroused at the SSNS Conference) and may or may not prove to be a possible assembly site.
8   This grant seems never to have been implemented. See Gilbert Markus' full discussion of the implications in his forthcoming study.
9   The way in which the different members of Somerled's family (the MacSorleys) responded to the difficult political situation in which they found themselves is rather remarkable; perhaps not surprisingly they chose different paths, according to how they felt their own personal position might benefit.
10 The name Ruadri suggests that he may have been a member of the MacSorleys, the descendants of Somerled.

References

Anderson, A O (ed) 1922 *Early Sources of Scottish History 500-1286 AD*, two vols (reprinted Stamford, 1990).
A-S Chron The Anglo-Saxon Chronicles New Edition, trans and ed by M Swanton 1996. London: Phoenix Press.
Barrow, G W S 1981 *Kingship and Unity. Scotland 1000-1306*. Edinburgh: Edinburgh University Press.
Beuermann, I 2002 *Man amongst kings and bishops*. Occasional paper, Skriftserie 4, Senter for studier i vikingtid og nordisk middelalder. Oslo: University of Oslo.

Beuermann, I 2007 *Masters of the Narrow Seas*. Oslo: University of Oslo.

Clancy, T O 2008 'The Gall-Ghaidheil and Galloway', *Journal of Scottish Name Studies* 2, 19–50.

Crawford, B E 1987 *Scandinavian Scotland*. Leicester: Leicester University Press.

Crawford, B E 1994 'The "Norse background" to the Govan Hogbacks', in Ritchie (ed), 103–12.

Crawford, B E (ed) 1995 *Scandinavian Settlement in Northern Britain*. Leicester University Press: Leicester.

Crawford, B E 2004 'Earldom Strategies in north Scotland', in Williams, G & Bibire, P (eds) *Sagas Saints and Settlements*, 105–24. Leiden: Brill.

Crawford, B E 2005 *The Govan Hogbacks and the Multi-Cultural Society of Tenth-century Scotland*. Govan: The Society of Friends of Govan Old.

Crawford, B E forthcoming 'Man in the Norse world', in *New History of the Isle of Man*.

Crawford, B E & Taylor, S 2003 'The Southern Frontier of Norse Settlement in North Scotland. Place-Names and History', *Northern Scotland* 23, 1–76.

Chron Mann Chronicles of the Kings of Man and the Isles, trans G Broderick, revised edition 1996. Douglas: Manx National Heritage.

Donaldson, G (ed) 1970 *Scottish Historical Documents*.

Duncan, A A M & Brown, A L 1957 'Argyll and the Isles in the earlier Middle Ages', *Proc Soc Antiq Scot* 90 (1956–7), 192–220.

Downham, C 2007 *Viking Kings of Britain and Ireland. The Dynasty of Ivarr to A.D.1014*. Edinburgh: Dunedin Academic Press.

Dumville, D 1997 *The Churches of North Britain in the First Viking Age*. Fifth Whithorn Lecture. Whithorn: Friends of the Whithorn Trust.

Etchingham, C 2001 'North Wales, Ireland and the Isles: the Insular Viking Zone', *Peritia* 15, 145–87.

Fisher, I 2001 *Early Medieval Sculpture in the West Highlands and Islands*. Edinburgh: RCAHMS/Society of Antiquaries of Scotland.

Graham-Campbell, J 1974 'The Viking-Age Silver and Gold Hoards of Scandinavian Character from Scotland', *Proc Soc Antiq Scot* 107 (1972–4), 114–35.

Graham-Campbell, J 1995 *The Viking-Age Gold and Silver of Scotland (AD 850–1100)*. Edinburgh: National Museum Scotland.

Graham-Campbell, J & Batey, C E 1998 *Vikings in Scotland*. Edinburgh: Edinburgh University Press.

Hacon's Saga The Saga of Hacon (Icelandic Sagas vol. IV), trans Sir G W Dasent, Chronicles and Memorials of Great Britain and Ireland during the Middle Ages, 1894. Rolls Series, London.

Heimskringla. The Sagas of the Norse Kings, trans S Laing. Everyman edition, 1960, 1964.

Holman, K & Adams, J (eds) 2004 *Scandinavia and Europe 800–1350: Contact, Conflict and Coexistence*. Turnhout: Brepols.

Hudson, B 1992 'Cnut and the Scottish kings', *English Hist Rev* 107, 350–60.

Hudson, B 2005 *Viking Pirates and Christian Princes*. Oxford: Oxford University Press.

Imsen, S (ed) 2010 *The Norwegian Domination and the Norse World c.1100–c.1400*. 'Norgesveldet', Occasional Papers 1. Trondheim: Tapir Academic Press.

Jennings, A 1996 'Historic and linguistic evidence for Gall-Gaedheil and Norse in Western Scotland', in Ureland, P Sture & Clarkson, I (eds) *Language Contact across the North Atlantic*, 61–73.

Jennings, A 2004 'Norse Place-Names of Kintyre', in Holman & Adams (eds), 109–19.

Kruse, A 2004 'Norse Topographical Settlement Names on the Western Littoral of Scotland', in Holman & Adams (eds), 97–107.

Lang, J 1974 'Hogback monuments in Scotland', *Proc Soc Antiq Scot* 105 (1972–4), 206–35.

Lowe, C 2008 *Inchmarnock. An Early Historic Island Monastery and its Archaeological Landscape*. Edinburgh: Society of Antiquaries of Scotland.

McDonald, R A 1997 *The Kingdom of the Isles. Scotland's Western Seaboard c.1100–c.1336*. East Linton: Scottish Historical Review Monographs Series 4.

McDonald, R A 2007 *Manx Kingship in its Irish Sea Setting 1187–1229*. Dublin: Four Courts Press.

MacNiven, A 2008 'Prehistory and Early History', in Caldwell, D *Islay. The Lands of the Lordship*, 15–32. Edinburgh: Birlinn.

Markus, G forthcoming *Introduction to the Place-Names of Bute* (Bute Landscape Project)

Megaw, B & E 1956 'The Norse Heritage in the Isle of Man', *Chadwick Memorial Studies*, 143–70.

Njal's Saga, trans M Magnusson & H Palsson, 1960. Harmondsworth: Penguin Books.

Oftedal, M 1955 'Norse place-names in the Hebrides', in Falck, K (ed) *Annen Viking Congress*, 107–12. Bergen.

Orkneyinga Saga. The History of the Earls of Orkney, trans H Palsson & P Edwards, 1978. London: The Hogarth Press.

Parker Pearson, M, Sharples, N & Symonds, J 2004a *South Uist, Archaeology and History of a Hebridean Island*. Stroud: Tempus.

Parker Pearson, M, Smith, H, Mulville, J & Brennand, M 2004b 'Cille Pheadair: the Life and Times of a Norse-period Farmstead c.1000-1300', in Hines, J, Lane, A & Redknap, M (eds) *Land, Home and Sea*, 235–54. Leeds: Society for Medieval Archaeology Monograph 20.

Power, R 1986 'Magnus Barelegs' Expeditions to the West', *Scottish Hist Rev* 65, 107–32.

Ritchie, A 2004 *Hogback Gravestones at Govan and Beyond*. Govan: The Friends of Govan Old.

Ritchie, A (ed) 1994 *Govan and its early Medieval Sculpture*. Stroud: Alan Sutton.

Stahl, A-B 2000 'Norse in the Place-names of Barra', *Northern Studies* 35, 95–113.

Williams, G 2003 'The *dabhach* reconsidered: pre-Norse or post-Norse?', *Northern Studies* 37, 17–32.

Woolf, A 2003 'The Diocese of Sudreyar', in Imsen, S (ed) *Ecclesia Nidrosiensis1153-1537*, 171–82. Trondheim: Senter for Middelalder Studier, NTNU, Skrifter nr.15.

Woolf, A 2004 'The Age of Sea Kings: 900–1300', in Omand, D (ed) *The Argyll Book*, 94–109. Edinburgh: Birlinn.

The Vikings came on very boldly, thinking the others were in a trap. Vigbjod asked who these men were who were so penned in. Thrand replied, "Here is my companion, Onund Treefoot".

The Vikings laughed and said:
May trolls take you, Tree-Foot,
May trolls break you all.

'It is quite a novelty for us to see men going into battle who are so utterly helpless". Onund said they could not be sure of that until it had been put to the test.

After that they brought their ships together, and a fierce battle began, with both sides fighting well. When the battle was in full swing Onund let his ship drift towards the cliff, and as soon as the Vikings noticed this they thought he was trying to escape, and so they closed on him and came under the cliff as quickly as they could. At that moment the men who had been left on the cliff came forward to the edge. They hurled such big stones down at the Vikings that no resistance was possible. Many of the Vikings were killed and others hurt and put out of the fight. They wanted to get away but were unable to, because their ships were then in the narrowest part of the channel. They were caught by the other ships and the heavy current.

When the crew on Vigbjod's ship dwindled, Onund and his men attempted to board her. Vigbjod saw this and urged on his men fiercely. Then he turned towards Onund and many retreated before him. Onund who was a powerful man, told his followers to observe how it would turn out for the two of them. They pushed a log under his knee so he stood solidly. The Viking came aft along the ship until he reached Onund. Then he struck at him with his sword, hitting the shield and slicing a piece off, but the sword ran into the log under Onund's knee and stuck fast. Vigbjod stooped to jerk the sword free, and just then Onund struck at his shoulder, cutting off his arm, and the Viking was out of the fight.

When Vestmar saw that his companion had fallen, he leapt into the ship that lay furthest out and fled away, and so did all who could. After that Onund and his men searched among the dead. Vigbjod was at the point of death. Onund went up to him and said:

Watch your wounds bleed
And think if you've ever
Seen me flinch. On a single leg,
I dodged the blows you dealt me.
Some men are full of boasts
Brainless though they be.

(*Grettir's Saga*, 7–9)

There is much that could be said of this passage. Note the short sentences suggestive of action. The dialogue cannot be historical though it can be used to make historical points. The viking mode of naval battle was to bring the ships side by side to create a sort of platform or floating battlefield. Both sides think they can read the sea, the currents and the topography but if so would one be able to trap the other so successfully? Would they not expect some such attack with missiles if they approached the cliffs too closely? In this battle Onund truly earns his soubriquet of 'treeleg'. The one-on-one combat is skillfully depicted. We might assume a man was out of a fight once his arm was cut off but the statement of the obvious was not alien to the saga genre. The poetic banter reminds us that skill in words was almost as important as physical ability. The precise location of the encounter remains problematical; a *Bódach* with good local knowledge is required to work out the site of the conflict. It is noteworthy that all of the vikings clearly had a reasonable knowledge of the Clyde and the Kyles of Bute (fig 4.1) which should remind us that the vikings had been acquainted with the western approaches for a very long time. By 1263, when Hakon's expedition reached Largs, the Norwegians had accumulated four and a half centuries of experience in Scottish waters, which they undoubtedly knew much better than most landlubbers on the mainland. There can be little question that the Scots were apprehensive about attacks from the isles. The castles of Wigtown and Ayr were garrisoned in anticipation of Hakon's attack and the counties of Wigtown, Ayr and Renfrew are richly fringed with fortifications all the way from the Rhinns of Galloway to Glasgow, from Dunskey to Dumbarton, structures facing west on the lookout for incursions by a second Somerled.

The earlier phase of Viking contact with Scotland has been usefully summarised by two archaeologists (Graham-Campbell & Batey 1998) who do not have a great deal to impart about Bute, but the finds from Inchmarnock have generated great excitement with the

Fig 4.1 The Kyles of Bute from Badlia Hill in Bute (DP 067125, © Crown Copyright: RCAHMS. Licensor www.rcahms.gov.uk).

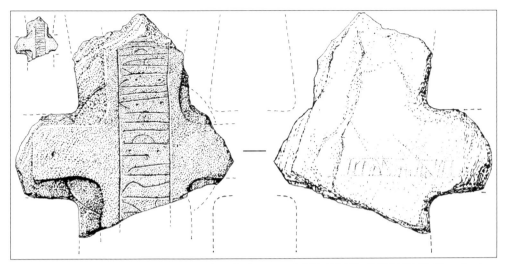

Fig 4.2 Rune-inscribed Norse stone cross from Inchmarnock (SC 403491, © RCAHMS. Drawing by Ian G Scott. Licensor www.rcahms.gov.uk).

discovery of a possible illustration of a viking raid, scratched on a stone (Lowe 2008: fig 6.27, no 46a) (fig 3.2). Inchmarnock has always been intriguing for it is also the site of one of the very few surviving runic inscriptions in the Western Isles. It has been read as containing recognisable words such as 'cross' and the name 'Guthleif' or 'Guthleik' (Hewison 1893, I: 223; Fisher 2001: 79) (fig 4.2). Otherwise the current Scottish historical school of what did *not* happen was well represented at the Royal Society Conference on the impact and influence of the vikings upon Scotland, where of three speakers on the early Vikings, one talked about the English church during the viking era, another discussed the richer sources for Ireland in the period, and a third concentrated on the difficulty of actually assessing the viking impact upon Scotland, in the present state of knowledge. So far DNA evidence throws little light on the genetic make-up of Bute (RSE 2006: 5–10).

The key to what little is known of Bute in the thirteenth century lies in the activities of the descendants of Somerled, the last of whose sons was killed with three of his own offspring in 1210. By whom is not recorded though the MacSorley kindred were engaged in battles with one another, as well as with people who had a claim to Man. It is known that Alexander II of Scotland led an expedition to Argyll in 1221–2, an event sufficiently alarming to prompt some Hebrideans to petition Hakon on 'the needs of their lands' (*Hacon's Saga* i, 89–90). Alan of Galloway complicated the situation by entering the fray in 1228–9 to harry Man and the Isles. Meanwhile the MacSorleys were in revolt against Hakon (Cowan 1990: 112–15).

The saga mentions three grandsons of Somerled who were active in this drama, the sons of Dugald mac Somerled: Dugald, Duncan and Uspak. The last-named is the warrior who attacked Rothesay Castle in 1230. He is said to have long fought as one of the Birchshanks (*Birkibeinar*) alongside Hakon in his drawn-out struggle for the kingship, but 'it came out that he was Dugald's son' (*Hacon's Saga* I, 150). He was obviously much more of a Norwegian than his stay-at-home brothers, but the saga language may suggest he was illegitimate, which was no great bar to achievement in either Gaelic or Norse society. He was known as the 'South-islander' or the 'Hebridean'. Hakon gave him the title of king [*konungr*] and the name, Hakon;

hence his designation of Uspak-Hakon, a mark of special royal favour not incompatible with the possibility that he had been fostered by the king.

While Uspak was preparing his fleet of eleven ships, at Bergen, King Olaf of Man arrived, seeking help. He reported Alan of Galloway's boast that the sea was no more difficult to cross from Scotland to Norway than in the opposite direction, a hollow threat, so far as the Norwegians were concerned, dismissed by the saga laconically and effectively, with the words, 'that was said not done' (*Hacon's Saga* i, 152). King Uspak's task was to sort out his own kindred, whom he met in the Sound of Islay. A MacSorley invitation to a feast, accompanied by strong wine, was sensibly declined since, notoriously, the climax of Hebridean banquets, then and for several generations, was the butchering of the guests. Each side prepared for the worst, 'for neither trusted the other'. Duncan slept on Uspak's ship and so was safe when the Norwegians captured Dugald, subsequently placing him in the safekeeping of Uspak, who took no part in the attack. With the original eleven ships somehow increased to eighty, an unbelievable number, Uspak sailed down the west of Kintyre and up the Firth of Clyde. Bute was the first target of this king of the Isles.

For three days they besieged the castle, which was under the control of a steward, who was probably in fact the constable of the castle and a member of the Stewart family. 'The Scots defended themselves well, pouring down boiling pitch and lead on the attackers', many of whom were wounded or killed. The Northmen armed themselves with wooden shields while they hacked at the soft stone of the castle wall until it crumbled. The constable was killed and the castle fell; much booty was seized and a Scottish knight (probably a Stewart) was ransomed for 300 silver marks, a colossal sum. Some 300 of the victors also died. Learning that Alan was to the south with 150 ships they sailed round the Mull of Kintyre and north along the coast. Uspak was overtaken by an unexplained illness, and died (*Hacon's Saga* i,

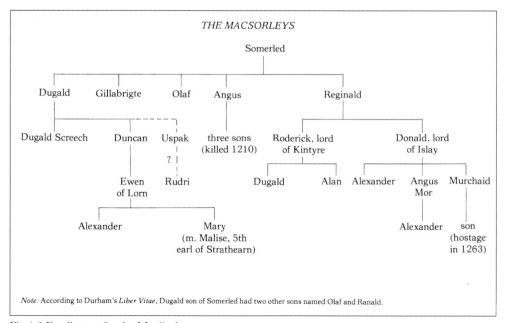

Fig 4.3 Family tree for the MacSorleys.

152–3). According to the *Chronicle of Man* he had been wounded by a stone during the siege. Clearly stones were the favoured weapons in Bute!

There is no further mention of the island in the saga until Hakon mounted his ambitious expedition to the Hebrides in 1263, as he attempted to consolidate his hold on the archipelago. Having arrived at Kerrera, Hakon despatched to Bute, 'a ship's captain whose name was Rudri – he was thought to have some claim to Bute' (*Hacon's Saga* ii, 351). The suggestion, long ago made, that Rudri was the son of the late Uspak Hakon, remains attractive and plausible (Duncan & Brown 1959: 203, n 5). He was assigned fifteen ships commanded by such captains as Erlend the Red, Andrew Nicholasson, Simon the Short, Ivar the Young and two Sudreyars, Eyfari and Guttorm. 'Because Rudri did not get the island from the Scots, he strove fiercely against them, slaying many, for which actions he was outlawed by the Scottish king' (*Hacon's Saga* ii, 351). According to saga information, additional men were sent to reinforce Rudri's troops in Bute but when they arrived the castle had already surrendered, in return for an agreement of peace. However Rudri, claiming to know nothing of peace, treacherously pursued them, killing nine men. Thereafter the island fell to Hakon, a triumph celebrated in verse:

> The dauntless henchmen of the king,
> The man of war so worshipful,
> Broad Bute conquered for their lord
> From the God-detested race.
> The soaring raven thrust his sword
> His cloven beak in Southern isles,
> Into the bodies of the fallen;
> So fell Hakon's enemies.

'Then Rudri fared far and wide with many slaughters and robberies and did all the harm that he could', when, to paraphrase another verse, farms were harried and burned as the hot-raged, hall-crusher ravaged Scotland's west coast and death-doomed warriors fell in the wasted isle of Skye (*Hacon's Saga* ii, 351). When Hakon retreated after the encounter at Largs, he officially granted 'Broad Bute' to Rudri. He was not part of the expeditionary force which portaged from Loch Long into Loch Lomond to harry its shores and raid 'almost across Scotland' but he definitely benefited, or might have done, since, as I have previously suggested, these adventurers were targeting the Stewart estates of Strathearn and Menteith (Cowan 1990: 117, 120–2). As it turned out Rudri was too late. The Stewarts returned to Bute as the Norwegian sun set over the Clyde with the Treaty of Perth in 1266.

Modern Norwegian historians, however, have a different take on all of this. No longer do they recognise that the death of Hakon in Orkney and the subsequent surrender of the Hebrides at Perth represent the death knells of medieval Norway. The *Norgesveldet*, the Norwegian Dominion of the area north of Orkney, continued (Helle 2003: 387). Norwegian foreign policy remained much as it had been before 1266, 'the loss of the Hebrides and Man having been compensated by the gain of Iceland and Greenland' (Bagge 2010: 100). An entire volume of essays, helpfully devoted to the investigation of *Norgesveldet*, has recently been published (Imsen 2010). One must defer to a nation's historians. Had I written the piece on Hakon's last campaign today, I would not have used the metaphor of Norwegian sunset. Attractive as I find them, metaphors can very often mislead. However, viewed from Perth or

Largs, or anywhere else in Scotland, the treaty of 1266 marks a conjuncture and the end of an era.

One other helpful Norwegian suggestion is to look at the 'project' or 'idea' that successive rulers had for their kingdom, a fairly necessary recourse for a nation whose documented early history, aside from the sagas, is even more impoverished than that of Scotland. Thus we have Harald Fairhair's project of unification through tyranny, as he stripped away the freedoms from his subjects, contrasting with that of Hakon the Good's policy of 'tentative christianisation', while his idea changed from force to the consent of the people. Olaf Tryggvason followed with a project of national unification through religion. The model works well for Norway as successive reigns establish evolving layers of experience, and it is persuasive because Norwegian historians do not shy away from writing nationalist history, while the Norwegian people of today find it easy to identify with, and even relate with, the folk of their past. Torgrim Titlestad's idea of Norway clearly embraces his hero, Erling Skjalggsson, the supreme *hersir* of West Norway, embodiment of generous lordship (for some), an international trader, possibly a pioneer of the commercial fishing industry, a summer viking par excellence, a man who freed his thralls if only out of self interest, owner of a ship capable of holding 240 men, christianiser and 'king among earls'. Unfortunately for him he fell out with his king, Olaf the Saint, against whom he fought his last battle in 1028. He was one of Snorri Sturluson's paragons as he faced the inevitable. 'Face to face should eagles fight' he said, while standing alone in the stern of his ship as, bloody but unbowed, he greeted Olaf, who, impressed by his martial prowess, offered him mercy. Erling accepted, removing his helmet, but Olaf could not resist marking him on the cheek with his battle-axe: 'a mark he shall bear, betrayer of his king'. A kingsman nearby sank his axe in Erling's head. 'With that blow' said the king, 'you struck Norway out of my hand' (*Heimskringla*, 467; Titlestad 2008: 129–313). It could be said that with the battle of Largs, and hindsight, the Hebrides were struck from the hand of the kings of Norway.

Gael, Norse and Scot all crossed paths in Bute. The island may have been part of the spawning ground of the Gall-Ghàidheil, Gaelic speakers of mixed Norse and Gaelic descent (Clancy 2008: 31). It was obviously seen as a place of great strategic significance, controlling, as it did, access to the Firth of Clyde and the sea lochs of its estuary, placing Glasgow and Dumbarton within reach, as also Loch Lomond via the Leven or Loch Long (Loch of the Ships), and Argyll by way of Loch Fyne. From Bute it was no great distance to the portage across Kintyre between West and East Loch Tarbert, though the saga implies that most of the voyages it records took the south Kintyre route around the Mull. Hence the appeal of the vikings' Bute project: first, an excellent harbour at Rothesay, (*Baile Bhoid* in Gaelic, possibly renamed by the Norse in honour of Rudri); second, potential control of the Clyde for its ease of communication and its vast resources. A third aim, made explicit by the 1230 raid, was the control of Rothesay Castle and the urgent expulsion of the Stewarts for it was in Bute that Scotland and Norway truly came face to face, so to speak. From a Norwegian point of view the Stewarts were the aggressors and if they triumphed in Bute then the whole of the Hebrides might be in danger of a Scottish takeover. Had Uspak lived, the process of attrition might have been delayed, though probably not for long. Rudri mac Uspak clearly thought it was worth his while having another go in 1263. He may have spent the previous thirty years attempting to regain what he considered to be his patrimony; we have no way of knowing. He is depicted in the saga as a wild, merciless character but he fits the mould of many Hebrideans in the period who were trapped between the millstones of Norway and Scotland and who were attempting the best for their kindreds. Bute was thus an important player in this particular story which ended with the Treaty of Perth.

References

Clancy, T O (ed) 1998 *The Triumph Tree Scotland's Earliest Poetry AD 550-1350*. Edinburgh: Canongate.

Clancy, T O 2008 'The Gall-Ghàidheil and Galloway', *J Scottish Name Studies* 2, 19–50.

Clanranald 1894 Cameron, A '*The Book of Clanranald*', in MacBain, A & Kennedy, J (eds) *Reliqiae Celticae: Texts, Papers and Studies in Gaelic Literature and Philology*, 2 vols. Inverness.

Chron Man 1973 *Chronicle of the Kings of Man and the Isles*, Broderick, G & Stowell, B (eds). Edinburgh.

Grettir's Saga 1974 *Grettir's Saga*, Fox, D & Palsson, H (trans). Toronto: University of Toronto Press.

Heimskringla 1967 *Sturluson, Snorri, Heimskringla History of the Kings of Norway*. Austin: University of Texas Press.

Hacon's Saga 1894 *Icelandic Sagas*, trans Sir G W Dasent, 4 vols, Rolls Series, London; partially reprinted 1997 as *The Saga of Hacon and a Fragment of The Saga of Magnus with appendices*, 2 vols. Felin Fach: Llanerch Publishers.

Bagge, S 2010 *From Viking Stronghold to Christian Kingdom State Formation in Norway, c. 900-1350*. Copenhagen: Museum Tusculanum Press.

Cowan, E J 1990 'Norwegian Sunset – Scottish Dawn: Hakon IV and Alexander III', in Reid, N H (ed) *Scotland in the Reign of Alexander III 1249-1286*, 103–31. Edinburgh: John Donald.

Cowan, E J 1998 *Scottish History and Scottish Folk, Inaugural Lecture Chair of Scottish History and Literature 1995*. Glasgow: Glasgow University, Scottish History.

Cowan, E J 2011 'The Worldview of Scottish Vikings in the Age of the Sagas', in Cowan, E J & Henderson, L (eds) *A History of Everyday Life in Medieval Scotland, 1000 to 1600*, 36–66. Edinburgh: Edinburgh University Press.

Duncan, A A M & Brown, A L 1959 'Argyll and the Isles in the Earlier Middle Ages', *Proc Soc Antiq Scot* 90, 190–220.

Fisher, I 2001 *Early Medieval Sculpture in the West Highlands and Islands*. Edinburgh: Society of Antiquaries of Scotland/ RCAHMS.

Graham-Campbell, J & Batey, C E 1998 *Vikings in Scotland An Archaeological Survey*. Edinburgh: Edinburgh University Press.

Helle, K 2003 'The Norwegian kingdom: succession disputes and consolidation', in Helle, K (ed) *The Cambridge History of Scandinavia Volume 1 Prehistory to 1520*. Cambridge: Cambridge University Press.

Hewison, J K 1893 *The Isle of Bute in the Olden Time*, 2 vols. Edinburgh: William Blackwood.

Imsen, S (ed) 2010 *The Norwegian Domination and the Norse World c.1100-c.1400*. "Norgesveldet' Occasional Papers No. 1. Trondheim: Tapir Academic Press.

Lowe, C 2008 *Inchmarnock: an Early Historic island monastery and its archaeological landscape*. Edinburgh: Society of Antiquaries of Scotland.

McDonald, R A 1997 *The Kingdom of the Isles: Scotland's Western Seaboard in the Central Middle Ages, c.1000–1336*. Scottish Historical Review Monograph 4. East Linton: Tuckwell Press.

Palsson, H 1973 'Hakonair Saga – Portrait of a King', *Orkney Miscellany King Hakon Commemorative Number*, vol 5, 49–56. Kirkwall: Orkney County Library.

RSE Royal Society of Edinburgh 2006 *The Vikings and Scotland – Impact and Influence, Report of a Conference organized by the Royal Society of Edinburgh 20–22 September 2006*. Edinburgh: Royal Society of Edinburgh.

Titlestad, T 2008 *Viking Norway Personalities, Power and Politics*. Stavanger: Sagabok.

Woolf, A 2007 *From Pictland to Alba 789–1070. The New Edinburgh History of Scotland*, vol 2. Edinburgh: Edinburgh University Press.

Chapter 5

A Casualty of War?
The cult of Kentigern of Glasgow,
Scottish patron saints and
the Bruce/Comyn conflict

Tom Turpie
University of Stirling

SAINTS and their shrines played a vital role in the prosecution of warfare during the middle ages. Before embarking upon a campaign the combatants prayed for victory and presented gifts at appropriate shrines. Belligerent English monarchs, such as Edward I (1272–1307) and Edward III (1327–77), had well-trodden pilgrimage circuits which preceded military action (Webb 2000: 111–40). The Scottish monarch James IV (1488–1513) valued the blessing of St Duthac, visiting his shrine at Tain on the eve of his ill-fated invasion of England in 1513 (Dickson 1887–1916, vol iv: 419, 36), while his predecessor Robert I (1306–29) favoured St Fillan (Taylor 2001). To the battle itself armies carried the symbols and relics of their patrons. At Neville's Cross in 1346 the Scots, bearing the Black Rood of St Margaret, were faced by an English army carrying a banner depicting St Cuthbert (Rollason 1998). Finally, when returning from the battlefield the victors made further gifts to shrines and religious houses in gratitude for their success. Richard Neville, believing that St Cuthbert had interceded to aid the English victory at Neville's Cross, presented the captured Black Rood to the custodians of the saint's relics at Durham (Rollason 1998). The association of a particular saint with victory, or defeat, and the political changes that resulted from warfare could therefore have a considerable influence on the popularity of a saint and its shrine. This article will explore the impact of the political changes that accompanied the Anglo-Scottish wars of the late thirteenth and early fourteenth century upon the cult of the west of Scotland saint, Kentigern of Glasgow.

The twelfth and thirteenth centuries, in which the Kentigern cult arguably reached the zenith of its popularity, were a period of considerable political, social and economic transition in the kingdom of Scotland. The story of how Andrew and Margaret became the patron saints of the Scottish church, royal dynasty and kingdom during this period is reasonably well known. St Andrews was a pilgrimage centre of international repute and the apostle had played an important role as a symbol of the independence of the northern kingdom in the conflict between the Scottish bishops and York over ecclesiastical superiority in the twelfth century (Ash & Broun 1994). The somewhat belated canonisation of St Margaret in 1250 provided the royal house with a source of prestige and dash of the sacred, placing the

MacMalcolm dynasty on something of a par with its neighbouring polities in the British Isles and Western Europe (Bartlett 2003; Baker 1978). The development of these two cults led to the gradual eclipse of earlier patrons of the national church and royal house, Columba and Cuthbert. However, this narrative presents too clean cut an image of the complex processes at work in this period. A fifth saint, Kentigern of Glasgow, had developed into a viable alternative for the role of royal patron, at least, in the late twelfth and thirteenth centuries. It would be the political circumstances of the Wars of Independence and conflict between the opposing Bruce and Comyn parties that would put an end to this process and cement Andrew and Margaret's position as the undisputed formal patrons of Scotland and its royal house.

The cult of Kentigern of Glasgow was one of the saintly success stories of the central middle ages in Scotland. The only contemporary record for the career of the saint is the obit of his death recorded in a Welsh annal under the year AD 612, which suggests little else other than that he was considered to be a bishop (cited in Macquarrie 1997: 117). Whilst there may have been a local cult devoted to the saint in the former Kingdom of Strathclyde, and perhaps Lothian, in the early middle ages, recent works by John Reuben Davies (2009) and Dauvit Broun (2007: 124–8) have shown that there is little evidence of widespread interest in Kentigern prior to the twelfth century. The cult that developed from the early 1100s was the result of the promotional activities of a series of bishops who, following the creation of the reformed diocese of Glasgow by David I (1124–53), encouraged the cult of their patron with building campaigns, translations and the production of two new *Vitae* (Duncan 1998; Shead 1970).

The first of these new hagiographical works, of which only a fragment survives (Forbes 1874: 123–33), was produced during the episcopate of Herbert (1147–64). The purpose of this new life was to raise the saint's profile and emphasise his place within the wider canon of Scottish saints. This aim is also evident in another extant document from the end of Herbert's occupancy of the see, the *Carmen de Morte Sumerledi* (cited in Howlett 2000: 24–9). The subject of this fascinating poem is the rebellion of Somerled of the Isles in 1164. It ends dramatically with Herbert brandishing Somerled's severed head and attributing victory to the intercession of St Kentigern. Within the poem the saint is firmly identified as both a local and national protector, and as a central figure amongst the saints of Scotland (Clancy 2002: 397–9).

In spite of these promotional activities the cult still seems to have been regional in character in the 1170s and, as Duncan (1998: 11) has suggested, charter evidence from the reign of Malcolm IV (1153–64) show the possessions of Glasgow being treated in 'somewhat cavalier fashion' by the Crown. The final catalyst for the transformation of Kentigern into a figure of national significance, closely associated with the Scottish royal house, was the transfer of Jocelin (1174–99) to Glasgow in 1174. Jocelin had built up a reputation as a keen promoter of in-house cults in his previous position as abbot of Melrose (Birkett 2010a). Whilst at Melrose he had championed the cult of an earlier abbot Waltheof, who was also the stepson of David I. Support for this saint with a connection to the royal house won him the favour of William I (1164–1214) and resulted in his elevation to Glasgow, to whose patron saint Jocelin transferred his promotional zeal.

Jocelin embarked on a three pronged promotional campaign at Glasgow, using as his model the recently martyred English saint Thomas Becket (d 1170, canonised 1173). The

Fig 5.1 View of Glasgow Cathedral from the Necroplis.

first step in this process was an ambitious building programme, successfully completed by 1197 (Stevenson 1835, 103). The second was the commissioning of a new and up to date life of the saint which was firmly in the European tradition of the late twelfth century. For this purpose Jocelin employed the well known Cistercian hagiographer Jocelin of Furness, a professional who was also responsible for lives of SS Patrick, Helen and Waltheof (Birkett 2010b). Although the exact dating of the *Vita Kentegerni* is unclear, it must have been finished in time for Bishop Jocelin's triumphant consecration of the cathedral on 6 July 1197 (fig 5.1). On that day the third stage in the promotional campaign was completed with the translation of Kentigern's relics to an elaborate new tomb in the cathedral (Stones & Hay 1967). This date coincided with the annual fair, granted to the burgh by William I, to be held 'for 8 days one week after 29 June' (Barrow 1971: 308). As a practical matter this translation was of considerable importance to Jocelin who was attempting to switch the focus of the cult from the intemperate 13 January, the official feast day of the saint, to a more practical summer date in July. This action mirrored the behaviour of the custodians of the shrine of Thomas Becket in 1220, a saint who had also inconveniently died in the depths of winter (Nilson 1998: 15–24).[2]

Jocelin's activities may have been intended as the prelude to a canonisation process (Duncan 1998: 16–17). The presence of an officially sanctified cult at Glasgow would have played an important role in any pretensions towards archiepiscopal status that the bishops may have had during this period. However, this process never appears to have been carried out. Jocelin's notable success was in developing a close relationship between the saint and the royal house. For William I, Kentigern was a personal intercessor second only to his commitment to Thomas Becket, to whom his new foundation at Arbroath was dedicated. The relationship between Kentigern and the Crown may have been intended to mirror the bond between the kings of France and the abbey of St Denis. As Duncan (1998: 18–19) has shown, the gift by William of a symbolic tribute of four pence to the cathedral was remarkably similar to the four bezants presented annually by the French monarchs to St Denis. Precedence for this special bond is provided by the *Vita Kentegerni* in which King Rederech conceded 'the dominium and princedom over all his Kingdom' to Kentigern, in a deliberate parallel of the Donation of Constantine (Forbes 1874: 94–6).

The relationship between William and Kentigern may have been further strengthened by the birth of an heir, the future Alexander II (1214–49), in 1198. Duncan (1998, 13–15) suggests that William attributed the belated birth of a legitimate heir to the intercession of St Kentigern and the blessing of the marriage bed by Bishop Jocelin. In a story from the *Vita Kentegerni* (Forbes 1874: 95–6) the saint had helped Queen Langovereth 'long bowed down by the disgrace of continued barrenness' to conceive a child called Constantine, the heir of King Rederech. William and Ermegarde's child was baptised by Jocelin and the king continued to make grants of land, money and serfs to Kentigern and the see of Glasgow throughout the remainder of his reign (Barrow 1971: 216, 283, 426, 217).

Although it has been suggested that royal interest in the saint began to wane after William's death (Shead 1970: 14), Alexander II and his successor Alexander III (1249–86) continued to be major patrons of Glasgow cathedral (Scoular 1959: 232; Simpson 1960: 148). In 1284 Alexander III indicated his personal commitment to the saint by founding an altar dedicated to Kentigern in the nave of the cathedral (Innes 1843, vol i: 235) (fig 5.2). This poignant

Fig 5.2 Chapel and tomb of St Mungo in Glasgow Cathedral.

Fig 5.3 Thirteenth-century carved architectural fragment from the tomb of St Kentigern, on display in Glasgow Cathedral.

dedication was made in the midst of a period of personal tragedy for the king who lost his eldest son in January 1284 and his youngest son and daughter in 1280 and 1283. The altar was intended as a family commemoration, providing prayers for the souls of his ancestors and family, most notably his recently deceased children (Durkan 1970: 65). Acts such as this on the eve of the Wars of Independence would have helped to fuel the confidence of the bishops of Glasgow in the strength of their relationship with the royal house. The manner in which they perceived this bond can be seen in a seal belonging to Robert Wishart (1271–1316). Wishart's counter seal was divided into three niches with Kentigern at the top, a royal couple in the middle and a praying bishop underneath, emphasising Glasgow's perception of the special relationship between their saint, his successor bishop and the royal house (Stevenson & Wood 1940, vol i: 110).

The successful revival of the cult, and the increasing power and influence of the diocese of Glasgow, was also reflected in the dedication of a series of churches to the saint across southern Scotland and in Cumbria during this period (Davies 2009: 72–82; Mackinlay 1914; Watson 1926). Whilst as Davies has shown (2009: 72–82), dating these, and other early commemorations of the saint, is problematic, they give a strong sense of the geography of the cult prior to the fourteenth century. The impact of the twelfth-century promotional campaigns and royal patronage can also be seen in the explosion of interest in the cult amongst the Scottish nobility during the period. Kentigern developed a strong following amongst the Anglo-Norman incomers of the twelfth century, especially those with a landed interest in the south west. Some of the earliest benefactors were the Bruces of Annandale and Walter fitz Alan, the High Steward, who gifted a number of churches and monies to the cathedral (Innes 1843, vol i: 72, 20). In the thirteenth century the most regular and generous patrons of the cult were the Comyn and Balliol kindreds. Individual benefactors from these families included Dervoguilla de Balliol, who granted lands to Kentigern in 1277, and her son John I (1292–6), who showed an interest in the saint during his brief reign (Innes 1843, vol i: 230; Simpson 1960: 369, 380). Patronage from the Comyn kindred came from William, earl of Buchan (d 1233), who contributed to the altar of St Kentigern in 1223, and Isabella de Valognes, who granted lands for her soul and the soul of her husband, David Comyn of Badenoch, in about 1250 (Innes 1843, vol i: 117, 199). John Comyn, probably one of the Kilbride branch, also made a grant to the cathedral in 1279 (Innes 1843, vol i: 233). In this period patronage also came from a number of less high profile families like the Somervilles, Vaus, Oliffards and de Moravias (Innes 1843, vol i: 16, 100, 184, 219, 120, 126, 203).

The saint and his shrine were not exclusively identified with twelfth century incomers, and received further patronage from the native earls of Lennox and Carrick (Innes 1843, vol i: 101, 108, 177, 187). Alexander fitz William sheriff of Stirling, who was a descendant of Thorald, the native sheriff of Lothian for David I, also gifted monies to the saint in the mid-thirteenth century (Innes 1843, vol i: 121) On the whole aristocratic patronage of the saint and shrine came almost exclusively from individuals and families with a strong territorial interest in the diocese of Glasgow and neighbouring lands. By the late thirteenth century, the bishops of Glasgow had managed to create a strong connection between the exercise of temporal lordship in the region and reverence, whether genuine or emblematic, for the cult of St Kentigern. This process is best illustrated by the example of the Comyn kindreds, whose expanding landed interest in the Glasgow area during the thirteenth century corresponded with their increasing patronage of the cult (Young 1998: 19–20). At the end of the thirteenth century with an established relationship with the Scottish royal house and strong aristocratic support, the future looked bright for the cult of St Kentigern.

Things started to go wrong for St Kentigern shortly after the death of Alexander III in 1286. The Scottish political community reacted to the unexpected death of the king by setting up an interim government run by six guardians (Barrow 2005). A new seal was commissioned for the guardians featuring a conventional depiction of a monarch on the front, but displaying on the reverse an image of the apostle surrounded by the legend 'St Andrew be leader of the Scots, your fellow countryman' (Stevenson & Wood 1940, vol i: 18). As one commentator has suggested, the image and legend purported to show continuity with the past (Barrow 2005: 17). However, this was the past from a particular perspective. The placing of the apostle on the seal emphasised the informal position of the bishops of St Andrews as the '*episcopatus Scottorum*', 'bishops of the Scots', a status they had been claiming since the twelfth century (Barrow 1994: 2–3). The decision to directly connect the apostle to the Scottish realm in this manner can be attributed to one of the guardians, the bishop of St Andrews, William Fraser (1279–97). As Ash has shown (1990: 47), the episcopates of Fraser and his direct predecessors were characterised by sustained promotion of their diocesan saint. This included the development of the final elaborate version of the St Andrews origin legend and the depiction of the apostle on episcopal seals. It was the image of the saint from Fraser's personal seal that was transferred onto the seal of the guardians in 1286 (Stevenson & Wood 1940, vol i: 85).

Although as a universal saint Andrew appears to have been a non-partisan figure around which to unite national sentiment, he was figuratively, and literally in the case of his relics, the property of the diocese of St Andrews. It is likely that there was some disquiet at the promotion of Andrew in this manner from the bishops of Glasgow who, as we have seen, had a clear perception of the close relationship between their saint and the Crown. The bishops of Dunkeld may also have had concerns over the use of Andrean imagery in 1286. Although their diocesan patron had been displaced as a dynastic and church patron by Margaret and Andrew in the twelfth and thirteenth centuries, Columban imagery continued to play an important role in royal ceremonials such as the inauguration of Alexander III in 1249 (Bannerman 1989; Duncan 2003; Broun 2003). Neither of these groups would have expected to see their patrons sidelined in 1286.

The concept of Andrew as regnal patron was turned into a reality during the propaganda battles of the Wars of Independence. As with the conflict between the Scottish bishops and York over primacy in the earlier period, the diplomacy of the Anglo-Scottish wars required a stronger and more internationally recognisable patron for the Scots, a role much better suited to Andrew than Columba or Kentigern. As early as 1301, the connection between Andrew and the kingdom was emphasised by Baldred Bisset (d 1311) who, during a mission to the Papacy, reiterated the Scottish argument against the primacy of York, describing the apostle as 'protector of the Kingdom' (Watt 1987–99, vol vi: 135–69). This role was fully elaborated in the 1320 Declaration of Arbroath. In the Declaration Andrew was presented as the patron of the small kingdom located at the 'uttermost ends of the earth' (Barrow 2003: xiii–v). The letter, with its papal audience in mind, argued that the being under the patronage of the apostle was one of several factors that proved the sovereignty of the kingdom (Barrow 2003: xiii–v). In the 1320 document Andrew was presented as the sole patron, with alternative symbolic figures like Columba, Kentigern, and even dynastic patron Margaret, effectively sidelined.

The Declaration of Arbroath was the work of Robert I's promotional team and as Barrow has commented he was the first Scottish king 'known to have invoked (…) Andrew publicly as the nation's patron' (2005: 218). It seems that Robert associated his victory at Bannockburn in 1314 with the intercession of the saint, granting an annual stipend of 100 merks to the cathedral priory at St Andrews in gratitude, and taking centre stage at the consecration of the rebuilt church in 1318 (Barrow 2005: 318; Watt 1987–99, vol ii: 271–2). This ceremony has been described by one commentator (Cant 1976: 26–7) as the 'vindication of Scottish independence', and is viewed by Ash and Broun as a 'thanksgiving by the whole nation' for the victory over the English (1994: 16, 20). This notion is based upon Bower's account of the ceremony written in the 1440s. Bower (Watt 1987–99, vol vi: 363–6) described the presence of Robert I, Bishop William Lamberton (1297–1328) and Duncan, earl of Fife (d 1353) at the consecration, symbolising the involvement of the three estates, and therefore of the whole kingdom, in showing appreciation for the role of St Andrew in Scottish victories. While Bower's latent diocesan loyalties mean that we must treat his description of events with a degree of caution, the abbot having been born and spending his whole career in the diocese of St Andrews, the consecration does appear to have been some form of national event. The ceremony emphasised the bond between the patronage of St Andrew and Scottish regnal independence, a theme evident in the Declaration of Arbroath just two years later.

The controversial manner in which Robert I had seized the throne meant that the decision to identify his kingship with Andrew was a logical, and perhaps necessary, step. While his faith in Andrew as an intercessor may also have played a role, Robert would have been keen to attach himself to the apostle as a figure who had come to be associated with the independence of the Scottish realm. By the early fourteenth century this connection was coming to be recognised beyond Scotland. An English political song from about 1300, whose subject was the ousting of John Balliol, referred to Andrew as the '*leader*' of the Scots (Wright 1839: 181). St Andrews was not the only cult centre that had political value for a king whose accession to the throne had come in highly unusual circumstances. The search for legitimacy was also a strong motivation behind Robert's high profile patronage of Dunfermline Abbey, where he was buried in 1329. As Boardman has shown (2005: 144), with this act Robert was consciously identifying himself with both the patron saint and burial place of much of the dynasty through which he claimed the throne.

Whilst the cult centres of SS Andrew and Margaret benefited from the succession of the new dynasty, Kentigern and Glasgow did not. The carefully cultivated relationship between the saint and royal house did not survive the Wars of Independence, with the Bruce dynasty displaying little interest in Kentigern (Duncan 1986: 50, 52–4; Webster 1982: 82, 87, 91, 443).[3] This is surprising as Robert Wishart had been a key supporter of the Bruce regime. Dubbed the '*bad bishop*' by the English, he was eventually captured and imprisoned by Edward I, and was only released after Bannockburn (Bain 1881, vol ii: 1286; Barrow 2005: 106, 193, 197). Wishart had exhorted his flock to support Bruce, regardless of the sacrilegious murder of John Comyn within his diocese, and had even used wood intended for his cathedral to make siege engines. However, Wishart was dead by 1316 and his cathedral would not receive the same patronage from the king as that of his contemporary, Lamberton of St Andrews. The early Stewart kings also had a traditional ancestral interest in the saint dating back to the twelfth century. This interest appears to have been continued by the future Robert II (1371–90), who in 1364 confirmed an annuity of £40 from his lands near Stirling to found an altar dedicated to Kentigern in Glasgow cathedral (Innes 1843, vol i: 302). However, this was not a personal dedication. It was part of the cost of the legitimisation of Robert's marriage to Elizabeth Mure which had been arranged in 1347 by the bishop of Glasgow, William Rae (1339–67) (Penman 2004: 312; Boardman 1996: 20). Like the Bruce monarchs, the Stewart kings showed little interest in the saint prior to the reign of James II (1437–60).

This decline in royal veneration has been noted by Shead (1970: 16) and Yeoman (1999: 28), with the latter tentatively suggesting that patronage of the shrine by Edward I may have led to this distancing by the Bruce and Stewart dynasties. Edward visited Glasgow in August and September 1301, making four separate offerings at the tomb (Bain 1881, vol iv: 448–9). The suggestion that the shrine was considered to have been polluted is an intriguing one. However, similar visits by the English monarch and his son to Whithorn, Dunfermline and St Andrews appear to have had little effect on their popularity with the Scottish public or royal house (Bain 1881, vol ii: 8 & 1225: vol iv: 448, 486, 487). A more compelling explanation is that the break with Glasgow resulted from the conflict between the Bruce and Comyn kindreds. Although members of the Bruce family had been patrons of the shrine in the twelfth century, Glasgow Cathedral had never been a primary focus of their patronage. As Ruth Blakely (2005: 167–80) has shown, disputes over the control of churches in Annandale had also led to tensions between the family and Glasgow bishops in the late twelfth century. As we have seen the main patrons of the cathedral in the thirteenth century had been the Comyn and Balliol kindreds. It is possible that the association with these groups, who had opposed the Bruce succession, made the cult too controversial for the new regime, breaking the personal relationship between crown and saint which had existed from the reign of William I.

This decline in royal veneration was matched by a considerable reduction in aristocratic interest in the cult. Between 1296 and 1450 the only dedications by nobles of comital rank came from the future Robert II and members of the Douglas kindred. The Black Douglases had acquired a considerable landed stake in the diocese of Glasgow in the late fourteenth century, through the marriage of Joanna Murray to Archibald Douglas (d 1401) (Brown 1998: 96–7).[1] Evidence of Douglas interest in the cult during this period is limited to gifts to the saint and shrine by William Douglas of Liddesdale in 1340, Joanna Murray in 1401 and the erection of his church of Cambuslang into a prebend of the cathedral by Archibald, the fifth earl in 1429 (Innes 1843, vol i: 290, 321; vol ii: 335). The lack of dedications by the top rank of the nobility is marked when compared to the thirteenth century when patronage came from the families of three earls and other major kindreds. However, of the main twelfth and thirteenth century patrons only the Stewarts would survive into the fifteenth, with families like the Bruces, Comyns, Balliols, Murrays and the native earls of Lennox and Carrick failing due to the politics of the wars or the lottery of dynastic succession. The main heirs to the territorial interest of these groups were the royal Stewarts and the Douglas kindred. Whilst the Douglases were well aware of the political cachet of well directed religious patronage, their broad property portfolio meant that this was distributed over a wide range of regional saints from Duthac in the north, to Cuthbert and Ninian in the south (Brown 1998: 183–98).

Although dedications to the saint from earls were rare in this period, a number of the lesser nobility continued to show an interest in the cult. Apart from the earl of Douglas, the other five prebends created in 1429 were under the patronage of John Stewart of Darnley, Alexander Montgomery of Eglinton, John Colquhoun of Luss, Patrick Graham of Killearn and John Forester (Innes 1843, vol ii: 340, 346). Grants to the saint were also made by emerging regional families like the Hamiltons in 1361, and the Stewarts of Lennox, who gifted a set of vestments to the cathedral chapter in 1429 (Innes 1843, vol ii: 297, 337). Further grants were made by minor local nobles Duncan Wallace and John Danielston (Innes 1843, vol ii: 308, 315). The somewhat token devotions of the Douglases and the continuing interest of the regional nobility in the cult suggest that the institutionalised relationship between local secular lordship and the diocesan saint continued into the fourteenth and fifteenth centuries. However, there was a considerable disparity in value between the foundation of a chaplaincy and a gift of vestments, which characterised the post-1300 devotions, and the granting of churches or wax that were typical of the earlier period.

The decline in crown and aristocratic interest in the cult seems to have had a concomitant impact on wider interest in the saint during this period. There were no new altars dedicated to Kentigern in major Scottish churches prior to 1451, and the saint's feast day fails to appear in any of the extant liturgical fragments from the late thirteenth or fourteenth centuries (Turpie 2011: 17–22). The absence from a calendar based at Culross (Forbes 1872: 50–64) is perhaps the most surprising. The patron of the local church was St Serf, who was presented in the hagiographical tradition as Kentigern's mentor and teacher. In the late fourteenth century

Fig 5.4 Symbols of St Mungo in the streets of modern Glasgow.

the invocation of the saint by a group of Scots was recorded by an English chronicler. In 1379 Thomas Walsingham described a strange ritual carried out by Scots raiding the plague-ridden north of England. The senior man would lead them in praying to '*God and St Kentigern*' to save them from the '*foul death*' that was killing the English (Taylor 2003: 310–11). In the fourteenth and fifteenth centuries the cult of the Kentigern seems to have declined to one of regional rather than national importance with the reference to the invocation of the saint by Walsingham, and continued interest in the shrine by the minor nobility, underlining his enduring patronal role in the Glasgow area. In the fifteenth century the custodians of the shrine of St Kentigern would attempt to address this situation with a concerted promotional campaign based around their patron saint (Turpie 2011: 191–7). However, that is another story.

This paper has argued that Kentigern emerged in the late twelfth and thirteenth centuries as a viable alternative to the dominance of the Fife-based saints. The success of the cult was based upon promotion by the bishops of Glasgow and the personal relationship between the saint and the royal house. However, the civil wars of the early fourteenth century led to the extinction of a number of elite patrons of the cult, while the succession of the Bruce and later Stewart dynasties broke the connection between the saint and royal house that had lasted since the reign of William I. Had John Balliol and his Comyn supporters emerged victorious from the wars, Kentigern would surely have benefited. It is even possible that the saint of Glasgow, with crown support, might have assumed the role of official national patron in the later middle ages rather than Andrew. Unfortunately for the bishops of Glasgow their patron saint became a casualty of the Bruce/Comyn conflict. When the parliament at Holyrood made the feast day of the patron saint of Scotland an optional bank holiday in 2008, it would be on 30 November, rather than 13 January, that the Scottish national day would be celebrated.

Notes

1. A charter of Malcolm IV and an early charter of William I mention recompense for 'transgressions' against the see of Glasgow.
2. Thomas was killed on 29 December. The translation was on 7 July 1220 and was subsequently celebrated as the main feast day of the saint, which was a common occurrence as the date of translation was open to manipulation whereas the death or martyr date was not.
3. Robert I made no new grants to the cathedral or saint, merely confirming the traditional royal stipends from Rutherglen and Cadzow which had presumably gone into abeyance during the interregnum. David II also showed little interest in the saint and re-assigned the payment from Cadzow to the Hamilton family in 1369.
4. Joanne was the heir of Maurice Murray of Drumsagard, a prominent supporter of David II who was killed at Neville's Cross in 1346. The inheritance fell to the Douglas family in 1408 and included twenty six estates in northern and central Scotland, including the barony of Bothwell.

References

Ash, M 1990 'The Church in the Reign of Alexander III', in Reid, N (ed) *Scotland in the Reign of Alexander III, 1249–86*, 31–52. Edinburgh: John Donald.
Ash, M & Broun, D 1994 'The Adoption of St Andrew as patron saint of Scotland', in Higgitt (ed), 16–24.

Baker, D 1978 ' "A nursery of Saints" St Margaret of Scotland reconsidered', in Ash, M (ed) *Medieval Women*, 119–41. Oxford: Blackwell.

Bain, J et al (eds) 1881–1986 *Calendar of Documents relating to Scotland*. Edinburgh: H M General Register House.

Bannerman, J 1989 'The Kings Poet and the Inauguration of Alexander III', *Innes Review* 68, 120–50.

Barrow, G W S (ed) 1971 *The acts of William I: King of Scots, 1165–1214*. Regesta Regum Scottorum 2. Edinburgh: Edinburgh University Press.

Barrow, G W S 1994 'The Medieval Diocese of St Andrews', in Higgitt (ed), 1–7.

Barrow, G W S 2005 *Robert Bruce and the community of the realm of Scotland*. Edinburgh: Edinburgh University Press.

Barrow, G W S (ed) 2003 *The Declaration of Arbroath. History, Significance, Setting*. Edinburgh: Society of Antiquaries of Scotland.

Bartlett, R (ed) 2003 *The Miracles of Saint Aebbe of Coldingham and Saint Margaret of Scotland*. Oxford: Clarendon Press.

Birkett, H 2010a 'The struggle for sanctity: St Waltheof of Melrose, Cistercian in-house cults and canonisation procedure at the turn of the thirteenth century', in Boardman, S & Williamson, E (eds) *The Cult of Saints and the Virgin Mary in Medieval Scotland*, 43–60. Woodbridge: Boydell Press.

Birkett, H 2010b *The saints' lives of Jocelin of Furness: hagiography, patronage and ecclesiastical politics*. Woodbridge: York Medieval Press.

Blakely, R M 2005 *The Brus Family In England and Scotland, 1100–1295*. Woodbridge: Boydell Press.

Boardman, S 1996 *The Early Stewart Kings. Robert II and Robert III, 1371–1406*. East Linton: Tuckwell Press.

Boardman, S 2005 'Dunfermline as a Royal Mausoleum', in Fawcett, R (ed) *Royal Dunfermline*, 139–54. Edinburgh: Society of Antiquaries of Scotland.

Broun, D 2003 'The Origin of the Stone of Scone as a National Icon', in Welander et al (eds), 182–97.

Broun, D 2007 *Scottish Independence and the Idea of Britain from the Picts to Alexander III*. Edinburgh: Edinburgh University Press.

Brown, M 1998 *The Black Douglases*. East Linton: Tuckwell Press.

Cant, R G 1976 'The Building of St Andrews Cathedral', in McRoberts, D (ed) *The Medieval Church of St Andrews*, 11–33. Glasgow: Burns.

Clancy, T O 2002 'Scottish Saints and National Identities in the Early Middle Ages', in Thacker, A & Sharpe, R (eds) *Local saints and local churches in the early medieval West*, 397–420. Oxford: Oxford University Press.

Davies, J R 2009 'Bishop Kentigern among the Britons', in Boardman, S & Williamson, E (eds) *Saints' Cults in the Celtic World*, 66–90. Woodbridge: Boydell Press.

Dickson, T (ed) 1877–1916 *Accounts of the Lord High Treasurer of Scotland*. Edinburgh: H.M. General Register House.

Duncan, A A M (ed) 1986 *The Acts of Robert I, 1306–29*. Regesta Regum Scottorum 5. Edinburgh: Edinburgh University Press.

Duncan, A A M 1998 'St Kentigern at Glasgow Cathedral in the Twelfth Century', in Fawcett, R (ed) *Medieval Art and Architecture in the Diocese of Glasgow*, 9–22. Leeds: British Archaeological Association.

Duncan, A A M 2003 'Before Coronation; Making a King at Scone in the thirteenth century', in Welander et al (eds), 1399–68.

Durkan, J 1970 'Notes on Glasgow Cathedral', *Innes Review* 21, 46–76.

Forbes, A P (ed) 1872 *Kalenders of Scottish Saints*. Edinburgh: Edmonston and Douglas.

Forbes, A P (ed) 1874 *Lives of S. Ninian and S. Kentigern*. Edinburgh.

Innes, C (ed) 1843 *Registrum Episcopatus Glasguensis*. Edinburgh: Bannatyne Club.

Higgitt, J (ed) 1994 *Medieval art and architecture in the diocese of St Andrews*. Tring: British Archaeological Association.

Howlett, D 2000 *Caledonian Craftsmanship. The Scottish Latin Tradition*. Dublin: Four Courts Press.

Mackinlay, J 1914 *Ancient Church Dedications in Scotland. Non-Scriptural Dedications*. Edinburgh.

Macquarrie, A 1997 *The Saints of Scotland. Essays in Scottish Church History, AD 450-1093*. Edinburgh: John Donald.

Nilson, B 1998 *Cathedral Shrines of Medieval England*. Woodbridge: Boydell Press.

Penman, M 2004 *David II, 1329–71*. East Linton: Tuckwell Press.

Rollason, L 1998 'Spoils of War? Durham Cathedral and the Black Rood of Scotland', in Rollason, D & Prestwich, M (eds) *The Battle of Neville's Cross, 1346*, 57–65. Stamford: Shaun Tyas Press.

Scoular, J M (ed) 1959 *Handlist of the Acts of Alexander II, 1214–1249*. Regesta Regum Scottorum 3. Edinburgh: Edinburgh University Press.

Shead, N 1970 'Benefactions to the Medieval Cathedral and See of Glasgow', *Innes Review* 21, 3–16.

Simpson, G G (ed) 1960 *Handlist of the Acts of Alexander III, Guardians and John, 1249–1296*. Regesta Regum Scottorum 4. Edinburgh: Edinburgh University Press.

Stevenson, J (ed) 1835 *Chronica de Mailros*. Edinburgh: Bannatyne Club.

Stevenson, J & Wood, M (eds) 1940 *Scottish Heraldic Seals*. Glasgow.

Stones, E L G & Hay, G 1967 'Notes on Glasgow Cathedral', *Innes Review* 18, 88–99.

Taylor, S 2001 'The Cult of St Fillan in Scotland', in Luiszka, T R & Walker, E M (eds) *The North Sea World in the Middle Ages – Studies in the Cultural History of North West Europe*, 175–211. Dublin: Four Courts Press.

Taylor, J (ed) 2003 *The St Albans Chronicle, Volume 1, 1376–94*. Oxford: Clarendon.

Turpie, T 2011 *Scottish Saints cults and Pilgrimage from the Black Death to the Reformation, c.1349–1560*. PhD thesis, University of Edinburgh.

Watson, W J 1926 *A History of Celtic Place names in* Scotland. Edinburgh: Blackwood and Sons.

Watt, D E R (ed) 1987–99 *Scotichronicon by Walter Bower in Latin and* English Aberdeen: Aberdeen University Press.

Webb, D 2000 *Pilgrimage in Medieval England*. London: Hambledon.

Webster, B (ed) 1982 *The Acts of David II, 1329–71*. Regesta Regum Scottorum 6. Edinburgh: Edinburgh University Press.

Welander, R, Breeze, D J & Clancy, T O (eds) *The Stone of Destiny, Artefact and Icon*. Edinburgh: Society of Antiquaries of Scotland.

Wright, T (ed) 1839 *Political Songs of England. From the Reign of John to that of Edward II*. London: Camden Society.

Yeoman, P 1999 *Pilgrimage in Medieval Scotland*. Edinburgh: Historic Scotland.

Young, A 1998 *Robert the Bruce's Rivals. The Comyns, 1212–1314*. East Linton: Tuckwell Press.

Chapter 6

The Bute or Bannatyne Mazer
– two different vessels

Dave H Caldwell, George Dalgleish,
Susy Kirk and Jim Tate
National Museums Scotland

THE medieval drinking vessel known as the Bute Mazer, or less commonly the Bannatyne Mazer, is a Scottish national treasure, prized for its supposed association with King Robert Bruce (fig 6.1). It is a large drinking bowl, 110mm high and 254 to 258mm in diameter, with a whale-bone lid. It takes its name from ownership by the Marquises of Bute as well as earlier associations with the Isle of Bute and the family of Bannatyne of Kames. Since 1998 it has been one of the pre-eminent items on exhibition in the National Museum of Scotland, Edinburgh, and before that was long displayed in the National Museum of Antiquities of Scotland.

Fig 6.1 The Bute Mazer (© National Museums of Scotland).

Fig 6. 2 Photo-montage of the inscription on the rim of the Bute Mazer (© National Museums of Scotland).

The Bute Mazer consists of a turned, maple wood bowl with a deep silver rim, plain inside but decorated on the exterior with an untidy inscription reserved against a cross-hatched background: NINIAN [mullet] bANNAChTYN [ihs] LARD OF YE CAMIS [cinquefoil] SOUN TO UMQhIL RObaRT bANNACRIN OI YE CAMISI [mullet] (fig 6. 2). The bowl is set on a rolled silver foot connected to the rim by six hinged and pinned straps. In the interior is a large silver-gilt print or boss set with six enamelled medallions containing shields around a lion couchant in full relief (fig 6. 3). The shields are heater-shaped (like an old-fashioned flat iron) and are described here clockwise, starting with the one between the lion's fore paws. We have, however, preserved the numbering used by earlier commentators:

1. Or, a fess chequy azure and argent, for Stewart, High Steward of Scotland, prior to about 1369 when the Steward's arms were augmented by a royal tressure.

2. Argent, on a chief azure three stars of the field. These are the arms of Douglas prior to the addition of a heart in commemoration of James Douglas' death in Spain in 1330, where he had taken Bruce's heart in a crusade against the Moors.

5. Gules, three cinquefoils ermine, for Gilbertson/ FitzGilbert /Hamilton.

6. Gules, a chevron ermine between three cinquefoils or.

4. Gules, a fess ermine, for Crawford.

3. Or, a bend chequy sable and argent, for Menteith, a branch of the Stewarts.

The lid consists of a disk of whale-bone carved on its top surface with an elaborate design of foliage and flowers, which is fitted with a central silver knop or handle (fig 6. 4).

Fig 6. 3 The silver-gilt print, with enamelled shields around a lion, in the base of the Bute Mazer (© National Museums of Scotland).

Fig 6. 4 The carved whale-bone lid of the Bute Mazer (© National Museums of Scotland).

Previous accounts of the Bute Mazer

The earliest record of the Bute Mazer is in a book on Ayrshire families by George Robertson published in 1823. Robertson identified it as an antique bowl, probably a baptismal bowl, then in the possession of Lord Bannatyne, and on the basis of the rim inscription, associated it with Ninian Bannatyne, Laird of Kames in Bute, whose father Robert had died in 1522. He assumed that shields three and four were those of the family, and that the other four related to Ninian's ancestry, thus:

> On the principle of an escutcheon, representing the alliances of the family, it is natural to suppose, that of the four upper, the two on the right represent the paternal arms of Ninian's mother and grandmother and the two on the left, the arms of their mothers; under which view it would appear that Ninian was the son of Robert, by his second wife, whose father had borne the name of Douglas, and her mother that of Crawford; and that Robert had been the son of a former Ninian, by a lady whose father carried the name of Stuart, and mother that of Menteith (Robertson 1823: 60–1).

Lord Bannatyne – Sir William Macleod Bannatyne – was a Lord of Session (judge), the son of Roderick Macleod and Isabel Bannatyne. He adopted the name Bannatyne on succeeding to the estate of Kames through his mother, from whom, no doubt, he also inherited the mazer. Robertson's explanation of its ownership by Ninian, son of Robert Bannatyne, in the sixteenth century has not been disputed. His heraldic interpretation is not unreasonable, but unproven. If shields five and six represented the Bannatynes they might be expected to have been charged with mullets in place of cinquefoils.

The most thorough report on the mazer was published in 1931 by the heraldic expert, John H Stevenson, with support from several other specialists. Stevenson identified it as a work of the early fourteenth century, remodelled for Ninian Bannatyne in the sixteenth century with the addition of the silver foot, straps and rim. He identified the lion in the centre of the print as representing King Robert Bruce and the shields roundabout as those of some of his leading barons. Since the arms of the Stewart are positioned between the lion's forepaws it is clear that he was regarded as the most important of the six and therefore the man for whom the mazer was made. Stevenson further believed that the mazer could be tied down in date to late 1314 – January 1317/8. It could not be any earlier than that given the presence of the Gilbertson arms, since prior to the Battle of Bannockburn in 1314, the head of that family, Walter son of Gilbert (of Hamilton), had commanded Bothwell Castle as a supporter of the English. It could not be later than January 1317/8 since on or about the fourth of that month the heiress of Sir Reginald Crawford of Loudoun, Sheriff of Ayr, executed by the English in February 1307/8, married Sir Duncan Campbell, and he retained a version of the Campbell arms for his own use.

Stevenson went on to speculate that the arms on the sixth shield, given their similarity to those of Gilbertson, might be those of John son of Gilbert, known to have been Bailie of Bute in or about 1322–5. In this role, or perhaps in another official capacity within the household of his master, the Steward, as Lord of Bute, it may have been incumbent upon John to supply a mazer for use at table in Rothesay Castle, the Stewart family residence in Bute. This line of reasoning, certainly the association with the Gilbertsons, was apparently strengthened by some of the other decoration on the print – three cinquefoils ('or' as on shield six rather than 'ermine' as on shield five) around the edge and scrolling, stylised, strawberry plants with leaves and fruits. Stevenson pointed out that the flower of the strawberry plant was one of the originals from which the heraldic cinquefoil was derived. Also, the mazer lid has a silver knop in the form of a cinquefoil and its overall decorative scheme includes a pentagon with five segments, comparable to a cinquefoil.

In appendices to Stevenson's paper Lionel Crichton, a respected London dealer in antique silver and a retail silversmith specialising in fine quality reproduction silver, opined that the mazer was Scottish work, while William Brook, an Edinburgh goldsmith, thought the print was of eastern origin but re-worked by a Scottish craftsman (Stevenson 1931: 35–7). Brook drew particular attention to the way the heraldic shields are on separate disks which have been soldered into holes cut into the print and saw this as evidence that the print and shields are from different sources. The view that the mazer is totally a Scottish work has prevailed.

Stevenson's paper has continued to form the basis of the National Museum of Scotland's view on the mazer as expressed in gallery texts, especially for an exhibition on Scottish medieval art in 1982 (Caldwell 1982: 37–8), and another on Scottish silver in 2008 (Dalgleish & Fothringham 2008: 32). In the latter case, a date of about 1565 was suggested for the rim, foot and straps, and attention was drawn to evidence for a relationship between Ninian Bannatyne and a Glasgow goldsmith, Peter Lymeburner, in whose house Ninian conducted business on 22 April 1567. So possibly Lymeburner was responsible for the present form of the mazer.

In a paper published in 1999 Professor Geoffrey Barrow looked in more detail at the social background of the mazer. He accepted Stevenson's suggestion that shield six bears the arms of John Gilbertson, the Bailie of Bute, and identified him as the son of Gilbert who was either the brother or nephew of that Walter who commanded Bothwell Castle for the English in 1314. Gilbert had acquired from Walter the Steward the lands of Kilmacholmac (now St Colmac) in Bute by 1312–13 and his son John was granted further lands in Bute. Barrow suggested that this John was the predecessor and, very probably, the ancestor of the Bannatynes of Kames. He speculated further that the inclusion of a chevron ermine in the arms on shield six is in honour of marriage with an important family, and he guessed that it might have been between John's father Gilbert and an heiress of Reginald Crawford of Crosbie in Ayrshire. That would also explain the presence of the Crawford arms on shield four. So for Barrow the heraldic scheme actually indicates John's ownership of the mazer, with his arms positioned between shields five and four, Gilbertson and Crawford, those of his paternal and maternal ancestors. The other three shields are understandable as those of his lord, the Steward, and the latter's close allies, Sir James Douglas and Sir John Menteith the younger, Lord of Arran and Knapdale. Given his particular identifications of the arms on shields three and four, Menteith and Crawford, Barrow only felt able to date the mazer to 1314–27. His reasoning for a start date in 1314 is the same as Stevenson's. The end date depends on the assumption that the Stewart arms are those of Walter the Steward who died in 1327, rather than his son Robert, still only 11 at the time of his father's death.

Barrow also called into question Stevenson's interpretation of the lion on the print as representing King Robert. In strict heraldic terms it should have been shown rampant rather than couchant. While not totally dismissing the royal symbolism he drew attention to the documentary evidence for one Leo son of Gilbert, one of the 28 esquires serving in Bothwell Castle in 1311–12 under the command of Walter son of Gilbert, and suggested the possibility should be kept open that the lion represents him. If that were to be the case, Leo might have been a brother of John the Bailie who died young, and the mazer might have been made to celebrate an important event in his life. It is not necessary to accept any more of Barrow's speculations on Gilbertson genealogy and heraldry than that the mazer was made for John the Bailie (or just possibly Leo) to understand his conclusion that the mazer is evidence for wealth amongst the lesser landed families of Scotland in the early fourteenth century. The mazer, indeed, may only be exceptional in having survived.

Barrow's analysis and views were followed in two accounts of the mazer by Virginia Glenn (1999 and 2003) which focussed on an artistic analysis. In the former she took issue with Brooks' assessment that the heraldic shields are from a different source than the print, giving as her reason the results of analytical analyses carried out in the research laboratory of National Museums Scotland (NMS). They show that the silver of the shields is virtually identical to the silver of the print. Also perhaps of relevance in this context is the fact that the red enamel of the eyes of the lion matches the red enamel in the shields. Glenn also, in her 1999 paper, drew attention to the conservative appearance of the lion, seeing it as being more like twelfth-century representations of lions rather than the more realistic shaggy beasts seen in fourteenth-century heraldry. The explanation, she suggested, is because the mazer was added to an existing collection of hanaps (drinking vessels) with similar lions; but the lion, she believed, must nevertheless have been of the same date and made in the same workshop as the rest since its silver is identical. Glenn's 2003 account covered the same ground. She added the assertion that the identification of the lion as King Robert Bruce is fanciful, and dated the rim, straps and lid to about 1500.

Ninian Bannatyne's Mazer

There are, then, differing views on the mazer and its significance. All are agreed that, at least to some extent, it is a work made or refashioned for Ninian Bannatyne in the sixteenth century. The word 'mazer' is dealt with in the following paper by Molly Rorke. Suffice it to record here that, while the word mazer was in use in Scotland in the sixteenth century and earlier, it is possible that many would have preferred to call a vessel like Ninian Bannatyne's mazer a tass, a generic term for a drinking cup that might be of a variety of materials including metal, wood and glass. Certainly the contexts in which tasses are encountered suggests as much – for instance, a 'litill tas of masar [maple wood] set in siluer' left to a daughter in a testament of 1575 and 'ane tas of trie [wood] with ane siluer fuit' mentioned in 1578 (both cited by DOST s.v. Tass).

The prevailing view is that it incorporates, or is mostly, work of the early fourteenth century but there is much less certainty on whether it is a noble piece of work that graced the table of the Stewart or is representative of what minor landowners and officials aspired to. These are issues which we hope to resolve here by a new examination of the piece. It may not be possible to clarify any further the speculations involved in identifying particular owners of the arms displayed on the print but a further consideration of the mazer's artistic context is overdue.

The first thing to notice is the finely turned wooden bowl itself, assumed to be of maple wood. It is remarkable that previous commentators have not drawn attention to a unique design feature, the lack of a base. Mazers at their simplest are turned wooden bowls with a slight base ring to allow them to stand steady on a table. Where they have been fitted with a print or boss these are invariably attached to the inner surface of the wooden bowl. In the case of the Bute Mazer the silver-gilt and enamelled print is in place of a wooden base. A visual examination of the underside of the mazer shows that its silver foot is added to a silver foot ring that forms the underside of the print (fig 6.5). It acts as a rim for a large basal opening in the wooden bowl. This unusual arrangement suggests that the bowl was fitted to the print, rather than vice versa.

So, if the print is essentially of fourteenth-century date, how old is the mazer itself? It has been noted, at least in the case of English mazers, that changes of shape in mazer bowls reflect changes in fashion with time, with those of fourteenth- and early fifteenth-century date generally being deeper than later ones (Hope 1887: 135). This, however, is clearly an inexact science. In fact, the bowl of the Bute Mazer does not look markedly different in appearance and profile from those of sixteenth-century Scottish mazers like the St Mary's Mazer of about 1556–8 or 1561–2 or the Fergusson Mazer of about 1576 (Dalgleish & Fothringham 2008: 35), albeit they are smaller. It is therefore not improbable that the mazer itself dates to the time of Ninian Bannatyne. The turning of wooden bowls as fine as this

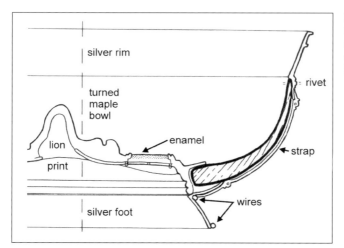

Fig 6. 5 Diagram showing the relationship between the silver foot, silver-gilt print and wooden bowl of the Bute Mazer (© David H Caldwell).

mazer demanded great skill and was no doubt in the hands of specialists, such as the copper (cupmaker), John Hunter in Newbattle, Midlothian, who was supplying cups to Mary Queen of Scots in 1562 (*TA* 11: 174).

Perhaps a goldsmith was commissioned by Ninian Bannatyne to create a mazer using an antique – the print – preserved by the family. It would seem more probable that an inscription so untidily and inaccurately rendered as that on the rim of the Bute Mazer would be the work of a goldsmith based in a provincial centre like Glasgow than one in Edinburgh or Canongate. Other Scottish mazers of the late sixteenth century with marks are all products of those latter two towns, have better quality engraving and are technically more competent. They include the Watson Mazer of about 1540 with a mark attributed to Adam Leys, Edinburgh; the Tulloch Mazer of about 1557 and the Galloway Mazer of about 1569, both by James Gray, Canongate; St Mary's Mazer by Alexander Auchinleck, Edinurgh, about 1556–8 or 1561–2; the Fergusson Mazer by John Mosman II, Edinburgh, about 1576; and the Craigievar Mazer, probably by either John Cok or John Cunningham, Edinburgh, possibly about 1575–91 (Dalgleish & Fothringham 2008: 32–6). All these mazers are of the standing variety, that is they are supported on tall stems. The bowl of the Bute Mazer may well have been considered too large for such treatment.

The actual date for the commission is difficult to pin down with any accuracy. The style of the lettering in the inscription ought to offer some clues as to date, except that there is nothing with a Scottish provenance that is directly comparable. Stevenson (1931: 227) believed the lettering indicated a date not long after Ninian succeeded his father as laird of Kames in 1522. It is not unreasonable to argue that the gothic lower case letters, for example b, c and h, should not be much later than 1522, and some of the capitals, especially I, M and N, with knops or bars mid-stroke, are likely to have been forms current in 1522. They might, however, especially if the work of a provincial goldsmith, be rather later.

About 1565 is the date of manufacture for the mazer previously suggested by Dalgleish and Fothringham (2008: 32). Given the way the rim and foot are secured together by six straps a case might even be made that the mazer is even later in date. This method of construction was commonly employed by Scottish goldsmiths when mounting coconuts and shells to form cups. The straps were fixed by hinges and pins to avoid damaging delicate nuts and shells by the application of solder. The earliest surviving Scottish examples of coconuts and shells so mounted date no earlier than the early seventeenth century. They include a coconut cup of about 1600 by Thomas Lindsay I, Dundee, in a private collection; a coconut cup of about 1610, possibly by James Hart, Canongate, in NMS; a coconut cup of the early seventeenth century, probably by Robert Gardyne II, Dundee, in a private collection; and the Heriot Loving cup (a mounted nautilus shell), 1611–13, by Robert Denneistoun, Edinburgh, on loan to NMS. On this basis a late sixteenth- or early seventeenth-century date might be considered more appropriate for the mazer. It is not known when Ninian died, but he was certainly still alive in 1587 (*RMS* 5, no 2160) and, for what it is worth, the Glasgow goldsmith, Peter Lymeburner, suggested as the possible maker, survived until 1606 x 1610 (Robertson 1823: 59; Dalgleish & Fothringham 2008: 224).

Whether Lymeburner or another, the goldsmith asked to mount the print in a mazer with a silver rim and foot may already have had experience of mounting coconuts and shells. He would have perceived the task of assembling and securing the different elements of the mazer to be a similar task, albeit on a larger scale. Straps are unusual on mazers and in Scotland unique to the Bute Mazer. It might even be considered as a possibility that the straps are not an original feature, although there is no evidence for that other than the composition of the metal. On the basis of recent X-ray fluorescence analyses (Tate & Kirk 2011) the straps are about 92% silver while the other main silver elements are about 95%. This may result from reusing metal from different sources, a point to which we shall return.

If the straps are indeed an original design feature, the goldsmith who mounted the mazer may have lacked confidence that the attachment of his rim would prove secure enough without this extra help. As on other mazers, the silver rim sits on top of the wooden rim of the bowl, not much more than 2mm in thickness, and is fixed with rivets. The goldsmith must certainly have been aware that the attachment of the bowl to the print was a botched job. It does appear that it is the straps that keep the bowl, print and foot together. Perhaps it was not just inexperience or incompetence that produced this result but a refusal by the client to allow too much tampering with his antique. To fit it effectively into a mazer the goldsmith would have had to remove its base ring.

Despite the obvious comparisons to be made with coconut cups this is not sufficient reason alone to date the mazer much later than 1522. There is plenty of evidence for early sixteenth-century and earlier coconut cups in England (Glanville 1987: 16–21) and it may be inferred that it is merely the accident of survival that has denied us comparable Scottish material. Two features of the inscription, not hitherto commented on, lead us to believe that a date between 1522 and 1560 is the most likely for the mazer.

First, there is the appearance in the inscription of a stop in the form of the sacred monogram of Christ, *ihs*, which post-1560 might have been seen as making a political or religious statement. Ninian had aligned himself with Clan Campbell, being granted a bond of maintenance by the Earl of Argyll in 1538 (Robertson 1823: 57; Wormald 2003: 123–5; Campbell 2002: 18), and is likely to have supported the protestant cause. The *ihs* may have appeared unfortunate after 1560, even if a gratuitous addition by the goldsmith.

Second, there is the insistence in the inscription that Ninian is the son of the late Robert. How long after 1522 would it have been relevant to record this piece of genealogy? There are no hard and fast rules, but it is certainly not a typical cognisance in recording ownership of objects, and one that might only have been used in the immediate aftermath of the father's death. So a date of 1522 for the Bute Mazer is perhaps most likely. In that case the attribution to Peter Lymeburner can be dismissed, though a Glasgow provenance is an attractive idea.

The date of the lid has always been in doubt. Stevenson (1931: 21) considered it to be early fourteenth-century while Glenn (2003: 191–2), has suggested the early sixteenth century, the date she assigned to rim, straps and foot. It seems most reasonable to the present authors that it belongs with the mazer made for Ninian Bannatyne about 1522. It is 240mm to 243mm in diameter and has eight rivet-holes around its rim to secure a now missing metal mount. It sits lightly within the rim of the mazer, an intentional arrangement, since its function may have been largely ritual. As it was passed around the table the lid would ceremoniously have been taken off by each guest prior to drinking a toast, and then put on again before being passed on to the next person. Mazer lids are now very rare, and there are none very comparable. A wooden one of about 1350 from St Nicholas' Hospital, Harbledown, Canterbury (Alexander & Binski 1987: 436–7), now in the Museum of Canterbury, may similarly have sat within the rim of a now missing mazer.

Whale-bone was used in the West Highlands to make tablemen and caskets, two of which, dating to the fifteenth century, survive, decorated all over with interlace designs (Glenn 2003: 184–5, 186–91). The angular leaf work on the lid is reminiscent of some on West Highland sculpture of the sixteenth century, like the tomb-chest of Alexander MacIver at Kilmichael Glassary in Knapdale and the lid of a tomb-chest at the medieval cathedral of Agyll, Lismore, both possibly by the same carver (Steer & Bannerman 1977: pl 29F&E). It is not close enough, however, to make a convincing case that the lid is by the same craftsman.

Its decoration also has similarities to the carving on two wooden caskets believed to be of Scottish origin, one of which is in the British Museum, the other long in the possession of the Forrester family of Corstorphine, Edinburgh (British Museum 1924: fig 173; Caldwell 1982: 72–5). Both include crowned Gothic Rs and Ms encompassed by intertwining ribbed bands, interspersed with four-petalled flowers and leaves and berries. It is particularly the ribbed bands which are reminiscent of the Bute Mazer lid, but not a compellingly close match. Neither West Highland art nor the two wooden caskets provide obvious parallels for the large flower-heads on the mazer lid.

The Forrester casket is said to have belonged to King James IV's queen, Margaret Tudor, and to have been given to an ancestor by Mary Queen of Scots. Just possibly of more relevance than this tradition is the fact that the Forrester family briefly had a west coast presence through the royal grant to Duncan Forrester of Corstorphine of the barony of Skipness with its castle, in Kintyre, in 1495, retained by him until 1502 (*RMS* 2: nos 2261, 2669). Could it be that the caskets and the mazer-lid are products of craftsmen, influenced to some extent by West Highland art, working in the Clyde region in the sixteenth century?

In having this mazer made for himself about 1522 Ninian Bannatyne would have been at the front end of fashion in Scotland, both in respect of mazers and in harking back to his ancestry. He would no doubt have seen his mazer as a status symbol, one that would have reflected his ability to keep a good table for entertaining guests. This was of considerable importance in a country where there was a notorious lack of inns, and visitors and travellers might expect to be entertained in private houses (Brown 1891: 89, 104–31). In the person of Ninian the Bannatynes of Kames acquired status as considerable landowners in Bute and Argyll and reached a social highpoint with good marriages, firstly to Janet, a daughter of the Stewart of Bute, and secondly, Margaret, a daughter of MacDougall of Raray (Robertson

1823: 56–9; Reid 1864: 246–9). It was very probably Ninian who built or remodelled the family residence on Bute, Kames Castle.

None of the other surviving Scottish mazers overtly commemorates ancestors as the Bute Mazer does with its heraldry. Some English mazers which belonged to religious houses retained the names of dead members of their communities and perhaps were a deliberate focus for commemoration (Sweetinburgh 2010). Although the Bannatyne family had lost the meaning of their mazer's heraldry by the early nineteenth century it must have been of importance to Ninian Bannatyne when he had it done. How exactly he wished the print to be interpreted will probably never be known, but his act in incorporating it in the mazer bears comparison with the way some weapons were 'improved' with inscriptions in the sixteenth and early seventeenth century to link them with heroes of old or worthy ancestors (Caldwell forthcoming).

An early fourteenth-century covered cup?

We doubt that the print was originally designed for a mazer. Molly Rorke, in the paper that follows, notes evidence for four mazers that had belonged to Robert Bruce, in the collection of King James III at the time of his death in 1488. We can only conclude that they were not directly related to the Bute Mazer. We suggest that the print in the Bute Mazer was designed to be the lid of a silver-gilt cup. That would explain both the foot ring and the rim, together creating a tight fit on the lip of a silver vessel. The rim is now angled upwards to fit it to the wooden bowl (fig 6.5). The form of that silver vessel cannot even be guessed with any confidence but its metal may possibly have been used to fashion the mazer's rim and foot. This could not, however, be confirmed by recent analysis of the silver mounts of the mazer made in the NMS Analytical Research Laboratory (Tate & Kirk 2011).

This research was limited to non-destructive surface analysis of the silver by X-ray fluorescence. The rim, foot and print were all shown to contain similar levels of silver, around 95%. The straps are slightly less pure, about 92%, while the decorative wires applied to the straps and around the foot are about 91% silver. Gold was present in all the mounts, about 0.8% on the print (underside where not gilt) and the bases of the heraldic medallions; about 1.2% and 0.3% on the rim and straps respectively, and 1.5% on the foot. The straps and wire thus conform reasonably well to the traditional Scottish standard of 91.6% purity (Dalgleish & Fothringham 2008: 13, 15–17) while the rim, foot and print are significantly purer. Analysis of the base of the print and the underside of the enamelled shields and lion confirm the earlier analyses carried out by NMS in the 1990s, which indicated that the silver of the medallions and of the base is virtually identical.

We agree with Glenn that the print, including the lion, enamelled shields and their decoration, all appear to be of one phase of workmanship, assignable to the early fourteenth century. X-ray fluorescence analysis of gilding on the lion found significant amounts of mercury, indicating that the print had been fire gilded (Tate & Kirk 2011). X-rays also suggest that the print itself is made from two sheets of silver, one on top of the other. The heraldic medallions were set into circular holes cut through both layers of the print, held in place at the top by a lip and secured beneath by crudely cut and soldered wire tags. Small centrally located holes in the centre of the silver disks on the underside of the medallions might have been for the escape of superfluous cement when they were mounted in place.

The lion itself is composite, its front legs attached separately, and has clearly been made by a craftsman with limited understanding of what a lion looked like. He may have been reliant on images in books, on carvings, etc. A particularly apt comparison is the lion at the feet of the joint effigy of Walter, Earl of Menteith and his Countess, Mary, at the Priory of Inchmahome on an island in the Lake of Menteith. Barrow (1999: 128) dates it to either 1293–6 or 1298–1304. Earl Walter was the grandfather of Sir John Menteith the younger, whose arms are believed to be represented on shield number three of the print. Stevenson (1931: 15) drew attention to a similar lion, this time rampant, on the reverse of the first seal of Roger de Quincy, Earl of Winchester, Lord of Galloway and Constable of Scotland (1220–64) (Stevenson & Wood 1940: vol 3, 551).

An interesting feature of the Bute Mazer lion is the way its mane has been represented by rows of tightly packed annulets, impressed into the metal with a punch. Such a punch was also used to decorate the berries on a number of silver ring brooches of the late thirteenth and early fourteenth centuries which have a distribution covering Scotland and the north of England (Callander 1924: 172–3) and also the spines of the six wyverns around a gold brooch with a particular association with the Bute Mazer. The so-called Kames Brooch, now in National Museums Scotland, was for long kept with the mazer, also having belonged to the Bannatynes of Kames (Glenn 2003: 67). The eyes of the wyverns, like the lion on the Bute Mazer, are set with red enamel. The brooch may date to the late thirteenth century.

Writing in 1931 the goldsmith, William Brook, thought that the enamelled shields were made by a different craftsman from the goldsmith who made the print, and that their incorporation in the print represented a radical adaptation of an existing scheme of decoration. Brook may well have been right about the enamels being the work of a different craftsman but we can detect no evidence that they were not part of the original scheme of decoration. There is good reason for them to have been produced separately. Firstly, enamelling of this quality may only have been produced by a specialist, perhaps working in a separate workshop. Secondly, if the shields had been done as one with the print it would have been technically difficult to bake the enamel to a sufficiently high temperature without damaging the rest of the work.

The enamelling is of a high quality. The shields themselves are examples of *champlevé* work, the opaque enamel being set in hollows in the silver. Charges and fields required to be *argent* (silver), *or* (gold) or *ermine* (black marks against a silver background) are represented by silver, or silver gilt, as appropriate. The surrounds to the shields have *basse-taille* work, consisting of translucent enamel laid over foliage and geometric designs engraved in the silver base-plates.

These enamels are not the only examples of Scottish enamelling dating to the early fourteenth century. The Savernake Horn in the British Museum has a baldric with champlevé enamel arms of a Randolph Earl of Moray, probably the first, King Robert Bruce's nephew, companion and leading general, who died in 1322. Two of his sons succeeded to the earldom, the first dying within weeks, the second in 1346. Although the horn, which is carved from an elephant's tusk, has been claimed as English work and has long been associated with the wardenship of the Forest of Savernake, the presence of the arms on the baldric must surely indicate an earlier Scottish provenance (Caldwell 1982: 36–7). The most recent scholarship on it dates the medieval mounts on the horn to about 1325–50 (Robinson 2008: 261). They are silver, decorated with *basse-taille* enamelled hunting scenes, a huntsman and a king with a bishop.

Remarkably, further copper-gilt enamelled mounts associated with a Randolph Earl of Moray, including the arms of the Earldom of Moray, have turned up in excavations at Dunstaffnage Castle near Oban. They may be from a horse harness (Caldwell 1996: 579–8). It is also worth recalling the account of King Robert I's death in 1329 given by John Barbour in his famous epic poem on the king's life. It describes how Sir James Douglas had a fine silver case, cunningly enamelled, made to contain the king's heart, which he could then wear around his neck when he took it on pilgrimage (Duncan 1999: 759).

This account and the surviving pieces demonstrate that leading Scots could command fine silver and enamelled work for themselves. The most likely explanation for its origin is one or more Scottish workshops in the early fourteenth century, perhaps also the source for silver and gold brooches, and more ambitious work like the print of the Bute Mazer. Barbour's *Bruce*, the Savernake Horn and the Dunstaffnage mounts are witnesses to the patronage of King Robert's right hand men, those closest to him and at the very top of Scottish society, but what about the mazer print? Who commissioned it?

The answer given to that question by Professor Barrow (1999), on the basis of the heraldic scheme, is John Gilbertson, the Bailie of Bute. Shield six, presumed to be his, includes *cinquefoils or*, and others feature in the design of the print, three of them alternating with wyverns. Gilbertson thus showed due deference to his lord, the Steward, by having the latter's arms placed between the paws of the lion, and added arms of his own forebears and Stewart allies to make up the design. Barrow, however, was not prepared to extend arguments for heraldic respect to the lion and recognise it as the Scottish king.

We would like to propose a different explanation for ownership and patronage, basically that first propounded by Stevenson in 1931. Firstly, we see no problem with identifying the lion as King Robert Bruce, in an allegorical sense. Heraldically it should have been represented as rampant, but it was clearly easier for the goldsmith to incorporate a lion couchant in his design. The Steward's shield is in the most honourable position in the design and he was the most important person by far in terms of status and landed wealth, also son-in-law of the king. That would make it most probable that he commissioned the work, having incorporated in the design the arms of leading supporters. We could envisage that the vessel represented here was one of a set that incorporated a variety of such heraldic references. In this case the vessel has been purloined by, or passed down to descendants of the Gilbertsons featured in the design.

An obvious objection to this hypothesis is the apparent inclusion of Gilbertson heraldic references in the print, primarily in the form of cinquefoils or, less certainly in the scrolling plant identified as strawberry and claimed to be the origin of heraldic cinquefoils. Identifying these cinquefoils with John Gilbertson's patronage or interest is not necessary. Cinquefoils are a common enough motif in medieval art with no apparent heraldic significance, like, for instance, the cinquefoils that decorate the obverse of the second common seal matrix of Inchaffray Abbey, perhaps not too different in date from the mazer print (Stevenson & Wood 1940: vol 1, 184; Robinson 2008: 61). It would seem to us more reasonable to associate the mazer print with the patronage of a great man like the Steward rather than speculate that a relatively minor figure like John Gilbertson could aspire to such riches.

Conclusions

As, no doubt, this paper has demonstrated, certainty on anything to do with the Bute Mazer is impossible to achieve. We propose, however, that it was made for Ninian Bannatyne of Kames in about 1522 by a goldsmith working in Glasgow or some other centre about the Firth of Clyde. Bannatyne required that an earlier piece of gilt and enamelled metalwork should be incorporated in his mazer as the print, because he believed it reflected on his ancestry or was an object of importance. That object was originally the lid of some other vessel commissioned by Walter the Steward in the period 1314-27, perhaps specifically for use in Rothesay Castle in Bute, or to commemorate an event there. The lion in the centre of the print surely represents King Robert Bruce himself.

Acknowledgements

Several colleagues have helped with advice and comments, including Stuart Campbell, Godfrey Evans, Jacquie Moran and Molly Rorke. David Caldwell is grateful to the owners of the mazers (from Hambledown Hospital) in the Museum of Canterbury and museum staff there for access and assistance in studying them. We offer our gratitude while absolving them of all blame for the end result.

References

Alexander, J & Binski, P 1987 (eds) *Age of Chivalry: Art in Plantagenet England 1200-1400*. London: Royal Academy of Arts.

Barrow, G W S 1999 'The Social Background to the Bute Mazer', in Fawcett, R (ed), *Medieval Art and Architecture in the Diocese of Glasgow*, 122–32. The British Archaeological Association Conference Transactions XXIII.

British Museum 1924 *Guide to Mediaeval Antiquities*. London: British Museum.

Brown, P H 1891 *Early Travellers in Scotland*. Edinburgh: David Douglas.

Caldwell, D H (ed) 1982 *Angels, Nobles & Unicorns: Art and Patronage in Medieval Scotland*. Edinburgh: National Museum of Scotland.

Caldwell, D H 1996 'Small Finds', in Lewis, J H, 'Dunstaffnage Castle, Argyll & Bute: excavations in the north tower and east range, 1987-94', *Proc Soc Antiq Scot* 126 , 579–87.

Caldwell, D H forthcoming 'Collecting Scottish Weapons', in a volume of papers from a Society of Antiquaries of Scotland conference on transatlantic craftsmanship held at Winterthur, USA, in 2009.

Callander, J G 1924 'Fourteenth-century Brooches and other ornaments in the national Museum of Antiquities of Scotland', *Proc Soc Antiq Scot* 58 (1923–4), 160–84.

Campbell, A 2002 *A History of Clan Campbell Volume 2: From Flodden to the Restoration*. Edinburgh: Edinburgh University Press.

Dalgleish, G & Fothringham, H S 2008 *Silver Made in Scotland*. Edinburgh: National Museums of Scotland.

DOST Dictionary of the Older Scottish Tongue http://www.dsl.ac.uk, accessed 27 February 2010.

Duncan, A A M (ed) 1999 *John Barbour: The Bruce*. Edinburgh: Canongate.

Glanville, P 1987 *Silver in England*. London: Unwin Hyman.

Glenn, V 1999 'Court Patronage in Scotland 1240-1340', in Fawcett, R (ed), *Medieval Art and Architecture in the Diocese of Glasgow*, 111–21. The British Archaeological Association Conference Transactions XXIII.

Glenn, V 2003 *Romanesque & Gothic Decorative Metalwork and Ivory Carvings in the Museum of Scotland*. Edinburgh: National Museums of Scotland.

Hope, W H St J 1887 'On the English Medieval Drinking Bowls Called Mazers', *Archaeologia* 50, 129–93.

Reid, J. E. 1864 *History of the County of Bute and families connected therewith*. Glasgow: Murray.

Richardson, C & Hamling, T (eds) 2010 *Medieval and Early Modern Material Culture and its Meanings*, 257–66. Aldershot: Ashgate.

RMS Registrum Magni Sigilli Regum Scotorum, ed Thomson, J M et al. Edinburgh: General Register Office (1882–1914).

Robertson, G 1823 *A Genealogical Account of the Principal Families in Ayrshire, more particularly in Cunninghame*. Irvine: Cunninghame Press.

Robinson, J 2008 *Masterpieces Medieval Art*. London: The British Museum.

Steer, K A & Bannerman, J W M 1977 *Late Medieval Monumental Sculpture in the West Highlands*. Edinburgh: The Royal Commission on the Ancient & Historical Monuments of Scotland.

Stevenson, J H 1931 'The Bannatyne or Bute Mazer and its Carved Bone Cover', *Proc Soc Antiq Scot* 65 (1930–1), 217–55.

Stevenson, J H & Wood, M 1940 *Scottish Heraldic Seals*, 3 vols. Glasgow: Maclehose.

Sweetinburgh, S 2010 'Remembering the Dead at Dinner-Time', in Richardson, C & Hamling, T(eds) *Medieval and Early Modern Material Culture and its Meanings*, 257–66. Aldershot: Ashgate.

TA Accounts of the Lord High Treasurer of Scotland, ed Dickson, T et al. Edinburgh: H.M. General Register Office (1877–).

Tate, J & Kirk, S 2011 *Analysis of the silver on the Bute Mazer*. Analytical Research Section Report no AR 2011/61. Edinburgh: NMS.

Wormald, J 2003 *Lords and Men in Scotland: Bonds of Manrent 1442–1603*. Edinburgh: John Donald.

Fig 7.1 The Bute Mazer.

Chapter 7

Mazer? What's a 'mazer'?
A history of the word

Molly Rorke
University of Glasgow

MANY modern Scots probably first became acquainted with the word *mazer* during the Folk Revival when Ewan McColl's version of the *Ballad of Gil Morris* was an integral part of the repertoire. In this song, Lord Barnard intercepts a message sent to his wife by a young man who is waiting to see her in the woods; he assumes this is a lovers' assignation, and is naturally furious.

> *Then up and sprang the bold baron, and an angry man was he,*
> *He's taen the table wi his foot and likewise wi his knee,*
> *Till siller cup and mazer dish in flinders he garred flee.*

And immediately *he's awa' tae the gude greenwood*, to decapitate his rival and bring the head back to his wife, only to discover that the youth he has killed is not, in fact, her lover, but her son. The plot has been used repeatedly, from John Home in his wildly popular eighteenth-century play, *Douglas ('Whaur's yer Wullie Shakespeare noo?'* cried an ecstatic Scot in the audience) to the twentieth-century Ellis Peters (of Brother Cadfael fame) in *Black is the Colour of my True love's Heart.*[1] A dictionary indicated that *mazer* meant maple wood.

Less commonly known is that the song seems to have been based on a Scottish ballad called *Childe Maurice,*[2] and that the testy Lord was originally called John Stuart. When it was printed by Bishop Percy in his *Reliques of Ancient Poetry* in 1765, John Stuart, the third earl of Bute, was a power in the land, and it is easy to see why both Percy, and even more , John Home, who became Bute's secretary, felt that it was advisable to change the nomenclature. In the ballad, the baron is called Lord Barnard; in the play, Lord Randolph.

Oddly, in the version printed by Percy the word *Mazer* does not occur. The baron vents his temper on a utensil called an *ezar dish*, and it is clear that the good Bishop had no idea what the word meant. In his glossary, he opined the meaning was probably *Azure* - blue,[3] which is only marginally more convincing than a modern web site of traditional song, where Leslie Nielson, 'the Contemplator',[4] gives it as *czar dish*, as in Czar of all the Russias.

More authoritative dictionaries were consulted: The Dictionary of the Older Scottish Tongue,[5] The Oxford Historical Thesaurus, and, of course, the magisterial Oxford English Dictionary, using online versions where available.[6]

The OED entry accessed was *mazer*, n.1, 'Draft Revision, Dec 2009'. The Oxford English Dictionary research is ongoing; like language itself, it is continually developing. In the past, in the days before printing and standardised spelling, language was even less static. As it stands, the OED lists thirty four different ways in which the word has been written at different times.[7] What seems clear etymologically, however, is that Germanic languages contained a form *mas* or *map* or *mad* (the final consonant varies) which means a scar, a spot, a swelling, an excrescence. In the forests of the north, this might apply to trees with burrs, knots, or a distinctive veining in the wood. One species which had these characteristics was called *maple* by the Anglo Saxons, *masdre* in those Old French dialects which derive from Frankish, essentially a Teutonic language.[8] Then the word became attached to a utensil typically made from that tree,[9] a drinking cup shaped perhaps from the hard burr,[10] or from curly grained wood. Old Icelandic had both the p and s forms. In several modern European languages the form survives; in French *madre;* German *maser;* Swedish *masur;* Danish, *mase*, all carrying the notion of whorls or curly graining in wood. Many other English words were derived from the same root, but they have since become obsolete. *Maple* clearly survived in English and established itself across the Atlantic, whereas other *mase-* derived vocabulary did not, for example, *mase* meaning a freckle, and *masers*, an obsolete word for measles. It was easy to blur *maselin,* an alternative spelling for mazer, with *mesel,* meaning leprous. Since such wood is particularly hard, mazer was used not only for drinking cups but for the thin slivers of wood inserted in people's skulls to replace shattered bone, and this gave *mazard,*[11] a colloquial word for head which had considerable staying power. Irish English retained it in the call for tossing coins until the nineteenth and twentieth centuries. But the word mazer itself, if not defunct, was thoroughly archaic by the eighteenth century.

It seems reasonable to assume that the word came first into England, and thence to Scotland, with the wine-imbibing Normans. Unlike ale, medieval wine could be highly acidic, and it was safer to drink from wood rather than metal. Examples of the word survive in the language, which was called *Inglis* before 1500 (to distinguish it from Erse, or Gaelic) and Scots thereafter.[12] In fact, Irish and Scottish Gaelic already had a word *mether,*[13] (Old Scots – *meddyr*[14]) for a wooden communal drinking cup. The Dunvegan Cup is one such. It is about ten inches tall and is 'quadrangularly formed at the top', in other words, it has four corners. Although it has been suggested that the name comes from the word for mead, the etymology is more likely to be derived from the concept of measuring, the corners making it much easier to pour an accurate measure of liquid or grain without spilling any. [15] *Meddyrs* [16] and, one presumes, *masers* might be made of yew, or alder. Similarly, in England, mazers were made from walnut, and in France from vine roots. What mattered was not botanical or etymological exactitude, but that the material was a hard impermeable wood which, properly seasoned, could hold liquids at room temperature without tainting, shrinking, furring up, or drying out and cracking, so beech, elm, or birch would probably also have been suitable.[17] In later centuries, native 'maple'[18] wood from the sycamore tree (called plane in Scotland) would have been available. Shaping mazers from enemy skulls seems to have been a practice restricted to the Scythians.[19]

As time went on the word mazer was applied differently north and south of the Border. In England, it could mean an alms bowl used, for example, by lepers. The word *mesel,* meaning leper, may account for this conflation of meaning. According to the Victoria and Albert Museum, by the end of the sixteenth century, mazers were standard inexpensive drinking vessels – a load of 200 imported into Exeter in 1493 cost only six shillings and sixpence.[20] In Scotland, however, mazers, either secular or religious, literal or metaphorical,[21] stayed more up-market. The beggars' bowl used by Henryson's leprous Cressida is called not a mazer, but *a cop*; the examples of mazers quoted in DOST usually emphasise is the value of the silver decoration. Indeed, the word is sometimes applied to 'a communal drinking cup or bowl, either silver gilt,[22] or made entirely of silver'.[23] DOST makes it clear that though such bowls were 'originally made of mazer-wood', by the fifteenth century a Scottish mazer was a 'costly vessel ornamented with, or having its single foot of gold or silver', and indeed the name was applied to 'vessels of similar design made entirely of metal'. In much the same way, we use the term 'plastic glasses' and the Americans talk about 'plastic silverware'[24] without any sense of linguistic anomaly.

But whatever the meaning, or the value, in both Scots and English, the word mazer is pretty well obsolete by the 1700s. Not a single example is recorded in eighteenth-century Scotland; what we now call the Bute Mazer features in an early nineteenth-century description simply as an 'antique cup'. Byron, who had no qualms about drinking out of a human cranium, was never described as toping from a mazer, but from a skull cup. Probably the sole example of the word in eighteenth-century English is in Ritson's introduction to *Scotish* (sic) *Song* where that vituperative antiquarian is crowing over Bishop Percy's inability to gloss *ezar* correctly. For *ezar* seems to be the word for 'maple' preferred in eighteenth-century Scots popular culture, as exemplified in the ballads. The words are similar enough to have caused a certain confusion, but they are etymologically quite different. Ezar never occurs in English, only in Scots, probably as a result of linguistic borrowing during the Auld Alliance, a practice particularly common from the fifteenth to mid sixteenth centuries, when France and Scotland were allies against England. Many such words were borrowed from French and remained in Scots (gigot, ashet, tassie, gardyloo etc),[25] but the late medieval/early modern forms came from Central French, a Romance rather than a Germanic language. In it the word for maple is derived from the Latin *acer*,[26] meaning not spots or pustules or burrs, but *sharp*, referring, presumably, to the shape of the leaf, rather than the characteristics of the timber. Modern Italian is *acero*; modern French *érable*, with an acute accent on the e, indicating that an s has been lost. The older French form, therefore, was *esrable*,[27] whence derives the Scots *ezar, easer*. An obvious parallel is the older French *estuver*, to steam. Modern French is *étuver* – e acute; the Scots version retained the older *estuver* form, which ultimately, in Modern Scots, became *stovies*.

And then, in late 1814, early 1815, the word *mazer* was resurrected. Credit for this must go to Walter Scott. Given that Scott was a high Tory, a unionist, an antiquarian, and an Edinburgh lawyer, his choice of the word was probably inevitable. In 1814, he was particularly strapped for cash, and chose a subject for a long poem that he thought was guaranteed to 'take': the wanderings of Robert the Bruce, culminating at Bannockburn. It was researched by a trip to the Northern and Western isles with Robert Lewis Stevenson's grandfather (who was inspecting potential sites for lighthouses), entitled 'The Lord of the Isles' to echo his blockbuster 'The Lady of the Lake' and written at frenetic speed. Although there are some stirring passages, like the part where Bruce's battle axe demolishes de Bohun,[28] it was not the happiest of subjects for Scott. As a Unionist he felt constrained to be somewhat apologetic to his English audience for the Scottish victory at Bannockburn; the Lord of the Isles, his name changed from Angus to Ronald (more acceptable to the educated ear) scarcely features except as part of a love story that might be described both literally and colloquially as pants, due to Scott's excessive enthusiasm for cross-dressing heroines. Bruce himself is anachronistically sensitive and quite unconvincingly chivalrous, while the antiquarian notes and appendices are longer than the poem, and the history is distinctly suspect.

In the poem Bruce celebrates his (completely fictitious) capture of Turnberry Castle, his ancestral home, thus:

> Bring here", he said, "the mazers four,
> My noble fathers loved of yore![29]

Scott does not use the Franco- Scots *ezar* form, though he could hardly have avoided knowing it. As a ballad collector, he was well acquainted with Percy's *Reliques*, and David Herd's *Scottish Songs* (1776), and indeed, the opinions of his quondam house guest Joseph Ritson. Moreover, the *ezar* form was in use in 1802, when the *Earl of Aboyne* ballad was first written down, and as late as 1860 in Aytoun's *Ballads of Scotland*, where it is glossed, correctly, as 'maple'. In the early nineteenth century, however, such colloquial Scots usages could well have been regarded by genteel society as vulgar, and less likely to 'take' with potential paying customers, while the republican and regicidal French and the threat of their '*invasion, and the thunder and the shout, and all the crash of onset*'[30] had been the nightmare of the British establishment for a quarter of a century. Nor does he use the Irish term *mether*; though the Dunvegan Cup itself merits a glowing description in the poem[31] (and seven pages of notes in the appendix), and one could hardly view the native Irish as loyal subjects of the British Crown circa 1800. Instead, Scott opts for the archaic term used by such eminently acceptable English poets as Spenser and Dryden, whose work Scott knew well, and by the Scots literati of bygone days – lawyers, churchmen and civil servants from the late medieval and early modern period.[32] Scott would certainly have known Lauder of Fountainhall's[33] use of the word in the Scots legal definition of 'vitious intromission'. His direct source is, however, is the Scottish Treasurer's Account of 1488, which includes the phrase: '*Foure masaris callit King Robert the Brocis with a couir*'.[34] With this as an excuse for shameless antiquarian padding, Scott includes the entire account in the appendix to the *Lord of the Isles*.

The position of the mazer couplet within the poem is thought provoking. Both Barbour's *Brus*[35] and the anonymous writer of the *Life of Edward II*[36] emphasise the amount of booty, including valuable gold and silver plate, captured on the field at Bannockburn. A reader might very well speculate about where the four mazers in the royal treasury had originated, but it seems that Scott, the Romantic Tory, simply could not conceive that a king like Robert I would have been so lost to chivalric values as to appropriate loot from a fellow monarch's baggage train. Thus, in a pre-emptive strike, a whole canto before Bannockburn, the four mazers are firmly emphasised as legally part of the Bruce family silver since time immemorial.

Although the poem did not make as much money as Scott had hoped – indeed, he subsequently took to novel writing instead – it was popular enough for the word mazer to go straight into literary and learned vocabulary, in which register it has stayed ever since. Thus the object under discussion is always referred to as The Bute Mazer.

The word *ezar* is now totally obsolete, and *mazer* regarded as archaic or historical, appropriate, for example, to Museum catalogues, or to C S Lewis's imaginary land, Narnia.[37] On the other side of the Atlantic, however, the word mazer is still going strong and, indeed, developing. In the USA, where they seem to imagine that mazers were for drinking mead, they have a highly successful Annual Mazer Cup International Mead Competition,[38] where

Mazers are presented as prizes for the best brew. But these attractive utensils are not carved from maser wood or ezar wood or indeed wood of any description. Rather more hygienically, they are made of glazed pottery.

Notes

1　Peters, E *Black is the Colour of my True Love's Heart.* Inspector Felse series, 1988.
2　Percy, Thomas, *Reliques of Ancient English Poetry…* Dublin 1766, Vol III p77, Eighteenth Century Collections Online, Gale, University of Glasgow Library.
3　Percy's *Reliques* , III.– A Glossary of the Obsolete and Scottish words in Volume the third., p81.
4　www.contemplator.com/folk Child Ballads#83 *Childe Maurice* verse 12.
5　DOST www.dsl.ac.uk
6　OED online, accessed in February 2010.
7　For the sake of consistency the spelling mazer has been retained throughout. It should be noted, however, that in DOST the headword spelling is maser.
8　OED *Mazer*,n.1 full entry, etymology.
9　OED *Mazer* 1b.
10　McNeill, F M 1981 *The Scots Cellar,*161. London: Granada.
11　OED *mazer*, 1c.
12　DOST on line accessed Feb 2010. *maser* (n) 1.Variety of wood 2. A sort of drinking bowl.
13　OED *mether.*
14　DOST *meddyr*, n.
15　The *mazies* mentioned in A Glossary of Perthshire Cant in *The Last of the Tinsmiths, the Life of Willie Macphee,* (Douglas, Sheila, Birlinn, Edinburgh 2006, pp14– 17), refer to wooden cups used by Travelling People, but given that Cant is likely to be Gaelic based, *mazie* seems more likely to derive from Gaelic, rather than Anglo Norman; like the Older Scots *Meddyr,* modern Gaelic *Measir* carries a sense of measuring. *Maclennan,Malcolm A Pronouncing and Etymological Dictionary of the Gaelic Language.* Acair 1988; see *measair*, p226.
16　Nineteenth-century antiquarians tended to confuse mazers, methers, and, indeed, surgical bleeding bowls. See T J Tenison, 'Of Methers and Other Ancient Drinking Vessels', *Kilkenny and south east of Ireland Archaeological Society,* 1860.
17　scottishwood.co.uk *All about hardwoods.* Some birch timber is 'masured'.
18　DOST *planetre* a 1. Note Sibbald's definition: '*acer majus –multis falso platanus.:* the great mapple, commonly yet falsly, the sycamore and plaintree'. (sic)
19　OED *maser*, n.2 1555.
20　www.vam.ac.uk/content/articles/m/mazer
21　DOST *maser* 2b fig. Zachary Boyd talks of *the cuppe of salvation, the great mazer of His mercie.*
22　DOST *maser* 1530.
23　DOST *maser* 1570.
24　www.nextag.com/reflection-plastic-silverware: 'Plastic Silverware. Reflections. Silverlike plastic silverware will give you the authentic look of real silverware, 200 Soup spoons $24.'
25　For an exhaustive list, see McNeil, F M 1932*The Scots Kitchen*, appendix. Edinburgh: Blackie.
26　See above note 18. DOST Sibbald's definition.
27　DOST *ezar.*
28　*High in his stirrups stood the King,*
　　And gave his battle-axe the swing…
　　… First of that fatal field, how soon,
　　How sudden fell the fierce de Boune!
　　Walter Scott Digital Archive Edinburgh University, *Lord of the Isles,* E text, Making of America Books, p238.

29 Walter Scott Digital Archive, Lord of the Isles, p214.
30 Coleridge. *Fears in Solitude.* (A poet, it should be noted, considerably to the left of Walter Scott.)
31 Walter Scott Digital Archive, *Lord of the Isles*, p58:

> *Fill me the mighty cup! he said,*
> *Erst own'd by mighty Somerled,*
> *Fill it, till on the studded brim*
> *In burning gold and bubbles swim,*
> *And every gem of varied shine*
> *Glows doubly bright in rosy wine!*

The provenance of the Dunvegan Cup is uncertain: traditionally, the fairies are involved; more recently, and prosaically, it is described as early modern, made of yew or alder, and set with coral or glass.
32 See the definitions given in DOST for *maser*.
33 DOST *maser*, 1698; Fountainhall's *Decisions*, II.27.
34 DOST *maser*; quoted also, at some length, in *Lord of the Isles*, Appendix, Note S, p346. See also the volume published by Scott's friend, Thomas Thompson, as *A collection of Inventories and other records of the Royal Wardrobe and Jewellhouse; and of the Artillery and other Munitions in some of the Royal Castles.* MDCCCLXXXVII – MDCVI, 8.
35 Duncan, A A M (ed) 1999 *The Bruce*, 502–3. Edinburgh: Canongate.
36 *Vita Edwardi Secundi.* www.deremilitari.org/resources/sources/bannockburn
37 OED *mazer*, 1951 *Prince Caspian*, xv 185.
38 www.mazercup.com

Chapter 8

Frontierland:
towards an environmental history
of Bute in the later Middle Ages

Richard Oram
University of Stirling

THE medieval history of Bute and the other Clyde islands has been presented traditionally as a series of isolated vignettes constructed from scattered, incidental references in narrative accounts which are not concerned primarily with Bute itself. Consisting mainly of references to military clashes in the long struggle for control of the wider Firth of Clyde between the Scottish crown and its agents on the one hand, and the rulers of Argyll and the Isles and their associates on the other, the story has been presented mainly as a succession of invasions, battles and raids. Other types of documentary source, principally charter materials which detail awards of land and office in the island, or financial accounts which record income drawn and expenditure incurred by Bute's Stewart lords, allow that traditional picture of conflict to be tempered by glimpses of the quieter routines of administration, peaceful inheritance of property, and the rhythms of agricultural life. Taken together, these two main groups of documentary evidence can be used to construct an image of island life which flowed along almost unchanging, disrupted only occasionally by brief episodes of violence which had few long-term consequences for the islanders. It is an appealing but hardly convincing image. Other forms of evidence which historians have not used traditionally, when combined with traditional parchment records, are revealing an altogether different experience. Palaeoclimate data (principally the record of past climate change represented by the isotopes trapped in the deep layers of the polar ice-caps, or revealed in tree-ring records), paleoenvironmental evidence (mainly analysis of pollen preserved in archaeological contexts, other plant remains, and the micro-faunal remnants of environmentally sensitive species), and geoarchaeological techniques (chiefly methods which explore the natural and anthropogenic processes of soil formation), have been combined with historical records to construct interdisciplinary environmental histories. While these can still only provide us with the broad themes in any historical narrative, together they provide context for the keynote events recorded in the documentary records. They can allow us to understand why events fell out as they did, or particular strategies were pursued, moving beyond the bare-bones catalogues of what happened and when.

This essay cannot provide a full environmental history of Bute, even just for the Middle Ages, but it can attempt to set out the broad context for events and consider some of the evidence which permits us to see the opportunities and problems which the ordinary islanders faced in their daily lives. It will begin with an overview of the current understanding of the broad environmental trends which were experienced in the North Atlantic region in the medieval period, and a general consideration of the impacts of natural agency, climatic, resource-based and pathogenic, on the human condition. This will be followed by a review of the evidence for weather and its impact on the western maritime zone of Scotland. These two sections set out some context for the final segment, which considers the significance of Bute within the Stewarts' domain and some of the evidence for environment-related stresses affecting the daily lives of its people.

Environmental change, famine and disease: the context

Growing contemporary awareness of environmental impacts on human culture and society, most commonly seen through the lens of the climate change debate, has helped to trigger an expansion of research into past climate trends. Within that new research, the study of the environmental history of the Middle Ages is helping us to gain greater awareness of how our ancestors coped with or collapsed in the face of climate change and long episodes of extreme weather. Their experience is helping us to model how resilient modern subsistence economies in environmentally marginal regions might be during a time of rapidly changing climate. For the historian, however, awareness of the nature and scale of the stresses which environmental change placed on the land- and sea-use regimes which supported the whole edifice of medieval society is helping to reconfigure our understanding of the underlying pressures which helped to drive political events. The fragmentary and largely qualitative nature of medieval record sources for climate, or more particularly weather events, for long rendered it impossible to talk in anything more than the broadest of generalisations about climatic trends. More recently, however, the greater availability of proxy data obtained from a range of scientific measures, such as analysis of the isotope record from cores taken from the Greenland ice-cap, has allowed climate variation across the Historic era to be expressed graphically in forms accessible to non-specialists. The result is that we can now reconstruct with some confidence a general picture of climatic variability in medieval Scotland from which we can identify both the likely long-term impacts on the human population of the country and the shorter-term effects of extreme weather events, especially those triggered by episodes of climatic instability. There is a danger of perhaps seeing environmental change as the primary agency for all changes in human society, political, societal, cultural and economic (neo-environmental determinism as that route is called), but recognition of the centrality of non-anthropogenic agency in defining the human experience encourages the re-evaluation of evidence for long-term change in how our ancestors exploited Scotland's natural resources. Environmental impacts on the medieval subsistence economy, it has been argued, forced major changes in the political and socio-economic structures of the kingdom (Oram & Adderley 2008; 2010a; 2010b).

The current scientific emphasis on the role of climate-related impacts in stimulating human societal change should not obscure the part played by other environmental factors. Epidemic disease, for example, is now widely recognised as having agency in the reconfiguration of economies, cultures and societies (Campbell 2009; Jillings 2003), with effects extending far beyond the obvious immediate impact of high human mortality. Indeed, the indirect consequences of epidemics may have had equally profound or even greater long-term impacts as high mortality rates did in the short-term. Research has suggested how high mortality rates might trigger fundamental shifts in devotional practice, human interpersonal relationships and wider social attitudes (Oram 2008). Epizootic diseases (widespread disease in particular animal species), such as the catastrophic pan-European cattle plague of the 1310s, also have been identified as significant factors in past human economic crises (Spinage 2003; Campbell & Newfield 2009). The consequences of such diseases for peasant economies that depended on meat and dairy products, wool, woolfells and hides, and on oxen for traction, cannot be overstated.

Famine and episodes of crop failure were also recurrent features of the environmental history of the pre-modern age. The most serious episode was the Great European Famine of 1315–22 (Kershaw 1973; Jordan 1996), but failure of the grain harvest dogged Scottish peasant society at regular intervals from at least the twelfth through to late seventeenth centuries and is widely recognised as contributing to high European mortality levels in urban and rural contexts throughout the late Medieval and Early Modern eras (Smout 1985; Gemmill & Mayhew 1995: 63–5; Appleby 1980; Sella 1991). Famines might have as many human as natural environmental factors contributing to them; if we recognise that fact we must also acknowledge that what are thought of conventionally as primarily human social actions can also have profound ramifications for the wider environment. The most obvious such action is warfare, specifically long-term disturbances like those experienced in Scotland during the Wars of Independence (Barrow 1976; 1978; Lomas 1996). Long-term political disturbance and the emergence of a raiding culture in the West Highlands and Hebrides in the later medieval period, however, produced as profound socio-economic upheaval as major episodes of international conflict (Oram & Adderley 2008; 2010a; 2010b). It is not just the immediate physical destruction of property and slaughter of human and livestock populations that resulted directly from human conflict that must be considered but, perhaps more importantly, also the long-term legacies of military campaigning. Depopulation and depressed agricultural economies were often consequences of epidemic disease which followed in the wake of armies (McKerral 1948; Stell 1991; Oram 2008). Long after the fighting was over, the destructive legacy of war and its associated diseases, social and economic dislocation, contrived to weaken the human population and the fabric of their society.

Confrontation with this catalogue of potential negative impacts of environmental and human-induced change on past societies certainly seems to confirm Thomas Hobbes' view of life for the bulk of the population as 'nasty, brutish and short'. But it must be remembered that there were also many positive outcomes from such changes. It was generally more benign climatic conditions spanning the period from the early tenth to later thirteenth centuries which stimulated a boom in the European economy and enabled the first major expansion of population in the medieval West since the collapse of the Roman Empire. Warmer and drier weather conditions in the developing kingdom of Scotland allowed arable agriculture to expand into more upland districts, helping to provide the economic platform upon which the apparatus of the state could be built. Longer growing seasons and the growth of abundant grass provided the fodder to maintain larger flocks and herds, from which the wool, dairy produce, meat and leather provided peasant communities with bulk produce to trade. Calmer seas and less frequent storms permitted the development of deep-water marine exploitation and the expansion of catches to a level where a commercial fish trade was possible for the communities down the Atlantic sea-board. It is in the balances and imbalances of these positives and negatives that the human settlement history of Bute and the wider Clyde estuary region was shaped.

Climate and weather in the Atlantic West

The contemporary climate change debate has stimulated new interrogation methods for palaeoclimate records, using data which could provide context for shifts in settlement patterns or modes of exploitation visible in the archaeological and historical record. Alongside material from historical documentary sources, proxy environmental measures which use ice-core, ocean sediment and tree-ring data can offer a long-term perspective on past climatic movement. Many of these data are region-specific but through synthesis of different types we can model likely climatic changes both over wider areas and longer periods. Climate change recorded in documentary sources has previously been discussed for various upland areas of Britain (Parry 1985), but Bute and the western margins of the British Isles generally experience a more temperate maritime climatic regime, and it is likely that long-term climatic shifts were mitigated considerably by the North Atlantic Ocean.

In respect of the climate for the period c1100 – c1600, various proxies have been resolved to annual or seasonal resolution (fig 8.1). These proxies, drawn from Ural and Siberian tree-ring data and the Greenland ice cap, are remote from the western Scottish context and should not be used as absolute indicators of climatic variability there. The method employed is to contrast Northern Hemisphere/North Atlantic summer temperatures from dendrochronological analyses, stable isotope records providing an index of relative winter 'severity' from ice core data, and for an annualised long-multi-proxy mean (for discussion and application of this method, see Oram & Adderley 2008). The annualised multi-proxy data indicates that a long period of higher annual mean temperatures commenced in the tenth century and extended through to the later thirteenth century, but within this timeframe both the proxy data and existing historical accounts reveal cold episodes and extreme weather events (Crowley & Lowery 2000). In addition to these longer term trends, year-on-year seasonal differences (ie between summer and winter) have also been identified as having significant consequences for landscape management in other North Atlantic territories including Iceland, Faroe, and southern Greenland (Simpson et al 2002; Edwards et al 2005; Adderley & Simpson 2005; 2006; Adderley et al 2008).

Synthesis of the various data exposes the general trend in weather events which were driven by these climatic shifts. The era commenced with a pronounced episode of cooling in the ninth and tenth centuries, attested for in record sources and in the evidence for a catastrophic volcanic eruption in southern Iceland which threw around 220 million tonnes of sulphate aerosols into the atmosphere which, combined with atmospheric water vapour, produced around 450 million tonnes of dilute sulphuric acid circulating the globe in the troposphere (Dawson 2009: 94-5). While we can only infer from more recent measured eruptions what the likely impact of such an event was on the global climate, the cooling effect produced by the 1991 eruption of Mt Pinatubo in the Philippines (less than one tenth of the scale of the tenth-century Icelandic eruption) suggests that there were perhaps decades of instability marked by colder winters and, probably, by wet summers memorable for acidic rainfall which stunted growing crops. As this episode faded, temperatures again climbed

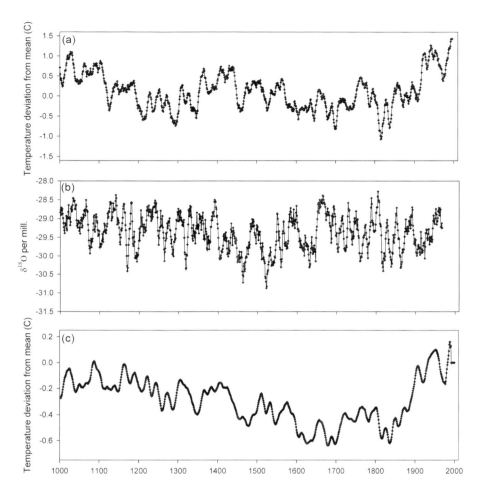

Fig 8.1 Long-term climate proxies AD 1000–AD 2000 for the exotropical Northern Hemisphere and North Atlantic: (a) normalised simple mean of four dendroclimate sequences showing deviation of summer temperature from mean (1601–1974) summer temperature (resampled data after Briffa et al 2000); (b) winter −18O data from DYE-3 ice core of Greenland Ice Cap Summit (Adderley & Simpson 2006; Vinther pers comm; Vinther et al 2003) and (c) unweighted aggregate of fifteen Northern Hemisphere proxies: annual deviations from long-term mean (Crowley & Lowery 2000). All data plotted as 10-Year Moving Averages.

to produce an era of milder conditions which spanned the eleventh and twelfth centuries, conditions which encouraged settlement spread and agricultural development in previously more marginal districts.

Twelfth- and thirteenth-century records reveal episodes of extreme environmental distress punctuating the generally more benign 1100s in Scotland. For example, the winters of 1124–5 and 1125–6 were especially cold. Prolonged winter rain, frost and snow, and cold and wet summer conditions resulted in harvest failure and famine, with many deaths reported from hunger and cold in winter 1125–6 (*Chron Bower* vol 4: 161). Some Irish annals suggest that the western British Isles experienced optimal growing conditions in 1199–1200, with 'a vast crop of mast and apples in abundance' noted in both years,[1] but others record 1200 as 'a cold, foodless year, the equal of which no man witnessed in that age'.[2] In Scotland, 1200 saw heavy summer rainfall, widespread flooding, destruction of property and deaths (*Chron Bower* vol 4: 423). Accounts of storm-damage and another dearth in 1205 indicate a harvest failure in 1204 and, perhaps, in 1205, and livestock was also badly hit by snow and frosts in winter 1204–1205 (*Chron Bower* vol 4: 437). Early sixteenth-century narratives drawing on thirteenth-century sources suggest that winter was one of the worst of the so-called 'medieval warm period' and Icelandic and Norwegian saga accounts of extensive sea ice off Greenland in 1203 provide a context for this cold episode (Stewart 1858: 61; Dawson 2009: 98). This same extension of the southward range of sea ice probably produced the anti-cyclonic conditions which brought the warm, dry summer followed by heavy rainfall in autumn which caused catastrophic flooding of the Tay in 1209 (*Chron Bower* vol 4: 457). Two mild, productive decades were followed after 1233 by another of severe winters. Conditions in this period are consistent with high surface air pressure, characterised by cold, icy and stormy winters moving in from the Atlantic, and punctuated by sharp droughts (*Chron Bower* vol 5: 149, 169). Drought conditions recurred for much of the British Isles through the 1250s, but a dramatic change occurred in 1258. High levels of volcanic sulphates in ice cores indicate another major volcanic eruption which triggered a second episode of climatic cooling which lasted for many years, if not decades. It is likely to have been this event, misdated to 1256, which the Lanercost chronicler described as 'great corruption of the air and inundation of rain' which destroyed cereal- and hay-crops that year (*Chron Lanercost*, 64; Dawson 2009: 99–100). A rapid southward extension of sea ice off Greenland again heralded severe winters for Britain in the 1260s, 1270s and 1280s, but bad though these episodes were far worse followed after 1300.

A combination of atmospheric and oceanic circulation systems drive climatic shifts like those experienced between 1000 and 1300. Changes in ocean surface temperatures affected the pattern of weather systems arriving in the British Isles from the Atlantic. In particular, ocean-surface warming increased atmospheric moisture and brought increased storminess with some extreme summer wind and rain events, and periods of extreme heat or coldness often seen in records of hot, wet summers and prolonged snow and ice in late winter. Conversely, extension of the southward range of sea ice increases the incidence of winter storms as cold surface temperatures bring the high surface air pressures associated with anti-cyclonic circulation. This draws cold air further south to collide with warmer moist air moving east across the Atlantic. The result is winter storm systems moving across the North Atlantic followed by late springs, adverse summer growing conditions, and wet and delayed harvests (Dawson 2009: 73). In contrast to the detailed records of the impact of this prolonged period of poor weather in the first quarter of the fourteenth century on England and Ireland (Jordan 1996: 7–39), little evidence survives of its direct impact on Scotland. This anomaly is attributable to the political upheavals which Scotland was experiencing at this time, with the existing records concentrating on the military and political struggle for survival. Dire accounts of conditions in Ireland and northern England, however, leave little room for doubt that Scotland experienced the same cycle of weather events, crop failures and famines that afflicted neighbouring regions, and administrative accounts relating to the

English garrisons in Scotland point to great difficulties locally in obtaining supplies of food and fodder (Dawson 2009: 101–2).

After 1300 there was marked shift towards colder annual temperatures in the northern hemisphere. Anti-cyclonic circulation established a seasonal pattern of bitterly cold winters, delayed and cool springs, hot and dry summers and warm, wet autumns from around 1308. Then in 1315 a further dramatic change occurred with the summers turning cold and delivering almost continual frontal systems which deposited seemingly endless rains. The result for much of England and Ireland was delayed harvests and shortages of both grain for human consumption and fodder for livestock, but the only contemporary account of similar conditions in Scotland is given by the Lanercost chronicler, who noted that in 1316 there was 'mortality of men through hunger and pestilence, unheard of in our times' (*Chron Lanercost*, 233). The later fourteenth-century *Gesta Annalia* also refers to a severe winter in 1321–2 'which was a sore trial to men and killed off nearly all their animals' (Fordun, ii: 341). Greenland ice core data point to this episode as stemming from a rapid summer-time rise in ocean surface temperatures in the North Atlantic, an overheating which continued through winter to maintain an upward spiral in temperatures and a consequent dramatic increase in atmospheric moisture (Dawson 2009: 102). These sea-ice conditions peaked around 1318–9 but it was only in 1325 that a further change occurred with a brief return of summer droughts, and by the early 1330s wet summer conditions had returned. This short episode was followed by a plunge to the lowest temperatures experienced in the North Atlantic region since well before 1000, with contemporary English and Irish sources chronicling a return of the conditions which had produced famine two decades earlier (Dawson 2009: 103) (no Scottish source mentions this event). While this plunge in temperatures has been described as 'a period of polar cooling that is minor by glacial standards', it was probably the final catalyst for a dramatic reconfiguration of social organisation and economic structures in Ireland, Scotland and Iceland, and the collapse of Norse colonies in Greenland (Mayeski et al 2004: 252; Oram & Adderley 2008: 80–82). The cumulative effect of these extended episodes over many years had been more pronounced than the traumas created by shorter periods of year-to-year variation.

While there is huge debate over the exact chronological range to which the term should be applied, the climatic cooling of the fourteenth century has been seen as the first stage of the so-called 'little ice age' which lasted through to the middle of the nineteenth century (Mann 2002; Fagan 2000). Like the 'medieval warm period', the 'little ice age' was not an era of consistent climatic conditions and it did not mean relentless cold weather. The 1350s did see unprecedented low temperatures but it was a severe episode soon after 1400 which perhaps saw the cold become more deeply entrenched. Winter storms in the North Atlantic were more regular, more violent and more prolonged, and the south-west to north-east circulation of warmer water which helped to give the British Isles their generally milder climate moved south as colder, polar circulation systems extended. One result was that the North Atlantic winter storm track which passed over Iceland and the Faeroe Islands became fixed instead over Britain. Storm systems fed in from the west off the Atlantic to collide with cold air drawn by anti-cyclonic circulation from Russia, and the result was often snow (Dawson 2009: 104–5). The sea ice retreated northward slightly mid-century but it is wrong to call this a period of warmer mean temperatures, rather it was less cold than what had preceded it.

Most evidence suggests that severe weather affected the Atlantic seaboard throughout the fifteenth century. An especially cold winter in 1431–2 was marked by ice and gales, and brought widespread deaths amongst livestock, but a second extreme winter in 1434–5 saw three-and-a-half months of unrelenting low temperatures which caused widespread shortages of food as mills were reportedly unable to grind grain due to the icing-up of water-courses (Chron Bower vol 8: 267, 293). The delayed spring in 1435 apparently was followed by a poor harvest and resulting food-shortages. Famine struck again in 1439 following a poor grain harvest; contemporary west of Scotland accounts suggest that the associated deaths were amongst the worst ever experienced (Auchinleck, 160). A re-advance of sea ice after about 1460 brought repeated cold winters, and from the 1490s these were accompanied by the hot dry summers and wet autumns which are characteristic of high pressure systems across northern Europe.

There is a dearth of detailed narrative accounts from Scotland for the central decades of the fifteenth century. This absence is only partly compensated for by parliamentary records which hint at poor harvests and resultant high food prices through the 1450s. Parliamentary legislation in January 1450 over supplies of food, hoarding and price inflation points to underlying problems with the harvest (RPS 1450/1/23; 1450/1/24). This was followed in August 1452 by similar legislation intended to force the release of hoarded grain into the market (RPS 1452/3). Favourable treatment of merchants who brought food to Scotland was ordained in the July 1454 parliament, again perhaps indicating that the harvest had been deficient (RPS 1454/3). Efforts to increase production levels, both to secure domestic supplies and reduce the drain on money through the importing of basic foodstuffs, can be seen in legislation of the March 1458 parliament, which instructed the sowing of minimum amounts of wheat and beans on any property where an eight-oxen plough was used (RPS 1458/3/29). A supply crisis was again the subject of legislation in June 1478 probably arising from a series of harsh winters and wet autumns in the mid-1470s, and 1482 legislation again giving favourable treatment to merchants importing foodstuffs suggests an extended period of shortages (RPS 1478/6/83; 1482/3/8; 1482/12/84).

From then down to about 1520 there was some recovery in annual temperatures, but there are indications of poor harvests along the Highland fringe in 1524–5 (*Chron Perth*, 21), and a return to colder and wetter circumstances in the middle of the sixteenth century. Winter 1554–5 was especially severe throughout the southern Highlands. Severe frosts began in November, but the main episode started with frosts between 13 December and 25 December, then snow began to fall lasting through to 17 January, 'it was the grettast snaw and storm that was sein in memorie of man lewand that tyme'. After a brief thaw, snowfall resumed and the coldest weather was experienced between 22 and 26 February (Taymouth, 21). Extreme weather accompanied these fluctuations in the annual mean temperatures; the 1540s saw severe winter storms, while the 1560s to mid 1570s experienced extremely cold winters and wet and windy summers, and from 1575 to 1582 eastern Scotland experienced near drought conditions summer and winter, while the west and central Highlands had unusually high levels of rainfall (Taymouth, 129, 135, 136, 137–8, 141–2). There was a short-term recovery again in the late sixteenth and early seventeenth century, but at its peak the annual mean temperature had barely returned to the levels experienced in the cold years of the mid fifteenth century. These, then, are the broad trends in northern hemisphere temperatures across the medieval period in the North Atlantic region. Long-term movement in the fortunes of the people of Bute and in the basis of their economic systems should be assessed in this context.

The catalogue of misery presented in the above account can only partly be offset by the reminder that in the years where no extreme or unusual events were recorded the people of Scotland were able to make a living at above subsistence level. Furthermore, despite the regular rehearsal of incidences of crisis triggered by severe weather events, principally expressed in terms of hunger-related deaths arising from harvest failures and consequent shortages and inflation in food prices, it is important to reflect on the fact that while society in Scotland clearly changed in the face of such challenges it did not collapse. What that suggests is that far from being static and inflexible (peasant conservatism is a term that is often expressed by modern scholars), the agricultural regimes upon which Scottish society was founded were responsive and resilient, and shifts in forms of social organisation and modes of exploitation should perhaps be thought of as positive reactions to climate change rather than always negative, rearguard defences of a failing system.

The Stewarts' bread basket?

Detailed historical records for most of the Clyde estuary are lacking before the mid twelfth century, from when it is possible to begin to reconstruct the course of events which saw the power of the Scottish crown intruded aggressively into the region by kings from David I (1124–53) to Alexander III (1249–86). For one hundred and fifty years, the narrative that can be recovered is one of prolonged political disturbance and a painfully slow progression towards stability. That century and a half of conflict to secure control of Bute and the other Clyde islands can be read as a straightforward political struggle driven by a simple desire for territorial aggrandisement. For the Scottish crown and the Stewarts, there was unquestionably a strategic case for westwards expansion, while for the members of the Argyll dynasty who opposed them there was an identical case for eastwards expansion to block Scottish encroachment. But territorial aggrandisement is only part of the issue, and the eagerness of all parties involved to secure control of Bute suggests additional motives. Of those motives, the most obvious is control of resources and expansion of their economic potential. The agricultural wealth of Bute would have expanded significantly the sources of income and ability to dispense patronage of whoever secured possession of the island.

Although there are no surviving records of the income obtained from Bute by its rulers before the fifteenth century, those later accounts of productivity from a time of extreme environmental stress point towards the likely agricultural potential of the island during the more benign twelfth and thirteenth centuries. In contrast to much of the land to its north and west, the geology of Bute produced a very sharp diversity in land form that encouraged a split in emphasis in agricultural practice north and south of the low-lying 'waist' of the island between Ettrick Bay on the west and Kames Bay on the east. While the Highland Boundary Fault which marks the division in the underlying solid geology which determines much of the landscape character lies to the south of the 'waist', the overlying drift geology makes the low ground of the east-west trench more suitable for agriculture (fig 8.2). North of the fault line, the solid geology is primarily metamorphic rock with igneous intrusions, producing a landscape of glacial rounded hills, craggy escarpments and trench-like valleys, supporting thin acid soils and areas of blanket peat. The highest point, Windy Hill, reaches

Fig 8.2 Aerial view of Bute looking towards Ettrick and St Ninian's Bay from Tormore Hill (DP 066199, © Crown Copyright: RCAHMS. Licensor www.rcahms.gov.uk).

a mere 278m above sea level, with most of the remaining hill country rarely exceeding 160m. Although there are pockets of land suitable for arable cultivation in this northern zone, especially in the Kames-Ettrick 'waist', much of this largely upland area was probably always exploited as rough pasture. Most of Bute's solid geology south of the line filled by Loch Fad and Loch Quien comprises sedimentary rocks overlain by deep, fertile soil, with the southernmost point of the island being primarily igneous in origin (fig 8.3). This tripartite split in underlying geology has determined the land-use strategies employed in the different zones throughout the human occupation of the island, but prevailing climatic conditions would have introduced further opportunities or constraints on the exploitation regimes in different periods. In contrast to the metamorphic rock and acid soil landscapes of Cowal to the north and northern Arran to the south, the southern districts of Bute would have been an island of fertility in a sea of impoverished grasslands. In short, Bute was a highly desirable piece of property.

Prehistoric settlement sites and early historic place-names in 'kerry-' (Gaelic *ceathramh* = a quarter(land)) on the fertile sedimentary zone indicate that this was already the location of important centres of agricultural production and tribute collection by the late tenth or early eleventh centuries (Oram forthcoming). In the more benign conditions of the 'medieval warm period', the settled and cultivated areas associated with such centres expanded and took in

Fig 8.3 Aerial view of Bute looking towards Glen Callum, taken from the south-east (DP 066098, ©
Crown Copyright: RCAHMS. Licensor www.rcahms.gov.uk).

more land that under colder and wetter conditions would have been incapable of sustaining agriculture or more intensive grazing. Even some areas of the less attractive metamorphic zone would have become more amenable to more rigorous exploitation. The brief episodes of extreme weather which punctuated the twelfth century aside, the climatic regime which encouraged this expansion of population and agriculture lasted through to the second half of the thirteenth century. Thus, when the Stewarts and the heirs of Somairle were competing for control of Bute in the 1200s, they were seeking to acquire one of the richest agricultural resource bases in the south-west Highland region. As their investment in building Rothesay Castle underscores, Bute became an important component of the Stewarts' lordship and was fully integrated into its economic structure.

How valuable Bute was to the Stewart descendents of Walter son of Alan we can only guess, for no detailed financial records survive from the Stewart lands earlier than the fifteenth century. No financial accounts, such as records of teind receipts from which a general view of the agricultural productivity of the island could be gained, survive from the diocese of the Isles under which the churches of Bute fell. It is only in the revaluation of land undertaken in 1366 for King David II as part of the process to better exploit the resources of the kingdom, where the Stewart lands in Bute, Cowal, Knapdale, Arran and the Cumbraes were valued collectively at £1000 'by the old assessment', that a relative impression of productivity can be achieved, but with no new value given it is not immediately obvious how Bute had been affected by the environmental crises of the fourteenth century (RPS 1366/7/18). For the rest of Scotland, outline analysis where both 'old assessment' and new valuation figures are provided reveals a fall of 44 percent north of the Tay and 52 percent south of it. The drops in both areas are sufficiently close, and the similarities in falls recorded in areas that had suffered heavily from military operations and areas remote from the main theatres of campaigning, to suggest that the sharp decline in land values was not solely a consequence of the impact of warfare (Grant 1984: 78). What the fall exposes clearest is a sharp decline in income received from rents, reversing what had been a generally upwards trend through the thirteenth century as rising population kept demand for tenancies high. A collapse in population during the famine and plague years reversed that demand and apparently sent rents into free-fall. It is perhaps as significant that the sharpest falls in values in the 1366 schedule are in central and western Highland or south-west mainland districts, where levels fell by between half and two thirds in most cases as against between one third and a half in the east. It is difficult to avoid the somewhat determinist conclusion that this marked divergence had additional factors behind it, the most obvious of which was the impact on agricultural productivity of poor weather associated with changes in the North Atlantic climatic patterns. Although no 'true value' figure was supplied for Bute, Arran and Cowal in 1366, the combined rentals from these districts which are obtainable for the 1440s suggest that there had been a drop of over three quarters from the suspiciously rounded £1000 of the thirteenth century to a mere £224 plus cattle and grain renders by 1445. The cumulative impact of late fourteenth-century price deflation, collapsing rents due to population decline, and a contraction in agricultural productivity through both falling population levels and environmental factors, resulted in a shift in Bute's position within the Stewarts' property portfolio from a central to more marginal role.

A closer look at the financial records permits identification of some general trends. The first surviving account was rendered at the Exchequer in June 1440 by the chamberlain of Bute and Arran. It included accounts for the period back to the harvest of 1438, but nothing earlier, and it is impossible to know whether or not the yields indicated in them are at a depressed level after the poor years of the 1430s. There are suggestions, however, that a new set of the royal lands in Bute, Arran and Cowal was made around the start of James II's reign, and it is probably safe to assume that the rents agreed on that occasion made allowance for the downwards movement in conditions reflected in the poor harvests experienced in recent years. The chamberlain's accounts record an annual rent comprising £141 16s money, and renders in produce (referred to as *grassums*) comprising11 chalders, 12 bolls and two firlots of barley[3], and 40 marts (ER v: 81). These *grassums* were paid at Martinmas (after the harvest was securely in) and were levied at a rate of one boll of barley for every merk of rent, and one mart for every five merks of rent. This weighting towards arable-derived income, a reflection of the relative fertility of the sedimentary rock areas of the island even during an era of extreme climatic disturbance, stands in sharp contrast to the Stewarts' other north and west Firth of Clyde properties, principally in Cowal, where the thin, acidic soils over the metamorphic rocks of the district produced little by way of arable crops. There, income from Dunoon and Glendaruel was in money and marts (see, for example, ER v: 246). While much of the barley received in Bute was disposed of as fees paid to royal officers there, more than half of it was transported to the mainland, possibly for sale at market or for onward transmission for consumption by the household. In 1440, for example, five chalders was shipped to Dumbarton and two to Irvine (ER v: 87). Even at the probably much-reduced levels of the mid-fifteenth century, Bute's grain surpluses were an important component of royal income. Indeed, the very fact that Bute was still capable of producing surpluses underscores the significance of the island and probably explains the attractiveness of the Clyde islands to other regional lords who sought to gain control of it in the fifteenth century.

This level of grain income from Bute was maintained through the whole of James II's reign, but in the 1460s the records of rents received include notice of significant arrears. In March 1460, the rents for one term accounted for £70 19s 3d, 11 marts and two quarters, and 11 chalders 15 bolls of barley, but there was also arrears of rents at £11 12s, 10 marts and three chalders, nine bolls and two firlots (ER vii: 11–14). This substantial level of arrears in money, barley and marts suggests that something significant had occurred to disturb the production regime or the rent collection mechanism. The receipts for the three terms from March 1460 to July 1462 continue at the same level as set in the preceding reign, yielding around £71 in money rents per term (ER vii: 107), but by that date arrears in marts had reached 43 and in barley over 14 chalders (ER vii: 109). It was not until 1462–4 that the rents returned to the levels taken in the 1440s, reaching over £140 per annum with no mention of arrears (ER vii: 272). This sudden but short-term emergence of high levels of arrears may be associated with the political disturbances which followed the death of James II, during which time John MacDonald, earl of Ross and lord of the Isles, had attempted to take control of the Clyde islands, and coincided with the death of the old chamberlain and a possible hiatus in the administrative mechanisms, but the arrears in 1460 relates to conditions dating back at least to 1459. It seems that, while the accumulation of arrears may have been worsened by political circumstances, other factors were at work. The records of poor weather conditions and bad harvests through the 1450s are perhaps being reflected here in the reality of tenants' inability to meet their rent obligations.

Alongside the money and grain rents, renders of cattle or marts, usually referred to in the accounts as *malemartis* (cattle rendered as part of the rental agreement), constituted an important component of Stewart income from the island. It emerges in the mid fifteenth century that these cattle were being driven live to supply the needs of the king's household. In 1440, allowance of 40s was made in the chamberlain of Bute and Arran's accounts for the costs of driving two groups of marts from Ardneil (Portencross) in Ayrshire, to where probably they had been carried from Kilchattan Bay in southern Bute, to Stirling (ER v: 85).[4] Twenty-nine Bute marts were driven from Ardneil to Stirling in 1443, thirty-two in 1444 and thirty-three in 1445, the beasts in this last year being taken on to Edinburgh (ER v: 64, 210). Reference in 1445–6 to the marts being taken to the Torwood, part of the royal hunting forest east of Stirling, suggests that the cattle were being grazed there to fatten them up before slaughter after the likely weight-loss of the long drive from the Ayrshire coast (ER v: 251). The number of cattle received in this way as rent remains fairly stable from the 1440s onwards, although there is again a significant episode of arrears noted in the early 1460s. The arrears of 43 marts, more than a year's render, points to a major disruption of the process in 1460–1 and was perhaps associated with raids on the island by John MacDonald, but could equally reflect the consequences of a weather event which had adversely affected the herds. There is a tendency to regard the pastoral component of medieval agricultural regimes as less exposed to the vagaries of climate than the arable, but the reduction in biomass production (growth of grass and other fodder) and contraction in the extent and altitudinal range of good-quality pasture that occurred across the medieval period, saw a progressive decline in the carrying capacity of the land. It is probable that the numbers of beasts evident in the records by the mid fifteenth century reflects a significant contraction from the pre-1300 levels. Surviving medieval chronicle entries, such as the 1321 *Gesta Annalia* reference to widespread livestock deaths, also reveal more immediate weather-related impacts. Winter deaths, especially among the breeding herds, would have taken years to recover from. Poor summer conditions, however, could be equally devastating, for in cold and wet conditions cattle expend calories on simply maintaining body-heat, calories that would otherwise have gone into body-mass or milk-production. Weaker animals are more likely to have died, pregnancies may have been less likely to reach full term, and calves faced under-nutrition from cows which were not producing adequate milk. By the mid fifteenth century, such long-term trends may have forced peasants to reduce the numbers of animals in their herds, adjusting the soums (the assessments of carrying capacity and, therefore, herd sizes placed on specific land) to reflect the reduced potential of the land.

It is likely that the downward trends in temperatures, increases in rainfall, also saw a resultant contraction in both growing seasons and altitudes at which viable grain crops could be grown. This factor led in turn to a slow withdrawal from the extended limits of agriculture which had been reached by 1300. We can assume that the area under cultivation contracted significantly in the north of the island and that arable crops became concentrated most heavily on the zone of sedimentary geology. Grain, and in particular barley, nevertheless continued to feature as the principal agricultural commodity being extracted from most properties in the southern parts of the lordship of Bute by the Stewart kings into the sixteenth century. For example, the 1512 charter of Farquhar McNeill to his son Donald of the twenty shillingland of 'Lapencaill' set out the rent due from the land to the king as 18s 6d in money, six firlots of barley, six firlots of oats, and 4s 6d for part of a mart (RMS iii: no 1083). Likewise, when in 1515 at Kingarth Gilchrist McCaw of Garrochty granted his cousin the twenty-five shillingland of South Garrochty, the rent due to the king from that property was given as 23s 2d in money, two bolls of barley, seven firlots of oats and 5s 7½d for part of a mart (RMS iii: no 819). Birgidale Knock, at the south end of Loch Fad, a twenty-five shillingland, yielded rent in 1517 of 25s, two bolls of barley, six firlots of oats, and the fourteenth and fifteenth parts of a mart (RMS iii: no 1376). The appearance of a component of oats in these later accounts is also perhaps significant, probably reflecting increasing investment in the cereal variety best-suited to the poor growing conditions of the era.

An indication of the overall scale and scope of arable productivity on the island at the end of the Middle Ages is obtained from the feu-charter of 1534, whereby King James V feued his property on the island to Colin Campbell of Ardkinglas. In addition to money rents of over £150, Campbell received 11 chalders and 15 bolls of barley, 10 chalders of oats, one chalder and eight bolls of 'flour', plus 41 and two quarter marts (RMS iii: no 1405). Rents, clearly, had been maintained at the low level reached a century earlier, suggesting that there had been neither a recovery in population levels to trigger inflationary movement in the economy nor an improvement in environmental conditions to boost yields and, hence, values. Livestock payments had disappeared, probably having been commuted for cash and incorporated in the money rent figure rather than signalling an abandonment of livestock rearing by the Stewarts' tenants. The more significant change, however, was the emergence of alternative crops in the cereal component of the rents. The presence of oats as a significant crop by the reign of James IV (1488–1513), which coincided with a return to the poorer growing conditions experienced in the early fifteenth century, possibly reflects a long-term shift by the tenants farmers into investment in crops better-suited to the climate regime which had become established across most of the maritime west. More work needs to be done on such financial data from the Exchequer Rolls across the fifteenth and sixteenth centuries, but from the sample evidence discussed here it seems that the climatic variability of the period down to the early 1460s had a significant impact on peasants' economies and their ability to pay rents to their lords, and that again by the 1490s it had encouraged them to shift into new exploitation strategies.

Conclusion

Political events, geography and geology combined to produce a unique set of circumstances which shaped the social and cultural development of Bute in the medieval period. Located in a political frontier zone between rival powers on opposite shores of the Clyde estuary, it was a strategic territory from which the peninsulas and sea-lochs of the south-western Highlands could be dominated or from where expansion into the mainland to the east could be launched. It occupied also something of a frontier position in terms of socio-economic structures, for its underlying geology allowed it to sustain an arable agricultural regime akin to that which prevailed across most of Lowland Scotland. Few parts of the mainland and islands to its north and west could support such intensive cultivation regimes at a similar level. Bute's agricultural potential was undoubtedly a key factor in its attractiveness to external powers over the centuries, for despite its relative smallness of scale it was capable of producing a disproportionately high level of agricultural yields. Its western maritime position did not shield Bute from the impact of climate change, although the shelter of Kintyre and

Knapdale to the west and the hills of Mid Argyll and Cowal to the north may have helped to ameliorate the worst effects of deteriorating weather conditions. Blessed with its Old Red Sandstone geology in the south part of the island, Bute was able to sustain an arable regime across an era where cultivation of cereals was in drastic decline in most of the western Highland and Hebridean zone. In common with the rest of Scotland, population levels may have collapsed as a consequence of famine and epidemic in the fourteenth century, but that fall enabled Bute's agricultural regime to remain viable and deliver surpluses for most of the time throughout an era of profound environmental change. To men like John MacDonald, whose Hebridean and West Highland domain had experienced the full force of climatic deterioration since the early 1300s, possession of Bute would have helped to offset the contraction of the resource base available to him from which he had to maintain the complex network of alliances, patronage and culture of conspicuous consumption upon which his Gaelic-style lordship was sustained. His attempts to take control of the island in the 1460s, used against him in the process of forfeiture brought before parliament in 1475, should be seen as the gamble of a man under pressure rather than a simple predatory act. The Stewarts' bread basket was too tempting a prize to ignore in such bleak times.

Notes

1   Annals of Innisfallen at http://www.ucc.ie/celt/published/T100004/index.html, Annals AI1199.6 and AI1200.5 (accessed 23/6/11).
2   Annals of Loch Cé at http://www.ucc.ie/celt/published/T100010A/index.html, Annal LC1200.5 (accessed 23/6/11).
3   One chalder = 16 bolls; 1 boll is equivalent to approximately 145 litres dry volume.
4   Ardneil was an important ferry-port on the route which linked the Stewarts' lands in Kyle, centred on Dundonald Castle, with their Bute properties. King Robert II, the first Stewart king, issued at least eight charters there between 1374 and 1390, presumably while waiting for suitable conditions for the voyage to the island: *RMS*, i: nos 466, 520, 692, 722, 777, 780, 799, 800. Robert III, who spent much of his reign (1390–1406) resident at Dundonald and Rothesay, also used the crossing from Ardneil: see, for example, National Archives of Scotland, GD1/19/1.

References

Adderley, W P & Simpson, I A 2005 'Early-Norse home-field productivity in the Faeroe Islands', *Human Ecology* 33, 711–36.

Adderley, W P, Simpson, I A & Vésteinsson, O 2008 'Local-scale adaptations: A modelled assessment of soil, landscape, microclimatic, and management factors in Norse home-field productivities', *Geoarchaeology* 23, 500–27.

Appleby, A 1980 'Epidemics and famine in the Little Ice Age', *J Interdisciplinary History* 10 pt 4, 643–63.

Auchinleck The Auchinleck Chronicle, printed in C A McGladdery, C A 1990 *James II*. Edinburgh: John Donald Ltd.

Barrow, G W S 1976 'Lothian in the War of Independence', *Scottish Historical Review* 55, 151–71.

Barrow, G W S 1978 'The aftermath of war: Scotland and England in the late thirteenth and early fourteenth century', *Trans Royal Historical Society*, 5th series 27, 103–26.

Campbell, B M S 2009 'Four famines and a pestilence: harvest, price and wage variations in England, 13th to 19th centuries', in B Liljewall, I A Flygare, U Lange, L Ljunggren & J Söderberg (eds) *Agrarhistoria på många sätt, 28 studies on manniskan och jorden. Festskrift till Janken Myrdal på hans 60-årsdag*, 23–56. Stockholm: Royal Swedish Academy of Agriculture and Forestry.

Campbell, B M S 2010 'Physical shocks, biological hazards, and human impacts: the crisis of the fourteenth century revisited', in S Cavaciocchi (ed) *Economic and Biological Interactions in Pre-Industrial Europe from the 13th to the 18th Centuries*, 13–32. Florence: Florence University Press.

Chron Bower Bower, Walter *Scotichronicon*, vol 4, 1994; vol 5, 1990; vol 8, 1987, ed D E R Watt and others. Aberdeen: Aberdeen University Press.

Chron Lanercost Chronicon de Lanercost, 1839. Edinburgh: Maitland Club.

Chron Perth The Chronicle of Perth, ed J Eagles, 1996. Llanerch: Llanerch Press.

Crowley, T J & Lowery, T S 2000 'How Warm Was the Medieval Warm Period?' *Ambio* 29, 51–4.

Dawson, A 2009 *So Foul and Fair a Day: A History of Scotland's Weather and Climate*. Edinburgh: Birlinn Ltd.

Edwards, K J, Borthwick, D, Cook, G, Dugmore, A J, Mairs, K-A, Church, M J, Simpson, I A & Adderley, W P 2005 'A Hypothesis-Based Approach to Landscape Change in Suðuroy, Faroe Islands', *Human Ecology* 33, 621–50.

ER *The Exchequer Rolls of Scotland*, 1878–1908, eds J Stuart, G Burnett and others. Edinburgh: HMSO.

Fagan, B 2000 *The Little Ice Age: How Climate Made History 1300-1850*. New York: Basic Books Ltd.

Fordun *John of Fordun's Chronicle of the Scottish Nation*, 1872, ed W F Skene. Edinburgh: William Paterson Ltd.

Gemmill, E & Mayhew, N 1995 *Changing Values in Medieval Scotland: A Study of Prices, Money, and Weights and Measures*. Cambridge: Cambridge University Press.

Grant, A 1984 *Independence and Nationhood: Scotland 1306-1469*. London: Edward Arnold.

Jillings, K 2003 *Scotland's Black Death: The Foul Death of the English*. Stroud: Tempus Publishing Ltd.

Jordan, W C 1996 *The Great Famine: Northern Europe in the Early Fourteenth Century*. Princeton: Princeton University Press.

Kershaw, I 1973 'The Great Famine and agrarian crisis in England 1315-22', *Past and Present* 59, 3–50.

Lomas, R 1996 'The impact of Border warfare: the Scots and South Tweedside, c.1290–c.1520', *Scottish Historical Review* 75, 143–67.

Mann, M E 2002 'Little Ice Age', in MacCracken, M C & Perry, J S (eds), *Encyclopedia of Global Environmental Change*, vol 1. Chichester: Wiley-Blackwell.

Mayeski, P A & others 2004 'Holocene Climate Variability', *Quaternary Research* 62, 243–55.

McKerral, A 1991 *Kintyre in the Seventeenth Century*. Edinburgh: Kintyre Antiquarian and Natural History Society.

Newfield, T P 2009 'A cattle panzootic in early fourteenth-century Europe', *Agricultural History Review* 57.2, 155–99.

Oram, R D 2008 "It cannot be decernit quha are clean and quha are foulle." Responses to epidemic disease in sixteenth- and seventeenth-century Scotland'. *Renaissance and Reformation* 30, 13–39.

Oram, R D forthcoming 'Ouncelands, Quarterlands and Pennylands in the Western Isles, Man and Galloway: Tribute Payments and Military Levies in the Norse West', in Imsen, S (ed), *The Realm of Norway and its Dependencies as a Political System: Tribute, Skatt and Skattlands*. Trondheim: Tapir Academic Press.

Oram, R D & Adderley, W P 2008 'Lordship and Environmental Change in Central Highland Scotland c.1300–c.1400', *J North Atlantic* 1, 74–84.

Oram, R D & Adderley, W P 2010a 'Innse Gall: Culture and Environment on a Norse Frontier in the Scottish Western Isles', in Imsen, S (ed). *The Norgesveldet in the Middle Ages*. Trondheim: Tapir Academic Press.

Oram, R D & Adderley, W P 2010b 'Lordship, Land and Environmental Change in West Highland and Hebridean Scotland c.1300–c.1450', in Cavacciocha, S (ed), *Economic and Biological Interactions in Pre-Industrial Europe from the Thirteenth to Eighteenth Centuries*. Florence: Florence University Press.

Parry, M L 1985 'The impact of climatic variations on agricultural margins', in Kates, T W, Ausubel, J H & Berberian, M (eds), *Climate Impact Assessment*, 351–67. Chichester: Wiley-Blackwell.

RMS *Registrum Magni Sigilli Regum Scotorum*, 1882–1914, eds J M Thompson and others. Edinburgh: HMSO.

RPS Records of the Parliaments of Scotland, www.rps.ac.uk.

Sella, D 1991 'Coping with famine: the changing demography of an Italian village in the 1590s', *Sixteenth Century Journal* 22 pt.2, 185–97.

Simpson, I A, Adderley, W P, Guðmundsson, G, Hallsdóttir, M, Sigurgeirsson, M A & Snæsdóttir, M 2002 'Land management for surplus grain production in early Iceland', *Human Ecology* 30, 423–43.

Simpson, I A 2006 'Soils and Palaeo-climate based evidence for past irrigation requirements in Norse Greenland', *J Archaeological Science* 33, 1666–79.

Smout, T C 1985 'Famine and Famine Relief in Scotland', in Cullen, L M & Smout, T C (eds) *Comparative Aspects of Scottish and Irish Economic and Social History 1600-1900*, 21–31. Edinburgh: John Donald Ltd.

Spinage, C A 2003 *Cattle Plague: A History*. London: Springer.

Stell, G 1991 'Destruction and Damage: a reassessment of the historical and architectural evidence', in MacDougall, N (ed) *Scotland and War AD79–1918*, 24–35. Edinburgh: John Donald Ltd.

Stewart, William *The Buik of the Croniclis of Scotland: or A Metrical Version of the History of Hector Boece*, 1858, ed W B Turnbull, iii. London: Rolls Series.

Taymouth *The Black Book of Taymouth* 1855 Edinburgh: Bannatyne Club.

Chapter 9

Bute from Norse times to the Improvements: some notes on landholdings and rural settlement patterns

Angus Hannah
Bute

LOW-LYING and sheltered, with many sandy bays and safe landings, Bute's fertility and accessibility have made it the least insular of islands. Dissected by the Highland Boundary Fault, it is at once highland and lowland. The ebb and flow of military, political and economic power has been a constant factor in island life, and British, Dalriadic, Norse, Gall-Ghàidheil, Anglo-Norman and Scots influences have all played a part in shaping the island's settlement history during the millennium under review.

For an island on the fringe of the highlands, Bute is relatively well documented, and particularly favoured with a fine collection of estate maps. Moreover, where farming is not too intensive, abundant evidence of former settlement survives in the landscape, recorded since 1990 by the Buteshire Natural History Society Deserted Settlement Survey (Proudfoot & Hannah 2000) and more recently through the Scotland's Rural Past project (RCAHMS 2011) and the full record revision undertaken by RCAHMS with the Discover Bute Landscape Partnership (Geddes & Hale 2010). My aim here is to bring together these diverse strands and see what they show about patterns of rural settlement and landholding from the coming of the Norsemen until the agricultural improvements in the eighteenth century.

The evidence of documents

Units of assessment

Aside from their actual meaning, which I have discussed elsewhere (Hannah 2004), the numeric values of Bute's Old Extent assessments reflect the underlying pattern of landholdings, testifying to an earlier landscape of larger fiscal units. Old Extents in merklands usually accompany farm names in documents such as exchequer rolls, charters, retours and rentals from the fifteenth century onwards. I have argued that these assessments were probably imposed in the late twelfth or early thirteenth centuries, with some respect for a pre-existing system (Hannah 2004).[1] Assessments became ossified at an early stage, meaning that new settlements could not be given any value unless by partition of an existing unit, so that some later changes and many minor ones remain invisible from this perspective. However, this very inflexibility has helped to preserve the older pattern.[2]

Pennylands were probably widespread and perhaps general on Bute in the Norse period and the immediately following centuries, but surviving references are scarce. They are found in the earliest extant charters (c1320: Bute 1945), and also in the names of Lenihall and Lenihuline, two farms in the north of the island. The first element of these names is *leth-pheighinn* 'half-penny', and it is likely that Lenihall, Old Extent 1½ merks, was a half-penny land. Lenihuline's Extent was three merks, but this farm had two foci of settlement and the name may have referred originally to only one of these. The farm figured in the Exchequer Rolls (ER v: 80) from its first appearance in 1440 until 1450 under a completely different name (Altone) which may have referred to the other settlement. Adding the charter evidence that Ardroscadale (later 12 merks) was five pennylands (MSA Cat, no. 2), while Kilmachalmaig (7½ merks) comprised three pennylands (Bute, Marquess of 1945), we may infer that in Bute 2½ or 3 merks of Old Extent equated roughly to a pennyland. This contrasts with six merks to twenty pennylands in Tiree (Dodgshon 1981: 79–81), Uist and Eigg (Raven 2005: 102) and a merk to two pennylands in Kintyre and elsewhere (McKerral 1943: 62).[3] However, merklands were a much later introduction in the Hebrides than in Bute, and often imposed more arbitrarily. In Bute, three merks is the most usual assessment for a single farm, while larger holdings were frequently 12 or 15 merks, corresponding to five pennylands.

Toponymic evidence

Place-name analysis helps to tease out successive strands of political control. Several of Bute's larger settlement units have names at least partially Norse in origin, including Ascog, Langal, Scalpsie, Birgidale, *Roscadale and possibly Scoulag, and must have existed or come into being during the period of Norse occupation (Márkus forthcoming; Márkus this volume). That Viking settlement constituted a significant 'land-grab' in the Clyde area is now widely acknowledged, though the Norse tongue was to prove much less durable here than in the Hebrides. Although Bute remained within the Norse sphere of influence for several centuries, it appears that the Gaelic language swiftly re-asserted itself. A few Gaelic names may be pre-Norse, but many belong to the Gall-Ghàidheil period, from shortly after 900 (Clancy 2008: 30), when Gaelic regained its dominance. Others, of course, are later still, as Gaelic continued to be spoken throughout the period under review. Almost all the smaller farms have Gaelic names, often referring to landscape features, though some names remain opaque.

Larger and older landholdings

I will now look briefly at a number of larger and older estates in order to sketch a history of the enduring framework of landholdings on the island (fig 9.1). Kingarth, being a twenty pound (30 merk) land, and so perhaps half an ounceland,[4] had the highest value of any single Bute property (only equalled later by the entire burgh lands of Rothesay), and it may also be the oldest surviving unit. The name is certainly pre-Norse, for it is recorded intermittently in the Annals of Ulster and Tigernach from 660 (Anderson 1922), and it may be pre-Gaelic in origin.[5] There is good evidence that the monastery dates from the sixth century and may initially have been a British rather than a Columban/Irish foundation, being dedicated to Blane, a British saint's name (Fraser 2005). It is impossible to say whether or for how long a secular estate pre-existed its establishment. Old Extents testify to subsequent division of the estate into four equal parts, three of which bore the names Garach, Kelspoke and Branser while the fourth was shared unequally between Lubas and Dunagoil. Most if not all of these names are Gaelic, albeit rather obscure in some cases, suggesting that this division did not take place in a Norse-speaking milieu. Before the end of the fifteenth century all four were further split into farms of between 1½ and 4 merks Extent, similar in size to those found elsewhere in Bute. A better grasp of the relationship between the monastery and the Dunagoil forts (Harding 2004) would clarify the history of settlement in this area, especially in the Norse and Gall-Ghàidheil periods. The surviving 'hall-type' buildings at Little Dunagoil, misleadingly classified as long-houses by their excavator (Marshall 1964), testify to significant Norse and early mediaeval occupation, though the succeeding farm of Dunagoil, sited some 300m inland, with only two merks of Old Extent is among the smaller farms of the island.

The postulated unit of *Roscadale, comprising 12 merks of Ardroscadale and 12 of Dunalunt, would have been next to Kingarth in value and possibly also in antiquity, since the name, whatever its exact

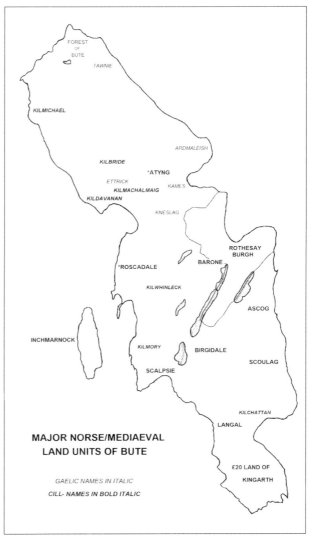

Fig 9.1 Location of the larger or older Bute landholdings, including those with Norse names, cill- names and a few with Gaelic names of topographical reference.

origin, is clearly Norse. This estate, too, would have been half an ounceland, since half of it was five pennylands in 1320, as mentioned above. When it was divided, the Gaelic *àird* (here signifying a slight promontory rising towards the sea from an inland valley) served to specify one half, while the other was named Dunalunt for a fortified hill on the landward side of the valley. This division therefore took place when Gaelic was again being spoken. Some time later further fission must have occurred, since Ardroscadale has comprised two 6 merk lands and Dunalunt four of 3 merks since documentation began. Nether Ardroscadale will serve as a case study later in this paper.

Scoulag may also have been valued at 24 merks, adding the five merks of *Scowlogmore* and three of Bruchag (an otherwise unattached adjacent unit) to the frequently mentioned 16 merklands of Scoulag which comprised four 4 merk farms. Of these, Kerrymoran and Kerryniven were Gaelic personal names prefixed by *Ceathramh*, quarter (Hannah 2000), while the other two simply prefixed *Scoulag* with Scots *Nether* and *Mid*. This pairing implies the existence of Upper Scoulag, a present-day farm not mentioned in older documents. Kerrymoran may have been an earlier name for this farm, leaving Kerryniven to make up the last quarter. Scowlogmore disappears from the record in the late fifteenth century, to be replaced by Kerrylamont, owned separately from the 16 merklands. At this period the names of smaller settlements could change more readily than their boundaries.

The name Barone is obscure, even its language being uncertain (Márkus forthcoming), evidence in itself of antiquity. This estate predated the burgh of Rothesay, as part lies within it, and part outside. Five merklands of the latter portion were divided in 1506 (RMS, vol 2: no.2987) among four tenants (with minor errors of arithmetic) in the ratios of one third, two quarters and one sixth. These extents correspond to the settlements of Balilone, Glenchromag, Chapelton and Achamor, all of which appear in the record within the next few years. It is hard to resist the conclusion that these townships had existed and been so named for a considerable time previously. Here is a substratum of settlement which slipped under the radar of official documents, and it may be that some other 'multiple tenancies' seemingly implied by charters should be similarly understood[6]. We can deduce that Barone (or this portion of it) was first split into two halves, each of which was again divided, one part equally and the other in a ratio of 2:1. These four settlements taken together are regularly referred to as Greater or Meikle Barone in seventeenth-century records, though confusingly this name was sometimes used later (eg on May's 1781 map, MSA BU) to designate the farm now called Barone Park or to contrast that farm with Little Barone, neither of which was included in the five merklands of the royal holding.

Cranslag[7] was a 12 merk land whose antiquity is affirmed by its long-standing division between royal (ie originally Stewart) and Bannatyne lands, indicating that it pre-existed the rise of these powers. It may well have originated in the Norse or pre-Norse periods. Two of the three quarters of this land held by Kames (earlier by Wester Kames) continued in its possession until that estate finally passed to the Bute family in 1863. The ownership history of the third quarter (Cranslagloan) is complex.

Kames became the largest estate with a Gaelic topographic name, but it only grew in power from the thirteenth century. The nuclei of Easter and Wester Kames were each three merks of Old Extent, bordering the bay on Bute's east coast which gave them their name (and later took it back). We may therefore postulate an older undivided Kames of six merks. These two Kames estates, of the Bannatyne and Spens families respectively, extended their control for some time up to Glenmore and across the island to Cranslag and Ardroscadale. The Sheriff's (Stewart of Bute) estate also grew steadily from the fifteenth century onwards and has dominated the island since the improvement period, reversing in one sense the earlier centuries of fission, while conserving the identities of individual farmsteads in an island-wide dispersed pattern.

Estates with Cill-names

Among the larger landholdings with Gaelic names, *Cill*- names predominate. The largest was Kilchattan with 14 merks, followed by Kilmory with 12. It is really impossible to know whether these names and their associated units in Bute go back to pre-Norse times, for there is as yet no convincing archaeological evidence (see Clancy 2008: 43, for a discussion of the situation in Galloway). The strong association of Catan with Blane makes it seem likely in Kilchattan's case.

Kilmory was divided unevenly into five merks of Over Kilmory and seven of Nether. Over (later Meikle) Kilmory remained a single unit despite still showing two distinct foci of settlement on May's map of 1780 (MSA BU), and indeed continued to be farmed as such until about four years ago, being judged one of the best farms on the island. Nether Kilmory was in three equal parts by about 1500, each having the unusual extent of 2⅓ merks.[8] The name of one, *Kilmory Chappelton*, retained for some time a reference to the eponymous chapel. This style probably fell into disuse after the reformation, when the chapel would have ceased to function, the farm later being known as Little Kilmory. The age of this chapel is unknown, though the dedication has been thought to tell against a first millennium date.[9]

A good case might be made for the antiquity of Kilmachalmaig (attested as a threepenny land in a charter of c.1313 (Bute 1945),[10] and subsequently comprising three farms of 2½ merks each). Evidence here includes a carved stone cross, thought to be engraved on a more ancient standing stone, and a cemetery of unknown period. The hypocoristic form of the dedication, while not conclusive, lends some support to an early date, while the pennyland valuation indicates Norse influence and may point towards a pre-Norse origin. In the case of Kildavanan, the hypocorism and 'celtic' dedication to Benén, in Latin Benignus (Watson 1926: 301), also argue for an early date, though this holding has only ever been a three merk land.

The dedications of Kilbride (a six merk land which has never been divided) and Kilmichael (five merks) imply little about dating, and arguments based on Kilmichael chapel's supposed inwardly corbelled gable (Hewison 1893: 114; Addyman 2008) have generally been discounted. Kilbride chapel is unlocated, though a nearby field is called *Kirkyaird Butt* on May's 1781 map. The name Kilwhinleck is too obscure to afford useful evidence, though we know from documents that its 5½ merk estate included a mill and at least four small outlying farmsteads which lasted well into the eighteenth century.

Some inferences

Where several neighbouring farms have the same fractional value, Old Extents by themselves can serve to infer an older, larger unit. An example is provided by the four adjacent lands of Rhu, Tawnie, Bronoch, and Bullochreg, along the East Kyle shore, each with a valuation of 1⅞ merks, which probably comprised a single £5 land when the valuation was undertaken. More speculatively, the next farms down the coast, Shalunt, Culnashambrug and Stuck, valued respectively at four, two and four merks, may have been once a single ten merk land.

Sometimes a combination of toponymic and assessment evidence allows less obvious conclusions to be reached with confidence. Four adjacent farms, now known as Dunalunt, Ballycaul, Ballianlay and Ballycurrie are shown to have formed a single unit by analysis of the place-name record (Hannah 2000), but the fact that each had a 3 merk Old Extent, making the whole Dunalunt unit worth 12 merks, provides additional confirmation. Its probable relation to the neighbouring 12 merk land of Ardroscadale has already been mentioned.

Another Norse estate of 12 merks was Langal, also comprising four farms of three merks each. Three of these (Langalchorad, [Langal]quochag, Langalbuinoch) have names consisting of Langal specified by Gaelic suffices which varied confusingly through the centuries, in the case of Quochag eventually dropping the generic entirely. The identity of the fourth part (Culevin) can only be inferred from its location and because we know that its Old Extent was three merks and it did not belong to any other large unit.

Bute's royal farms

Exchequer Rolls (ER v: 79ff) furnish the first extant list of Bute's royal farms, which in 1440 occupied about two thirds of the island. The remainder comprised Rothesay burgh (with extensive rural area), the two Kames estates, with ten farms,[11] the smaller estate of Ascog and three other units, of which the Sheriff held two. Forty farms are named in the list, ten of these having two or more parts, usually numbered sequentially, a scribal convenience used when the parts were equal in value. The Gaelic suffices *mòr and beag* are used three times and once the Latin *inferior/superior* (for *nether/over*). There is one example of repeated fission in the list, Kilchattan being divided into *mòr and beag*, and *Kīlchattan mòr* in turn having three numbered parts.

This list is repeated with minor changes in 1449 and 1450 (ER v: 359ff, 406ff), after which there is a gap of more than half a century before the next list in 1507 (ER xii: 509ff). Here names replace numbers, the estate name being usually retained as a generic, prefixed with such specifics as *uvir/nether*, *hidder/yonder*, *mekill/litell* (or Gaelic equivalents *mòr/beag*, etc) while *mid* or *meadhanach* is added where the unit splits into three. Occasionally the tenant's name serves this function, and rarely a previously undocumented name is invoked. Only on linguistic grounds can we guess how long such a name might have been in oral use. Fission since 1440 is evidenced only at Branser and Nether Kilmory, each now listed as three units.[12] This list is repeated with only slight changes in 1527 (ER xv: 302f). To emphasise continuity over five centuries and throughout the improvements, it is worth noting that all the farms in these lists apart from four in Kingarth parish and five in the north of the island were still being farmed as separate units in the mid twentieth century. Bute did not suffer the population explosion and subsequent wholesale clearance which afflicted so many highland areas.

In 1506, a charter (RMS, vol 2: no.2987) lists Bute royal farms for a different purpose, confirming in *feu-ferme* all the king's tenants on the island. 26 farms had a single feuar, six tenants held two or three units each, while 46 tenants shared the remaining 23 farms, in most cases equally. In general, this did not cause fresh division of the unit, but seems rather to have reflected its internal structure (cf Barone above). How the fields were shared out is not entirely clear, but no further fission occurred, new names were not created, and the original units continued as entire farms into the centuries that followed, despite being often held for long periods by two tenants or, on rare occasions, two different heritors. Dodgshon has discussed at some length how multiple tenancies operated in various parts of Scotland, but always in a context of open-field systems (1981: 149ff).[13]

Bute had been claimed by the Stewarts since around 1200 and along with Renfrew and parts of north Ayrshire came to comprise their demesne lands. After gaining the throne, their attachment to the island remained strong (Boardman 2006: 99), and it is clear from the Exchequer Rolls that Bute continued to furnish meal and marts for the royal table into the sixteenth century. But the setting of royal lands in *feu-ferme* under James IV marked a significant change, inaugurating a power struggle among the feuars which soon resulted in the emergence of several small estates, but ultimately in domination by the Stewarts of Bute, constables and hereditary keepers of Rothesay castle and sheriffs of Bute, who were initially granted just the two farms of Ardmaleish and Greenan along with these titles around 1380,[14] Barone being added in 1419 (MSA BU/1/1/15).

The evidence of estate maps

Using sources such as those mentioned above, we can infer that from around 1300 onwards there were some 80 farms[15] scattered fairly uniformly across the island, with the exception of the generally uncultivable shoreline and the inhospitable higher moorlands. Apart from Rothesay, which grew up around the medieval castle, there were no larger aggregations of settlement. It is likely that the rural population fluctuated between two and three thousand, roughly 20 to 40 persons per farm. But did these people live close together in a compact ferm-toun or in isolated cottages scattered among their fields? And is there evidence for change in this pattern, as in various Hebridean localities (Dodgshon 1993; Raven 2005)? From the middle of the eighteenth century, thanks to the third Earl's enthusiasm for agricultural improvement, Bute is furnished with several sets of high quality estate maps. The first of these, drawn by John Foulis in 1759, depicts buildings for the first time in enough detail to answer this question, at least for the immediately pre-improvement period.

Most farms are depicted as having a single focus of settlement, with up to half a dozen or even more buildings in a cluster, often aligned roughly in parallel down the slope, but without strict organisation and with the odd building at right angles. These of course include a variety of ancillary buildings as well as houses. Often there is an additional, isolated house towards the periphery of the unit, and these will be discussed in detail below. Exceptions to

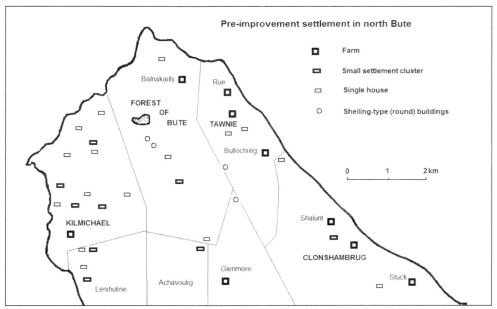

Fig 9.2 Composite map of settlement sites in north Bute, combining the results of field survey with an understanding of the larger settlement units derived from documentary evidence.

the usual unifocal layout occurred in the north of the island, in effectively highland country, where livestock farming was dominant. Here Lenihuline is shown to have had two foci of settlement, while the large farm of Kilmichael had several, apparently long-established sites within a mile of the main steading, but not extending further into the hinterland. Field survey has shown that at some earlier time even more houses were scattered across the hill country of north Bute (Proudfoot & Hannah 2000; Geddes & Hale 2010), and it would be unwise to assume that the pattern shown by Foulis had prevailed across the island in earlier centuries (fig 9.2).

Bute is too small for transhumance to be a major feature; just two groups of rather slight shieling huts are known (Proudfoot & Hannah 2000). These do not figure on estate maps, neither do many of the more frequent footings of sub-rectangular buildings, scattered singly or in pairs across the landscape in places where grazing might be found, but without accompanying cultivation. It seems reasonable to postulate that these represent an attempt to exploit the pastoral potential of the land when a market was developing for livestock, and at the same time crops were less dependable, during the 'little ice-age'. These buildings may well belong to that period, between the fourteenth and seventeenth centuries. In the Hebrides similar sub-rectangular huts with rounded gables have been dated to the later medieval period (Raven 2005: 380–1). Excavation might help to date the Bute houses, as well as determining whether their occupation was brief or seasonal, or if they reflect a more drastic albeit temporary change in farming practice.

Butts

There is one widespread exception to the clustered disposition of Bute's lowland farmsteads. We learn from documents that many farms had an associated 'butt', a term which seems almost peculiar to Bute when used in this way. Estate maps make clear that the reference is to a patch of land near the periphery of the farm, with its own isolated house, roughly equivalent to the more familiar *pendicle*.[16] *Buttmen* had a definite status, intermediate between tenants and cotters, reflected, for instance, in the sums they paid in hearth tax (BtM L04-1027 B41.4) and roads labour remission (BtM L04-1037 B41.5). Earlier, there may have

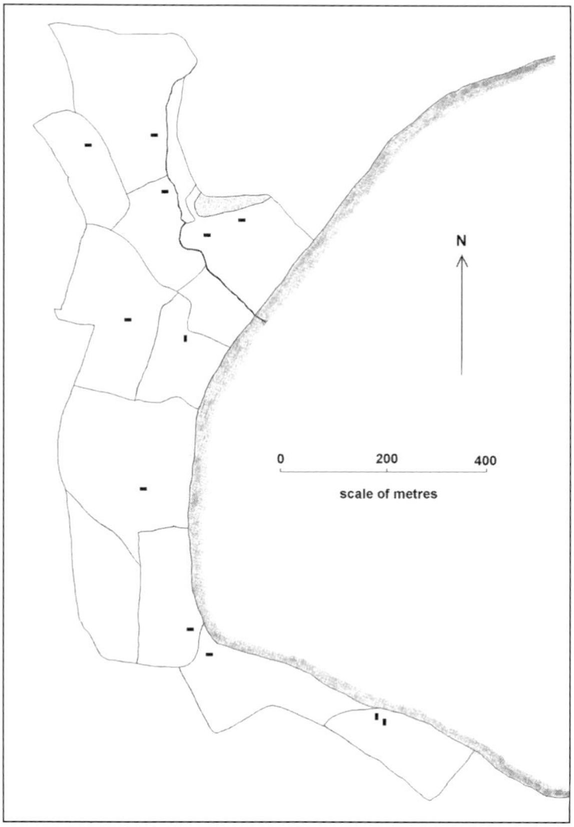

Fig 9.3 The 'hamlet' of contiguous butts around Kilchattan Bay in 1760, redrawn from Foulis' map (by kind permission of Mountstuart Archive).

been a commitment to some days' work on the main farm. The existence of butts provides additional confirmation that houses were otherwise clustered about the steading.

Detachment of the butt was an aspect of the fission process which never gave rise to full-scale farms, and was quite different from equal division into fully viable units. There is no evidence for when butts were first established, but in a few areas, notably around Kilchattan Bay, they were numerous by the late seventeenth century, in that area no longer associated with any farm, but let individually by the Estate on an annual or longer-term basis (James Stewart rental 1695–1700, MSA BU/ BE 1). Proliferation of butts probably depended on the availability of other work, as cultivation of the butt could barely have provided a livelihood on its own. Very locally their preponderance created a dispersed pattern of settlement, amounting to a scattered village, unique on the island and marking the culmination of a very specific fission process (fig 9.3).

A pre-improvement case study: Nether Ardroscadale

Figure 9.4 shows part of Nether Ardroscadale in 1781, a farm typical of many in Bute. Although north of the highland boundary fault, it is in some respects a lowland farm, occupying a low ridge between the sea and a glaciated valley, with some fine arable and pasture land, as well

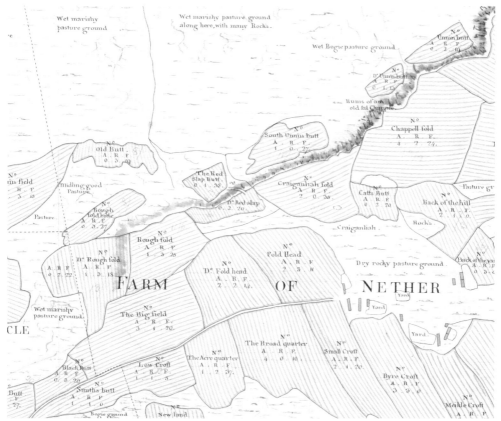

Fig 9.4 Part of Peter May's plan of Nether Ardroscadale, 1781 (RCAHMS DP075154; © The Bute Collection, Mountstuart Archive)

as rough grazing. May's plan depicts its immediately pre-improvement layout. The straight dashed line on the left shows where it was proposed to cut off a new pendicle.

The steadings occupy an area of elevated, rocky ground which could not be cultivated but would always be relatively well-drained. Below this to the east, the land slopes gently down to a broad valley, wet in the bottom. The slopes immediately below the farmstead were the best arable, comprising the infield of the farm, in Bute as elsewhere generally called *croft* land. These fields were long enough for a plough team to operate efficiently, but usually relatively narrow. They grew the oats which were the backbone of the lowland rural economy, feeding the people and the draft horses, and paying the bulk of teinds and rents, as well as barley, needed for feu-duty and for brewing or distilling and later as a cash crop. Above the cliff, on the higher ground to the north (right on the map), were *folds*. These often had a rounder shape, enclosed from hill or woodland for folding livestock. The usual boundary was a stone and earth dyke, topped by a fence or dead hedge. Once adequately manured, these outfields would be cultivated periodically.

After *croft* and *fold*, *butt* is by far the most frequent field-name generic on May's Bute maps (Hannah 2008). Butt fields are often peripheral, but they are not outfield, nor necessarily of recent origin. They are distinctive in being usually specified either by a personal name or an occupation, or by the use to which they were put. This is often a cash crop, here (unusually) onions (*Unnin Butt*), whilst other examples from Bute include hens, geese, potatoes and tobacco. Reference to a trade, as here the Smith's Butt, indicates that the butt field was cultivated by an individual for whom it furnished only part of an income, and relates this usage of 'butt' to the meaning of pendicle discussed above.

May's plan shows that here agricultural improvement has scarcely begun. The old landscape remains intact. But it does more than that. Both the forms and names of the fields add historical depth to the map. We see that some boundaries are older than others, and that subdivision of fields has taken place. For instance the large fold to the north of the steadings has been divided into three fields, perhaps in two stages. This may signify a division among tenants, or have been to facilitate rotation of folding and cropping. The map shows three separate steadings within the farm nucleus; these may represent successive stages of growth.[17] Nether Ardroscadale was among Bute's largest farms, six merks of Old Extent, and might have made three viable units, but was never split up.

The six crofts comprising the infield also seem to differ in age. Successive extension southwards is indicated by the shape of their boundaries, and probably again a subdivision of earlier, larger fields. Note also that some pairs or groups of adjacent fields have the same name, again suggesting that they were formerly a single field. However, this does not amount to evidence for an earlier open-field system, though a scaled-down version of the lowland medieval system may have operated on some of Bute's larger farms. Most farms were small, and held by a single tenant. Where two or more tenants were sharing they seem (as here) to have divided the fields with more or less permanent boundaries, unlike the Hebridean run-rig system of the immediately pre-improvement period.

Some phrases on the map define the historical dimension explicitly: 'Has been in tillage' indicates a change within living memory. This phrase describes an outset no longer needed, or found unsuitable for sustained cultivation, hinting that a peak of economic or population pressure may have passed. The South Onion Butt presupposes the Onion Butt; Old Butt and New Land appear self-explanatory.[18]

A large fold to the south west of the farm, above the road, has also been split into three smaller fields. This fold was bounded by an old head-dyke, and an outset beyond this, called the Rough Fold, has itself been subdivided. Beyond this, a further area, called the Rough Fold Brae, has been enclosed. We can thus see five phases of activity on this portion of the farm: first the large fields within the head-dyke, then the threefold division of these, followed by extension on to the rough ground, the subdivision of that field and finally a further outset on the steep slope below. It is impossible at present to attach a chronology to this sequence, which indicates a progressive attempt to increase production and may reflect some increase in population, though returns would diminish as ever-smaller areas of less good land were brought in.

Conclusions

For all the diversity of influences to which settlement in Bute has been subjected, a strong thread of continuity can be traced throughout. There is little evidence of drastic change in the organisation or distribution of rural settlement, and most farms have remained on or close to the same site for many centuries. At a finer scale, field survey suggests that significant changes may have occurred in the degree of settlement dispersion on at least some farms, and archaeological work is needed to help determine this issue. Some deserted sites have been identified where excavation might yield useful results. From the documentary side, the considerable resources of the Mountstuart archive remain largely untapped, affording an opportunity for greatly enhanced understanding of the pre-improvement rural economy. Bute's strategic significance and agricultural value made the island a contentious possession among neighbouring powers, and consequently work on any of the surrounding regions is likely to shed further light on Bute. Conversely, research focused on the island will have a broader impact on our understanding of the various political, economic and linguistic hegemonies which have held sway in the Firth of Clyde through the centuries.

Acknowledgements

Thanks are due to Andrew Maclean, Barbara McLean and Lynsey Nairn at Mountstuart and to Jean McMillan at Bute Museum for help in accessing archival material, to The Bute Archive for permission to reproduce figures 9.3 and 9.4, and to RCAHMS for access to digital imagery. I am indebted to Gilbert Márkus, George Geddes and John Raven for commenting most helpfully on drafts of this paper, and to John Baldwin for encouraging me to contribute in the first instance.

Notes

1. A full list of Bute Old Extents culled from a wide range of sources is given in Hannah 2004, Appendix.
2. Ross (2006: 66) draws attention to the value in this respect of similarly ancient *dabhach* assessments and boundaries in Moray.
3. Lamont (1957, 187) argues that this was a later imposition, in Islay at least, and that earlier a quarterland had been equated to 20 shillings, making an ounceland (20 pennylands) worth six merks as in the other cases.

4. Assuming the equivalence discussed above, that three merks on Bute make up a pennyland, 30 merks would be half of a twenty pence ounceland. 12 or 15 merks, frequently the assessment of a larger unit on Bute, would then correspond to a quarterland, an important ancient unit in some Hebridean and Irish contexts.

5. See Márkus (forthcoming) for a discussion of the evidence for an underlying Old Welsh name.

6. I know of no other instance where the sub-units had entirely separate names, but there are several cases where holdings were divided into discrete parts which acquired their own specifics. For instance, it is probable that the twentieth-century farms of East, West and Mid St Colmac were direct descendants of the three pennylands of Kilmachalmaig. Dodgshon (1981: 151) draws attention to the frequency of touns being shared among feuars, but without considering the case where each share comprised a discrete, pre-existent settlement. Later, however, he refers to cases where 'the township assessment appears to have been thrown around...a number of small dispersed sites' comprising 'a pattern of tenure and settlement...both more detailed and older than the framework of assessment embracing it' (Dodgshon 1998: 149). Barone seems to have been an example of this.

7. *Cnarsay* and *Knaslak* are among early forms of this rather obscure name (see Márkus forthcoming, for a full discussion).

8. This sum is equal to 41 shillings 1⅓ pence, and the threefold division explains this seemingly odd assessment.

9. This has been questioned by Márkus (pers comm), citing a Virgin Mary cult in eighth-century Iona.

10. Lord Bute dates this charter to c1320, but detailed analysis of witnesses may allow a more precise dating to 1313 (see Molly Rorke this volume).

11. The Bannatynes of Easter Kames held Kilmachalmaig, Ardroscadale, Ettrick, Kilbride and Glenmore, the Spens family of Wester Kames had Edinmore, Edinbeg, and three quarters of Cranslag (Cranslagmory, Cranslagloan and Acholter).

12. It is impossible to know whether this represents a real change or merely a greater attention to detail on the part of the authorities.

13. I have found no evidence for open field systems on Bute, which of course is not proof that they never existed, but it is clear from estate maps that across most of the island the fields were quite small enclosures in the immediately pre-improvement period. This is in striking contrast to the situation in Arran as described by Headrick (1807). See further discussion in main text.

14. No definite dating is known for this grant, and here I follow the fourth Marquess's comment 'about 20 years previously' (ie before Robert III's confirmation charter of 1400) in Bute 1945.

15. I use 'farm' here to mean an aggregate of rural settlement working a defined area and regarded as a fiscal unit for administrative purposes.

16. It is worth emphasising the primacy of land over house in this context. Estate maps name many *butt* fields (see discussion in main text), but relatively few have an associated house. In those cases, the house and field together acquire the title of *butt*, which then comes to have the meaning of pendicle or smallholding.

17. If so, this growth took place quite early, since the three pennylands which probably pertained to this farm in 1320 (out of five for the whole of Ardroscadale) may well correspond to these three nuclei, indicating that the process was complete before that date, and indeed before the imposition of merklands a century or so earlier.

18. Appearances may deceive. A draft version of this map bears the seeming oxymoron: 'new land known as the old butt'. Presumably, a former butt field had been let to go out of cultivation and was returned to it after a lengthy interval, but before the memory of its earlier use had been lost.

References

Archival sources

(MSA= Mountstuart Archive; BtM= Bute Museum)

BtM Hearth Tax rolls for Bute, 1693, Bute Museum Archive, BtM LO4-1027 B41.4.

Foulis, J 1759, a set of estate maps drawn for 3rd Earl of Bute, particularly of Kilchattan Bay, Lenihuline and Kilmichael, etc, MSA BU uncatalogued.

May, Peter, 1780–2, a series of maps of farms on the Bute estate, MSA BU uncatalogued. It seems likely that Peter's son Alexander assisted in the production of these maps.

MSA BU/1/1/15: Charter of Robert, Duke of Albany, granting 'all and haill the lands of Barone' with pertinents to John Stewart, sheriff of Bute, and his wife Janet Semple.

MSA BU/ BE1 Rental of James Stewart, 1695–1700.

MSA Cat Catalogue of the Fourth Marquess, no 2, a charter (c1320) of a grant by Walter, Steward of Scotland to John son of Gilbert the son of Gilbert and his heirs of the ... five penny land of Ardroscadale (*Ardrossigille*).

Statute Roads Labour Lists for Bute, from 1769, Bute Museum Archive, BtM LO4-1037 B41.5.

Printed sources

Addymann, T 2008 Unpublished report on Kilmichael Chapel prepared for HS and Discover Bute Landscape Partnership Scheme.

Anderson, A O 1922, *Early Sources of Scottish History, A.D. 500 to 1286*, 2 vols. Edinburgh: Oliver & Boyd.

Boardman, S 2006 'The Gaelic world and the early Stewart court', in Broun, D and Bute, Marquess of [fourth] 1945 'Isle of Bute charters, *Trans Bute Nat Hist Soc* 13, 7–25.

Clancy, T O 2008 'The Gall-Ghàidheil and Galloway', *J Scottish Name Studies* 2, 19–50.

Dodgshon, R A 1981 *Land and Society in Early Scotland*. Oxford: Clarendon Press.

Dodgshon, R A 1993 'West Highland and Hebridean settlement prior to crofting and the Clearances: a study in stability or change?' *Proc Soc Antiq Scot* 123, 419–38.

Dodgshon, R A 1998 *From Chiefs to Landlords*, EUP, Edinburgh.

ER *The Exchequer Rolls of Scotland*, Burnett, G et al (eds) 1882-95, vols. V, XII, XV, Edinburgh.

Fraser, J 2005 'Strangers on the Clyde: Cenél Comgaill, Clyde Rock and the bishops of Kingarth', *The Innes Review* 56, 102–20.

Geddes, G & Hale, A 2010 *The Archaeological Landscape of Bute*. RCAHMS, Edinburgh.

Hannah, A 2000 'Bute farm names with personal name elements', *Trans Bute Nat Hist Soc* 25, 61–7.

Hannah, A 2004 'Old Extent in Bute and the meaning of the Merkland', *Trans Bute Nat Hist Soc* 26, 28–38.

Hannah, A 2008 'Bute field names on the maps of Peter May', *Trans Bute Nat Hist Soc* 27, 52–5.

Harding, D W 2004 'Dunagoil, Bute, re-instated', *Trans Bute Nat Hist Soc* 26, 1–19.

Headrick, J 1807 *View of the mineralogy, agriculture, manufactures and fisheries of the island of Arran*. Edinburgh.

Hewison, J K 1893 *The Isle of Bute in the Olden Time*, vol 1. Edinburgh & London: W Blackwood & Sons.

Lamont, W D 1957 'Old land denominations and 'Old Extent' in Islay, part i', *Scottish Studies* 2, 183–203.

McKerral, A 1943 'Ancient denominations of land in Scotland', *Proc Soc Antiq Scot* 78, 39–80.

Márkus, G forthcoming *The Place Names of Bute*.

Marshall, D 1964 'Report on excavations at Little Dunagoil', *Trans Bute Nat Hist Soc* 16, 1–61.

Proudfoot, E & Hannah, A 2000 'Deserted Settlements on the Isle of Bute', *Trans Bute Nat Hist Soc* 25, 25–56.

Raven, J 2005 *Medieval landscape and Lordships in South Uist.* Unpublished PhD thesis, University of Glasgow.

RCAHMS 2011 *Scotland's Rural Past.* Edinburgh: RCAHMS.

RMS *Registrum Magni Sigilli Regum Scottorum* (Register of the Great Seal of the Kings of Scots) ed J M Thomson et al, 1882–1914, Edinburgh.

Ross, A 2006 'The Dabhach in Moray: a new look at an old tub', in Woolf, A (ed) *Landscape and Environment in Dark Age Scotland*, 57–74. St Andrews: St John's House Papers No11.

Watson, W 1926 *The Celtic place-names of Scotland* (reprinted 2004). Edinburgh: Birlinn.

Chapter 10

'An enormous expense enclosing and dividing'. Agricultural Improvement in eighteenth-century Bute

George F Geddes
Royal Commission on the Ancient and
Historical Monuments of Scotland

OVER 40 years ago the Royal Commission on the Ancient and Historical Monuments of Scotland (RCAHMS) began an archaeological and architectural survey of the county of Argyll. With the publication of seven volumes between 1971 and 1992, this turned out to be a project of wide scope, one that changed the organisation, and influenced our understanding of this part of Scotland to a great degree. It has long been a source of local frustration that other parts of Scotland have not been surveyed in such detail, though the reasons for this are complex and multiple. In the case of the Isle of Bute, it was simply out-with Argyllshire (fig 10.1).

With this in mind, it was with great pleasure that RCAHMS embarked on a detailed survey of Bute between 2009 and 2011, thanks largely to the sponsorship of the Discover Bute Landscape Partnership Scheme (DBLPS), a project that held at its root the principle of active engagement with the community of the island itself, as well as the wider community of interest. Considerably more detailed than a traditional Inventory survey, the project encompassed the revision of over 500 sites, as well as aerial sorties and documentary research. Over thirty measured surveys were undertaken in the same tried and tested way, but this time hand-in-hand with enthusiasts, and a small but well illustrated publication sold out within the first year (Geddes & Hale 2010).

Bute has a long and illustrious history of archaeological study, and it currently boasts two important organisations: the Buteshire Natural History Society and Bute Museum. Both were nurtured in their infancy by John Nairn Marshall (1860–1945) and his daughter Dorothy (1900–1992), and both continue to inspire and inform current generations. The Bute Settlement Survey project also deserves a particular mention as it has added greatly to our knowledge of the island's rural past, recording about 200 settlement sites, mainly dating from the eighteenth century (for a summary see Proudfoot & Hannah 2000). That project takes a well-deserved place as an early example of the currency of partnerships between professionals and local enthusiasts, and an exploration of the eighteenth-century rural landscape.

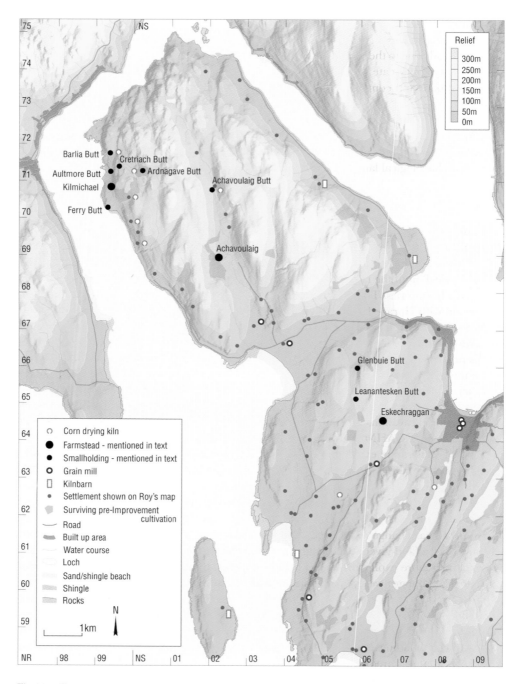

Fig 10.1 This map of south and central Bute depicts the farmsteads discussed in the text against areas where pre-Improvement cultivation remains are visible, derived from Historic Landuse Assessment data, and the settlement pattern in the mid eighteenth century, derived from Roy's Military Map (Crown Copyright RCAHMS GV004951).

It rapidly became apparent in 2009 that an all-island survey would highlight certain themes of interest and importance. The mid to late eighteenth century was naturally worthy of further study due to the surviving remains and the suite of documentary sources, including more than seventy estate maps. The central aim of this paper is to highlight these sources and to compare and contrast the archaeological and documentary evidence. After a short introduction to the theme of Improvement and summaries of the types of evidence available, there are three detailed case studies, all from the northern half of the island. A subsequent note on critical approaches draws much from a recent workshop held by the DBLPS. The examples presented here serve to illustrate the potential for further and detailed study of both the archaeological landscape and the Bute Collection at Mount Stuart Archive.

Documentary evidence

The Improvement period (c1750–1850) is better known through the discipline of history rather than archaeology, the latter undergoing something of an awakening in the last twenty years. Features of the later eighteenth and nineteenth centuries were not considered 'archaeological' until the later decades of the twentieth century and did not appear in early RCAHMS Inventories. The application of archaeology and map studies to the 1800s began in Scotland with Horace Fairhurst in the late 1960s (1968; 1969). The Improvement period tends not to feature in summaries of Scotland's archaeology, despite the fact that a high proportion of surviving sites and monuments are either a product of, or have been affected by, this process of change. Particularly appealing to enthusiast and professional alike, it is a period more readily understandable than much of what precedes it, and for many people it is a crucial theme in their own family histories. Only a small proportion of any archaeology syllabus tackles Improvement, and commercial archaeological projects (an important source of funding for excavations in particular) rarely include a thorough analysis of Improvement features. Recent RCAHMS publications have gone some way to exploring this theme in more detail, illustrating examples of the buildings and landscapes which are characteristic (Glendinning & Wade Martins 2008; RCAHMS 2007; RCAHMS 2008; Boyle 2009; RCAHMS 2011).

Surviving evidence for eighteenth-century rural landscapes has been affected by the essentially transforming nature of Improvement. Driven in part by the Scottish Enlightenment, there was a clear change in the attitude of landowners and their factors, a transition from acceptance of a God-given world to the development of one that could be actively moulded and exploited more explicitly. Adding further impetus, transport networks were improving, technological changes were revolutionising manufacturing, markets were opening up, and labour was readily available. There were great incentives for the creation of wealth.

In Bute, a landscape of irregular arable folds measuring no more than three acres disappeared to be replaced by larger, more regular fields enclosed by stone walls. Vernacular stone and clay buildings with thatched cruck-framed roofs were taken down and replaced by typical lime-mortared courtyard farms. Long established meadow, wood and pasture was rationalised. These features survive in some places, particularly in areas given over to sheep and in places where the high water mark of early Improvement was not economically sustainable in later periods. Coupled with this, the movement to a more efficient use of arable land tended to cause the abandonment of outfield that had previously been cultivated periodically, and there was an overall reduction both in arable cover and in settlement dispersal.

In the eighteenth century, most of the Isle of Bute was owned by the 3rd Earl, John Stuart (1713–1792). As the first Scottish Prime Minister of Britain, Bute was a highly educated and influential figure who spent part of his upbringing with the Dukes of Argyll, prime movers in Improvement (RCAHMS 1992: 32). The ownership of estates at Wortley, in Yorkshire, and Lutton Hoo, in Bedfordshire (where the house had been designed by Robert Adam, and the landscaping by Capability Brown), must have influenced both his expectations and his awareness of agricultural potential. Bute was also the first president of the Society of Antiquaries of Scotland in 1780 (Smellie 1792); interestingly, the pursuit of archaeology now extends beyond the forts and cairns that he was interested in, to the results of his own sponsorship of agricultural change (Geddes & Hale 2010: 3).

A good description of the state of agriculture in Bute during the eighteenth century comes from agricultural surveys (Smith 1798; Aiton 1816), the Statistical Account, and in particular the writing of Blain (Ross 1880). John Blain, who came to Bute in 1761 worked as a factor, town clerk, tax surveyor, custom collector, sheriff and magistrate. His papers represent an important source, complementing that of the estate. Old parish registers record the marriage of John Blain to minister's daughter Elizabeth Campbell in Rothesay in May 1768 (Rothesay Old Parish Registers). They went on to have ten children between 1769 and 1787.

In the middle of the eighteenth century, the rents of the Bute farms were generally paid partly in kind, partly in labour (Ross 1880: 269). Tenancy was 'at will', so either the landlord or the tenant could terminate the contract at any time, given a reasonable amount of notice. This system may have worked well when the tenants, factors and landlords had a close relationship, but in a situation where mistrust might develop it acted to prevent improvement in both building stock and land. The landlord also retained a 'steel-bow', a vested interest in each crop: if a tenant wished to move on, half the crop he sowed would go to the new tenant and half to the owner, hardly an incentive for an efficient changeover. Incoming tenants could rely on the harvest of their forebears and begin a tenancy with very little capital, clearly a good opportunity for some, but one that would not necessarily benefit the land holder.

By about 1748, the Earl of Bute had introduced a few farmers from others parts of the country, such as Annandale (Aiton 1816: 73; Ross 1880: 269), in order to stimulate new approaches to farming on the island. During 1759, he made a number of crucial changes to increase (and demand) the independence of the tenant, sweeping aside the previous arrangements. He gave up the steel-bow, stopped accepting rents in kind or labour, and changed the dates of exit and entry to Martinmas (11 November) and the subsequent Whitsunday (15 May), meaning that the incoming tenant would have to plant a new crop before harvest the following year (Ross 1880: 270). Leases were set at nineteen years, replacing the earlier system of tenancy at will. Estate plans of 1759 demonstrate that the farms around Mount Stuart (eg Kerrytonlia, Kerrylamont, Bruchag and New Farm) had already been reorganised to a great extent. In one case, the expense of enclosure may have equated to the value of over twenty years crop (RHP14107, 18).

The survey for the southern part of Roy's Military Map of Scotland (1752–55) provides an interesting and accessible snapshot of the whole island, which can be compared with more detailed estate sources. Initiated with some urgency after the '45, this national survey is nowadays referred to with some caution, since there are many areas where it cannot be relied upon as a true reflection of settlement. In Bute, however, it is complete, showing 178 named features, mostly small farmsteads, as well as roads, arable land and forest. About 81 of the 156 farmsteads were rebuilt in the nineteenth century and continued as farms into and beyond the Improvement period. Although ostensibly produced at a scale of 1:25,000, the surveyors gave considerably more attention to the town of Rothesay and the house and gardens at Mount Stuart than to the countryside in general. The level of detail reflects the intention of the sponsors, rather than the capability of the surveyors.

It is surely no coincidence that the next major phase of investment in Bute was about nineteen years later, during the tenure of factor Peter May (c1722–1795). By that time, much had already taken place, although there was concern at the cost and the manner of its execution. In 1777, Scottish politician James Stuart Mackenzie (c1719–1800) wrote to his brother Lord Bute that 'you were to be at no expense further than might be absolutely necessary, either for keeping up the present rents, or for an immediate return' (Adams 1979: 203). One of Scotland's most important early land managers and surveyors, May came to Bute as factor with Mackenzie's recommendation, having undertaken surveys for him from the 1750s. In fact Mackenzie was instrumental in his employment and it was Mackenzie as much as Lord Bute who drove Improvements, after experience in his estates in Perthshire, Angus and Ross and Cromarty. With his son Alexander (Sandy), Peter May quickly went about a re-survey of the estate farms, as well as the assessment and valuation of the estate building stock. In a letter dated January 1780, May explained the dynamic nature of agricultural improvements:

> The south side of the island is mostly a cornfield, and has cost Lord Bute an enormous expense inclosing and dividing the lands with ditch and hedge. But I must observe with regret that they are now in wretched order.
> (Adams 1979: 217)

Not long afterwards, it was clear that May has instituted a number of key changes and was well on the way to improving things for his employer:

> …As to the rents of the estate, I think Peter May has arranged things so that he will be able to raise some of them even next year and more the year after. In short all seems to be going well there…"
> Letter from J S Mackenzie to 3rd Earl of Bute, August 1780
> (Adams 1979: 219)

The case studies in this paper make use of three documentary sources in particular; the estate maps by John Foulis completed in 1759, the estate maps produced by the May family dated between 1781 and 1784, and the 'inventory and appreciation' of farmsteads begun by Alexander May in 1782.

The maps by Foulis, produced in 1759 and bound in a volume at Mount Stuart, include over forty surveys of individual or small groups of farms, each with a description of the character of the land, advice on improvements, and mention of particular issues, such as want of labour. Buildings were generally depicted with both the correct alignment and the correct size, although they were shown as idealised elevations, rather than in plan. A typical byre-house, for example, is depicted as a three-bay cottage with a central door, two windows and chimney stacks, but this bears little resemblance to the buildings described in later documents or archaeological remains. The occasional representation of a second storey is probably accurate, at Meikle Kilmory for example, and the symbol of a wheel by the gable indicates the presence of a grain mill. The depiction of arable is idealised, with straight rigs shown in patchworks filling the boundaries of farms, but meadow, pasture and woodland was also shown, with small hillocks indicating the presence of rough terrain. His plan of the farms and policies at Mount Stuart is considerably more detailed and the plan of the house and garden is a fine example of eighteenth-century survey (see Geddes & Hale 2010: 42), for the level of survey detail tends to reflect the level of improvement. Unfortunately, little is known about Foulis and, while it is likely that correspondence survives at Mount Stuart, there is only one other plan by him in the National Archives of Scotland.

Correspondence from throughout Peter May's career describes the theodolite, poles and chains that were used and something of the methodology tried and tested in different parts of Scotland (Adams 1979). Up to four boys were employed to assist, and local guides helped the surveyors with field names. Large scale general plans were produced to aid the locating of marches, while smaller scale maps depicted individual or small groups of farms. May wrote with clear instructions about the process of reducing plans, a task which had clearly vexed his apprentice in the 1760s. Presumably overseen by his father, Alexander's plans of Bute are extremely detailed, showing individual rigs, dykes, buildings and archaeological features, with names and comments as seemed appropriate. All but one of the May maps assessed as part of the project were fair copies, and the pencil grids used in their reduction are still visible as faint lines. Each field is numbered, presumably corresponding to a book of notes.

The results of the work by Alexander May include a series of about thirty estate maps of the highest quality, which depict and name individual areas of pasture, arable and individual buildings. Though long attributed to father Peter, who was a noted surveyor from the mid-eighteenth century, it seems likely that Alexander undertook the majority of the survey despite other pressures on his time, partly with assistance from Robert Johnson (Adams 1979: 232; 237). Peter May was probably about 60 years old by this time, and there is evidence that he directed others in their surveys as his responsibilities grew. On taking up the role as factor to the Earl of Findlater in 1767, he intended to 'give up entirely the business of surveying land' (Adams 1979: 86). Confirming Alexander's role, the Earl of Bute noted in 1784 that:

> I am ignorant whether Lady Mount Stuart ever mentioned the receipt of the tin roller enclosing a plan of Mount Stuart; if she did not I must do it, and express at the same time a strong commendation of the neat manner in which it was executed; but I am well acquainted with Mr Alexander May's various talents in that way.
> (Adams 1979: 242)

At the same time, the estate funded an 'inventory and appreciation' of the value of each of the agricultural buildings of the estate which was in some cases kept relatively up to date into the early nineteenth century. The book includes indexed entries for over 160 holdings in Bute, surveyed in 1782. Each entry provides a small sketch of the main and subsidiary farmsteads, detailing each building, its occupant and its function. The buildings are then described in detail, including information on the dimensions and the material of the walls, and the species and type of thatch. In some cases, it also includes information on doors and windows, where they were of value and not owned by the tenant.

The documentary evidence includes commentaries on the general scope and advance of Improvement, but with the addition of very specific details, particularly for the 1780s. Much research remains to be done, and it is likely the Bute collection at Mount Stuart will yield considerably more detail on both the early Improvements from the 1730s and the rebuilding of Bute's farmsteads in the early nineteenth century. It seems likely that analysis as detailed as that undertaken at Menstrie glen using the Wright of Loss papers (RCAHMS 2008) will be well within our grasp.

Archaeological evidence

The archaeological evidence for the second half of the eighteenth century is both complex and multi-faceted, including individual components, such as farmsteads, mills and kilns, as well as landscape features such as cultivation remains, dykes and plantations. Bute's countryside took its present form during the early nineteenth century in particular, but the crucial forces that shaped it had already been active for about a hundred years. The recognisable suite of compact farmsteads, rectangular fields with stone dykes, hedgerows and plantations often seems ubiquitous, but it is surprising how much survives beneath, and how many early features of Improvement have been retained.

Many of the eighteenth-century farmsteads, some of which were dispersed over quite a large area, were taken down and grubbed out as part of the nineteenth-century rebuilding of the farm steadings. Given that about half of those shown by Roy were abandoned, one would expect there to be many more substantial surviving remains. Those farmsteads that stood in the rich arable land have been completely removed, some no doubt surviving as archaeological sites beneath the current ground surface, whereas those that stood in ground that has been left to pasture generally remain as grass-grown footings. The island's complement of rural mills has also been decimated, with little evidence surviving at Ascog, Scalpsie, Drumachloy and Ettrick. At Greenan, a gable still stands, while the water-powered grain mill at Little Kilmory probably dates to the nineteenth century and has been subsequently altered.

Upstanding ruinous buildings do survive particularly well, for example at Ardnagave and Achavoulaig Butt, but they tend to represent peripheral land holdings rather than the principal farms. There are also a few cases of roofed buildings which may incorporate eighteenth-century elements. At Kerryfearn and Lubas, for example, there are structures that are squat and wide, and align with eighteenth-century map depictions. Other fragmentary remains of the larger farmsteads, such as the kiln barn at Ardmaleish, are particularly important. The barn, excavated by Milligan (1961; 1963) and planned by RCAHMS in 2009, was described in great detail in 1782 (fig 10.2). A building of 'stone and clay' that once stood to 13ft [4m] in height, it is now reduced to only 1m or so. Kiln-barns were once numerous on Bute, but very few survive. Corn drying kilns are more common survivors because they were attached to the smaller and more rural settlements. Good examples survive at Ardnagave, Achavoulaig Butt, and Kilwhinleck, the latter excavated in 1934 (Marshall 1934). Where eighteenth-century farmsteads survive as field monuments, they tend to comprise the footings of buildings. Well preserved farmsteads are found in the south of the island where the farms of Kelspoke, Branser, Kingavin and Glen Callum were amalgamated into an 800 acre farm before January 1780, when it was 'let at £200 a year for a sheep park' (Adams 1979: 218). Occasionally, as at Glen Callum and Cavin, we note the presence of nineteenth-century shepherd's cottages.

Elsewhere on the island, head-dykes enclose areas of cultivated ground, most notably at the head of Glen More. Sometimes standing to more than 1m in height, these turf-and-stone dykes were often depicted by May, but it is quite possible that some pre-date the eighteenth century, particularly when one notes Blain's reference to the Michaelmas Head Court in 1688 where it was decided that 'all head dykes should be built shoulder high'. The dykes were 'totally disregarded' by the time of his writing around 1800 (Ross 1880: 250). He also noted that 'in many places evidences of cultivation appear where not a furrow has been turned over for more than a century past' (Ross 1880: 258). Although a survey of cultivation remains was out-with the scope of the RCAHMS Bute project, many areas of it have already been recorded through aerial survey since 1977, and the Historic Land-use Assessment project (Geddes & Hale 2010: 36; http://hla.rcahms.gov.uk/). The majority of the larger areas survive in the far north and south of the island, higher areas of the interior and areas of the coastal strip below the raised beach. The most substantial remains survive at the south-west tip of the island around Barr Hill.

Case studies

Eskechraggan

The farmstead of Eskechraggan lies just to the north-west of the Greenan Loch and it now comprises a nineteenth-century courtyard farm with large twentieth-century sheds. On the estate map of 1759 by Foulis it is depicted as four single-storey buildings and two enclosures clustered within a landscape of arable cultivation with rough pasture to the north (fig 10.3). At that time the whole farm was of 213 acres, of which 60 were arable, but another 40 could be ploughed 'for want of hands' (RHP14107, 47). Just to the north of Eskechraggan march, a smallholding of 20 acres labelled *But-leananteaechtan* is depicted as a rectangular area of 'moory pasture' and 'cold moory arable bank' with a single building and a yard. In the accompanying text it is described as 'well laid out' and 'has been a part of Escragan large farm' (RHP14107, 55), although it appears to be tied to North Largievrechtan in 1759. *But Glenbouie*, a smallholding of 17 acres with two buildings and 'an industrious tenant', was also described as if it was formerly part of Eskechraggan. Foulis recommended the addition of six more butts to the farm for the improvement of the land and the rents. In Bute, the term 'butt' or 'but' is used to refer to both individual fields and smallholdings attached to larger farms. It does not equate to a croft, which implies a specific form of legal tenure.

Great changes took place in the next 22 years and May's plan of 1781 shows a very different layout (fig 10.4). Limited to a smaller area near the loch, the field system of Eskechraggan had been partly improved, for long lines representing stone dykes overlay the globular arrangement of earlier fields. The main farm holding had been reduced in overall size to 119 acres, with nearly two thirds in arable. In order to achieve the increase in arable, some land had been added from neighbouring farms, including a distinct block from the adjacent farm of Barone. Elements from 1759 are recognisable on the later plan: the 'meikle

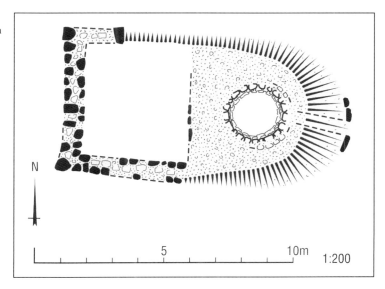

Fig 10.2 Plan of the kiln barn at Ardmaleish (NS06NE 3) (Crown Copyright RCAHMS GV004950).

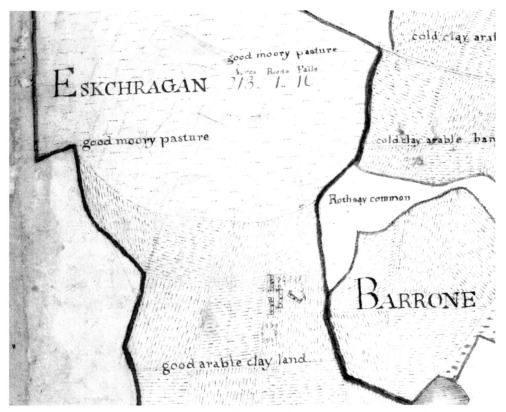

Fig 10.3 Extract of the plan of the farms of Eskchragan, Barrone and Leannymallach by John Foulis, 1759 (© The Bute Collection, Mountstuart Archive).

enclosure of Eskechraggan' appears to be the arable that was formerly part of Barone and its irregular boundary is partly overlain by a rectangular enclosure.

Butt Leninteskine was included in both the May survey and the appreciation, and it seems to have been considered a butt of Eskechraggan again by the 1780s. It had been increased in size to 69 acres, of which 29 were arable, a change that was facilitated by the addition of pasture taken from Eskechraggan, and the addition of at least a few new arable folds, probably to the east and north.

Elsewhere, other elements of the new field system split plots in half. May's plan does distinguish between different types of boundary, but thorough field survey and research is needed to clarify the symbols. Most of the field names are simply descriptive (eg heathery), but some include proper names (e.g. Nicol's/Johnston's fold) that do not appear to relate to the recorded tenants. The folds around Eskechraggan include some that are very large and pre-date the system of stone walls which has been laid out over them. At *Leninteskine*, the folds are a little smaller, and this is generally true of the butts which were on less favourable land with less available labour. There is no clear sign of a head-dyke at Eskechraggan, but some folds may have been formally enclosed by turf dykes, while other areas of cultivation depicted as folds may have had no visible upstanding boundary, instead simply marked by change in land use. There are also areas noted as 'has once been in tillage' and a plot of rig labelled 'wet land overgrown with rushes'.

In 1782 the farm was 'possessed' by the aforementioned John Blain and occupied by his subtenants. The four individual buildings function as ranges, the first comprising a byre and house (occupied by tenant John Mcfie). The second housed a stable, barn, sheep house and cottar house (occupied by James Duncan). The third was another byre and house (occupied by sub-tenant Robert Spence), while the fourth contained a milk house and a calves house. The gabled buildings were generally constructed in 'stone and clay', occasionally with the addition of turf to the upper part of the walls. Roofing couples were of oak, ash and alder with cabers and ribs (ie rafters and purlins) in similar species. The barn was a more substantial affair with hewn lintels and rebates, fir couples 'standing on the wall head', split oak cabers, and four doors with a given value. The whole farmstead at Eskechraggan was valued at £27, the butt of Leninteskine worth an additional £10. The same document records the 'amelioration' (improvement) of the houses by the tenant John MacPherson in 1832, over fifty years later. This is almost certainly the stage at which the old buildings of Eskechraggan were taken down and replaced by a U-plan courtyard steading, on the same site.

Leninteskine farmstead seems to have been completely abandoned by the 1860s, when it is depicted on the 1st edition of the Ordnance Survey 6-inch map in ruins (Buteshire 1869, Sheet CCIV), but further division did take place before the end of the nineteenth century (1897, Sheet CCIV.NW). The western fields of this butt were by that stage completed cleared, cultivated and bounded by stone walls, while those to the east, added in the late eighteenth century, are shown by the Ordnance Survey as cleared but are not enclosed and have probably been abandoned. This large eastern area is still notably green, with the remains of rig-and-furrow aligned east-to-west, as shown in 1781. The ruins of Butt Leninteskine survive today within an improved pasture field, and the footings of two buildings correspond in both orientation and length to those recorded in the 1782 inventory. Although supplemented by field clearance, there is some evidence that the buildings were not simple left to collapse and that some material was removed: the interiors are choked with a relatively small amount of rubble and it seems likely that the walls were robbed of stone, and the roofing timbers and thatch were removed to be re-used or spread as fertiliser, respectively.

Very little is now visible of Butt Glenbuie. Mature trees grow on fragments of bank that probably once enclosed the yard, a short section of track way survives, and two modern fields mirror the size and shape of the eighteenth-century holding.

Achavoulaig

The modern farmstead of Achavoulaig comprises a compact courtyard of buildings with the addition of some large modern sheds to the north-east. Two settlements are shown on Roy's military map at the west side of Glenmore Burn, between Drumachloy to the south and Loch Tarff (now known as the Bull Loch) to the north. These are Achavoulaig and the subsidiary Achavoulaig Butt, and it seems likely that Roy's surveyors noted them from the east side of the glen without finding out their proper names. Little if any cultivation is shown by the butt whilst a long swathe of it is shown around the main farm, and there is a definite distinction in Roy's symbols which reflects their relative status.

Foulis surveyed the farm of *Achavoulick* with High and Laigh Glenmore in 1758–9, stating the area at 384 acres of which 50 were ploughed (fig 10.5). His plan shows the principal farmstead of six buildings, surrounded by 'arable folds' and a 'shruby' birch wood to the north-west. Far up the glen, two isolated buildings and a smaller area of folds are depicted. In the accompanying text, Foulis described how it is 'very pleasant along the burn, where

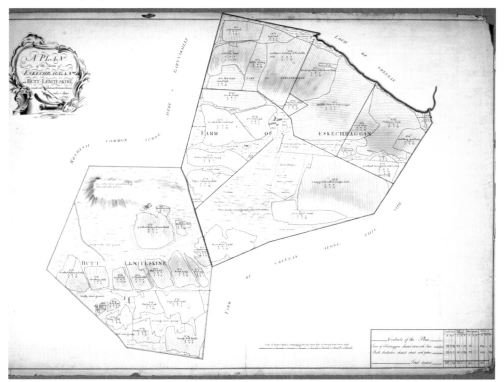

Fig 10.4 The May plan of the farms of Eskechraggan and Leninteskine, dated 1781 (© The Bute Collection, Mountstuart Archive).

half a score of those cottages called buts might be fixed, to the great improvement of the land and rents' (RHP14107, 64).

The boundaries and arrangement of land was similar when the farm was resurveyed by May twenty years later (fig 10.6). Around 1780 the farm was of 333 acres, of which only 41 acres were in arable, similar proportions to 1759. Over thirty individual plots of cultivation are depicted, of which the largest is about three acres. They are generally given English descriptive names, such as 'Meadow Rig'; 'Croft at the back of the yard'; 'Swine's butt', but some Gaelic derived names are less easily understood such as *Clanverpal*, and *Culnadallach* (perhaps 'back of the oak wood'). Each field had a distinct boundary marked by a thick line, but many have a second thick line above, probably indicating various phases of head dyke. Indeed, an analysis of both vertical aerial photographs and the contemporary and adjacent estate maps of Drumachloy and Kildavanan suggests that the marches of the farms had already been changed by 1780: the head-dyke continues south onto Drumachloy land, enclosing a large area of arable with Achavoulaig farmstead near the centre. The high and low 'clanverpal' arable folds shown on May's map are still extant just to the west of the farmstead remains, and a thorough survey of the area would perhaps tease out the detailed history.

In 1782 the main tenant Robert Maconachie stayed in a house and byre 'under one roof', and the choice of phrase may suggest that it was usual by that date for the house and byre to be separated by a mid-gable. Built of stone and mortar, with the upper part of the walls in turf, the building was roofed with seven ash couples and a heather thatch. A small cottar's house was attached to the end of this building, while another cottar occupied a large building (60ft long), but in 'very bad repair', and valued at just over £1.

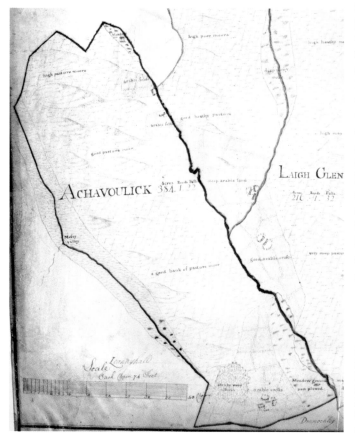

Fig 10.5 A plan of the farms of Achavoulick, High Glenmore and Laigh Glenmore by John Foulis 1759 (© The Bute Collection, Mountstuart Archive).

140

A sub-tenant, Robert Macalpin, stayed in Achavoulaig Butt, which lay much further up the glen. The stone-and-clay house and byre, over 40ft in length, was in 'very bad repair' in 1782, the four couples (3 of plane and 1 of alder) were supported on 8 remedial forks. A small barn with a heather thatch was in little better condition, whilst some 'old timber in a sheep house' was valued rather than the sheep house itself. The whole of the butt was only worth £1.17.4. Mention is made in 1784 and 1785 of timbers for the kiln, probably at the butt of Achavoulaig, though there may have been one at the main farm. In 1808, the ledger notes the 'amelioration' of the main farmstead, and the arrears of the outgoing tenant.

Little survives of Achavoulaig farmstead except the grass-grown footings of two buildings that can be found on either side of a small burn, in the positions shown on the farm plan, and up to 0.7m in height. The largest has a well-defined east end but is less well preserved at the west. This is likely to be the main 85ft long range, containing a house, byre and cottar house. A smaller building 7m to the south is probably that shown on May's plan, but not valued, while a third, another 13m to the south, may be the ephemeral remains of the barn and stable. The remainder of the farmstead has been removed for use elsewhere. In contrast, Achavoulaig Butt is one of the better preserved groups of eighteenth-century buildings in Bute and they still stand to gable height (fig 10.7). Sections of the bank of the adjacent burn have been revetted, presumably to protect the farmstead from spate, and there is a fragment of what may have been an earlier third building. A large farmyard bank extends from the barn to the south, returning along the stream edge, and another, later, bank hints at earlier phases. A kiln is situated over 60m to the north-west, and the remains of cultivation survive close to the west as well as further up hill.

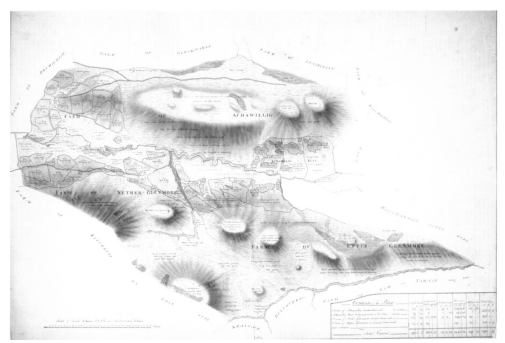

Fig 10.6 May's plan of the farms of Achawillig, Upper Glenmore and Nether Glenmore (© The Bute Collection, Mountstuart Archive).

High on the hill above, a very substantial turf and stone dyke encloses the arable of the butt, the overall size of which has been reduced at some point. Within this area, plots of cultivation are still visible, some still obvious as greener areas of furrows, but others now very damp and overgrown with vegetation. The dykes running north to south (as shown on the plan that divided this wider area into three parts) are less obvious on the ground and have been much less substantial features. There is no obvious evidence on the ground to reflect the position of the meadow, which lay immediately south of the modern forestry boundary.

Kilmichael

The farm of Kilmichael is one of the largest in Bute and is graced with both a beautiful aspect and a relatively grand suite of nineteenth-century buildings, including a farmstead that was listed in 1998. Roy's map shows four settlements, three of which were named as Barlia, *Kirrytriach* (Cretriach) and Kilmichael. The fourth, Ardnagave, is named but not depicted, perhaps because it lay high on the hill and relatively far to the east. The estate plans of Kilmichael are a little less detailed than some others as the surveyors wanted to depict the farms on sheets of a consistent size, although it is possible that the surveys were undertaken at the same scale, but a greater reduction was used for the final copies. The plan by John Foulis also shows four farmsteads and it is possible to accurately locate these thanks to their depiction in relation to features such as streams and meadows, as well as to each other (fig 10.8). They are Kilmichael itself (of five buildings) and the smallholdings of Barlia, Cretriach and Ardnagave (two buildings each).

In 1759, the whole farm covered 858 acres, of which 100 were arable, and the majority of the remainder was described as 'moory' hills and mosses, although there were areas of woodland and a meadow on the Aultmore Burn below Ardnagave. Foulis recommended that the coastal fringe from Ettrick Bay to Kilmichael be set out as smallholdings, while the hinterland should be devoted to breeding 'small black cattle and sheep'.

> For if the most were made of the spots of arable land…which in this part of Scotland is to be done in small possessions, it is needless to occupy a number of hands upon an un-improveable subject that can be done to as good purpose by one or two hands, while so much subject worthy of attention lyes uncultivated for want of hand.
> (RHP14107, 67)

The estate plan of Kilmichael produced by May has a slightly different colouring to that on the dated sheets, and it may date to slightly later in the eighteenth century (fig 10.9). Despite the larger size of the farm, the plan was produced with the same care giving the acreage of Kilmichael as 933 Scots acres, of which 57 were arable and 23 acres 'natural wood'. The plan shows settlements at the Ferry (two buildings), Kilmichael (five buildings), Aultmore (two buildings), and Cretriach and Ardnagave (three buildings each). Very unusually for May, two of the three buildings at Ardnagave are depicted despite being apparently in ruins. Although May does show areas that were formerly cultivated, the Ardnagave folds are shown with boundaries, rigs and names, as if they were still in use at this time. The 'North Park' of Kilmichael appears to have been enclosed by a stone dyke at this time, as does the arable ground at the main farmstead, and earlier field dykes are shown in the pasture ground on the slopes above the farmstead. Much of the pasture is annotated very specifically, such as 'midling good rough pasture for young cattle'. Two tracks are shown, both leading over to the meadow and presumably to peat grounds further into the hills. Both are still in use.

The farmstead of Kilmichael, 'possessed by Joseph Shankland', included five ranges with mixed uses: a dwelling house: a byre and calves house; a stable and two cottar houses; two barns and a chaff house; and a kiln barn. The dwelling house was more substantial than

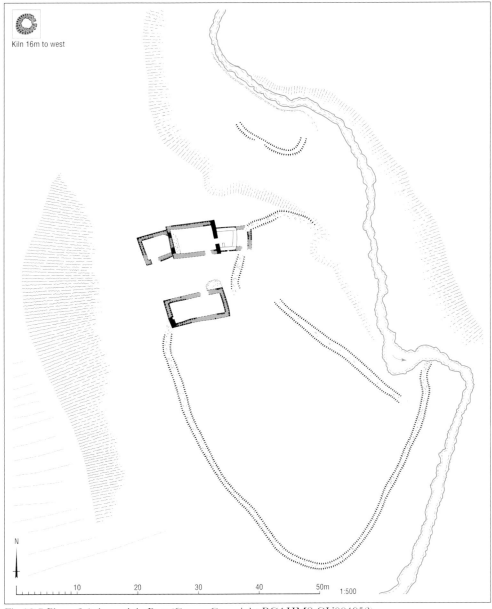

Kiln 16m to west

N

| 10 | 20 | 30 | 40 | 50m | 1:500 |

Fig 10.7 Plan of Achavoulaig Butt (Crown Copyright RCAHMS GV004953)

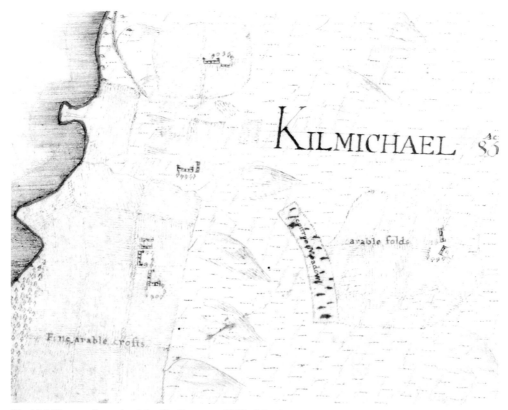

Fig 10.8 Extract from the John Foulis map of Kilmichael showing the area around the settlements (© The Bute Collection, Mountstuart Archive).

elsewhere, built of stone and clay with 'two outer gables and one inner gable built to the top'. Unusually, the house had three windows, with the upper half glass and the lower half timber, as well as timber doors that were individually valued. Roofed with twelve oak couples 'standing on the wall' (as opposed to crucks that rested on the floor), the building had a heather thatch that was a 'good deal wore but watertight'. If Smith's comments are anything to go by, a heather thatch might last up to 100 years (Smith 1798: 19). Other buildings in the group were built entirely of stone and clay, and had couples of other species (including ash and fir), and thatch of straw, heather, fern or a combination thereof. The valuation included a manger, forks to support weak couples, doors and their furniture and stakes for binding animals. Interestingly the valuation did not include a door 'owned by the tenant'. The most valuable buildings were the main house and the barn, valued at £11 each, and the whole farmstead was put at £34 15s 6d.

The smaller butts included the 'ferry butt lying northward of Joseph Shankland's farm', comprising only one building that was valued at £2 5s 4d. Butt Cretriach included a five-bay house with ash couples 'wore about the knees' and a fern thatch, and a barn, together valued at £4 4s 11d. Another ferry butt, to the south-west of Kilmichael farmstead, included a byre-house tenanted by a 'Widow Black', and a brew house which had walls 'built by the tenant'.

The farmstead at Ardnagave must have been abandoned at this time, and does not feature in the entry for Kilmichael or under its own name, despite featuring on a later larger scale estate map by Mackinlay in 1823.

Turning to archaeological evidence on Kilmichael farm, a rich suite of buildings survive, particularly at the northern end of the farm. They include both farmsteads set in areas of arable, and small huts that are probably related to the limited practice of shieling. Some of this may relate to cultivation in the medieval period, and some of the buildings must surely be earlier than eighteenth century in date. Substantial eighteenth-century remains survive at three of the five locations noted on May's map.

Lying just outside the nineteenth-century head-dyke, the eighteenth-century settlement of Barlia has been reduced to grass-grown footings of at least two buildings. The fields to the north were abandoned by c1780, but large areas of rig are still visible, some of which are enclosed by turf dykes. At Cretriach, there are the remains of three buildings. A knocking stone that would have been used for mashing and removing husks stands nearby. Two of the buildings were probably constructed after 1780 but all three were abandoned before the Ordnance Survey of 1864 (Argyllshire 1869, Sheet CCXIII). Two buildings are arranged in parallel, and both have been shortened.

Further down the hill, on the south side of the Aultmore burn, very little is left of the farmstead known as Aultmore or Ferry butt. The ruins of the ferry house and quay stand further to the west, but the outline of the three associated arable plots is recognisable in the current shape of the fields and the location of the mature trees.

The settlement at Ardnagave lies at an altitude of about 130m above sea level in a small hanging valley over 900m ENE of Kilmichael (fig 10.9). There are the remains of extensive rigged cultivation below a well preserved head-dyke which runs from the former meadow ground to the Aultmore Burn on the east. The largest building measures 13m by 5.7m over walls 0.6m in thickness and up to 2.4m in height. It has at least one entrance, in the east wall, and there may be a byre-drain within its lower (south) end (fig 10.10). A second, less well preserved building stands 10m to the north, in the south-east corner of a small, roughly triangular enclosure. It measures 12.8m by 4.5m transversely over stone walls 0.7m in thickness. A bedneuk projects from the west side of the building, presumably to house a box bed set into the wall, and there is an entrance in the east wall. This is the only known bedneuk in Bute, and there do not appear to be any others in Argyll (see RCAHMS 1971– 1992). Similar examples have been found during survey at farmsteads including Nether Benzieclett, Orkney (Fenton 1978), Strath Rusdale (eg Dalmore, Dalreoich) and Upper Strathnairn, Highland (RCAHMS 1994: 6–7), and Camserney, Perth, and it is clearly a widely distributed, if unusual, feature in eighteenth-century buildings.

An outshot at the north end of this same building seems to overlie an earlier building. The third building is situated 50m south-west of the first and is more ruinous still, measuring 8m by 5m over walls reduced to a rubble spread. The northern end of the building has been let into the natural slope and a large accumulation of stone at the south end may indicate the presence of a kiln. The fourth building lies 50m west of the largest, on the south-west side of a small enclosure. Rectangular in plan, it measures 10m by 5.5m over walls reduced to grass-grown footings. The corn-drying kiln is situated immediately east-north-east of the third building. It measures about 5m in diameter by 1m in height overall and the bowl (about 2m in diameter) is partly filled with debris.

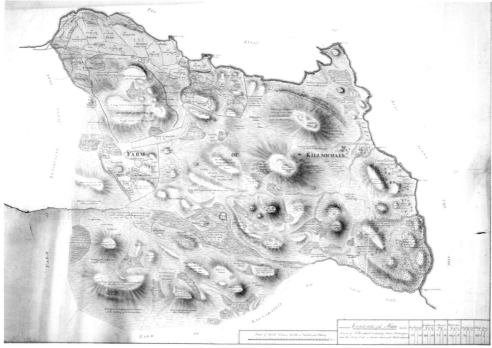

Fig 10.9 Extract of May's plan of Kilmichael c1784 (© The Bute Collection, Mountstuart Archive).

Nothing is now visible of the buildings of the eighteenth-century farmstead of Kilmichael, although it is possible that there are sub-surface remains of some structures, particularly in those areas that do not underlie the more substantial nineteenth-century buildings. To the south-west, at the site of another ferry port, the site of the eighteenth-century butt is now in a thick copse but the standing remains date to the nineteenth century, rather than 1769, when this new ferry terminal was created (Maclagan 1997: 18–21).

Eighteenth-century cultivation remains have generally survived best in the areas of the farmstead higher than the 40m contour, and they include large swathes of improved and formerly cultivated ground near Glenvoidean chambered cairn.

Discussion and conclusion

Much of the material presented above can seem to be a relatively straightforward representation of physical and documentary evidence. It is particularly useful as a measure of the accuracy of different eighteenth-century map sources, a guide to the vernacular architecture of Bute during the later eighteenth century, and as part of the wider story of change in eighteenth-century Scotland which affected rural society in particular. But history can be read in a number of different ways and it is important to recognise that the story of landscape change did not begin in 1750. Such a thorough survey as May's depicts many patterns of rig, enclosure and building that reflect longer term changes, and we should be careful to recognise the fragments of medieval as well as twentieth-century landscapes in the overall pattern, as noted by Angus Hannah in this volume.

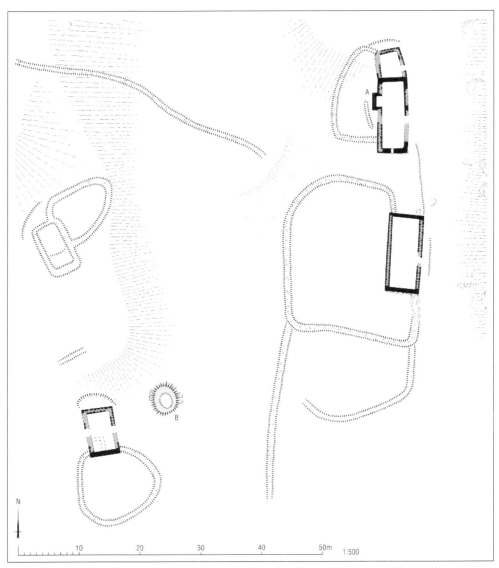

Fig 10.10 Plan of the two byre-houses, corn drying kiln and barn at Ardnagave (Crown Copyright, RCAHMS GV004728).

Improvement was not an inevitable and consistent event across Bute: there were dynamic processes that affected the rate and character of change. The farmsteads of south Bute were turned over to sheep before 1780, while some smallholdings in the north survived well into the twentieth century. Notably, Foulis consistently recommended that the number of smallholdings was increased on some farms. The story of the three case studies demonstrates how varied the situation was in each farm in the 1750s and how different the alterations made over the next 30 years were. Finally, and perhaps most importantly, we must appreciate

147

that this is a story about communities of people, some of whom benefited from Improvement and some of whom did not. It is an explicitly political story, but one in which people were individual agents (see Carter 1979; Dalglish 2010). Different families must have reacted differently to the pressures and opportunities that they experienced when land holdings changed, and a more holistic approach is recommended for future work, where archaeological and documentary approaches are subsumed within a socio-economic analysis.

Bute presents us with a fantastic opportunity to tie together both a comprehensive archaeological survey of the island's rural settlement over the last twenty years, and a very important collection of documents held in the Bute Collection at Mount Stuart. By combining these two sources, it is possible to present a remarkably clear picture of the changes that took place in the later part of the eighteenth century. We can see that the powers of the estate were far reaching and comprehensive efforts were made to change the landscape with productivity in mind. When viewed from 200 years later, these appear consistent, measured and thorough but a more detailed examination has shown us that they were piecemeal and complex, and that it is more productive to look through the prism of individual landholdings when one has the opportunity.

The rich documentary evidence allows one to begin to look at the people involved and to gain an understanding of the personal stories of owner, factor, tenant, sub-tenant and cottar, while the archaeological monuments inspire a deep and constant sense of place. The story of the eighteenth-century farms of the island is one of continuous change and effort, and it cannot be seen as static or as an inevitable result of overwhelming historical processes.

Acknowledgements

This essay was developed from a presentation given at the Scottish Society for Northern Studies conference in Rothesay in April 2010. Much of the fieldwork and research was funded through the DBLPS and RCAHMS Bute project, and my gratitude extends to both Bridget Patterson and Paul Duffy of the DBLPS. Particular thanks go to Andrew Maclean at Mount Stuart for access to the material held in the Bute collection at Mount Stuart, while the estate and tenants were gracious in allowing unhindered access to their land. The survey of Achavoulaig Butt was undertaken as an RCAHMS training exercise with local residents Isabell McArthur, Charles Murray and Donald Kinnear, whose humour and attention to detail was greatly appreciated. An earlier draft of this paper was also commented on by Angus Hannah and Paul Duffy.

The remaining surveys were undertaken by the author, Ian Parker, James Hepher, John Sherriff and Alan Leith of RCAHMS. The publication illustrations were created by Georgina Brown and Ian Parker. Editing duties at RCAHMS were adopted by John Sherriff and Robin Turner, with additional comments from Piers Dixon. The archive material at Mount Stuart was photographed by Stephen Wallace and Derek Smart.

References

Archival sources

Held at the Bute Collection Mount Stuart (© Bute Collection, Mountstuart Archive):
1. Estate plans by Alexander May c1780–1784
2. 'A Survey of the Island of Bute' by John Foulis 1759

3. The Inventory and Appreciation of Farmsteads by Alexander May, 1782–c1840
4. Estate map of North Bute by Joannes Mackinlay, 1823

Items 1, 2 and part of item 3 were photographed by RCAHMS as part of the DBLPS project. A copy of item 2 is also available at the National Archives of Scotland (RHP14107).

Printed sources

Adams, I H (ed) 1979 *Papers on Peter May Land Surveyor 1749–1793*. Edinburgh: Scottish History Society.

Aiton, W 1816 *General view of the agriculture of the county of Bute*. Glasgow: Board of Agriculture.

Boyle, S 2009 Mapping Landscapes of the Improvement Period: Surveys of North Lochtayside, 1769 and 2000, *Scot Geogr J* 125/ 1, 43–60.

Carter, I 1979 *Farm Life in Northeast Scotland 1840–1914, the poor man's country*. Edinburgh: John Donald.

Dalglish, C 2010 For the community: Scottish historical archaeology and the politics of land reform, *Inter J Hist Archaeol* 14.3, 374–397.

Fairhurst, H 1968 'Rosal: a Deserted Township in Strath Naver, Sutherland', *Proc Soc Antiq Scot* 100 (1967–8), 183–7.

Fairhurst, H 1969 'The Deserted Settlement at Lix, West Perthshire', *Proc Soc Antiq Scot* 101 (1968–9), 160–99.

Fenton, A 1978 *The Northern Isles: Orkney and Shetland*. Edinburgh: John Donald.

Geddes, G & Hale, A 2010 *The Archaeological Landscape of Bute*. Edinburgh: RCAHMS.

Glendinning, M & Wade Martins, S 2008 *Buildings of the Land, Scotland's Farms 1750-2000*. Edinburgh: RCAHMS.

Maclagan, I 1997 *The piers and ferries of Bute*. Rothesay: Bute Museum.

Marshall, J N 1934 'Old kiln at Kilwhinleck', *Trans Buteshire Natur Hist Soc* 11, 84–7.

Milligan, I D 1961 'Ardmaleish', *Discovery Excav Scot*, 27.

Milligan, I D 1963 'Corn kilns in Bute', *Trans Buteshire Natur Hist Soc 15*, 53–9.

Ordnance Survey 1869 1:10560 Map, Argyllshire Sheet CXCIII. http://maps.nls.uk/os/6inch/

Proudfoot, E & Hannah, A 2000 'Deserted Settlements on Bute', *Trans Buteshire Natural History Soc 25*, 25–56.

RCAHMS 1971–92 *Argyll, an inventory of the monuments, volumes 1–7*. Edinburgh: HMSO.

RCAHMS 1992 *Argyll, an inventory of the monuments. Vol 7, Mid Argyll & Cowal medieval & later monuments*. Edinburgh: HMSO.

RCAHMS 1994 *Upper Strathnairn, Inverness: an archaeological survey: summary report*. Edinburgh: RCAHMS.

RCAHMS 1997 *In the Shadow of Bennachie: The Field Archaeology of Deeside, Aberdeenshire*, Edinburgh: RCAHMS and the Society of Antiquaries of Scotland.

RCAHMS 2008 *'Well Shelterd & Watered' Menstrie Glen, a farming landscape near Stirling*. Edinburgh: RCAHMS.

RCAHMS 2011 *Scotland's Rural Past, community archaeology in action*. Edinburgh: RCAHMS.

Ross, W (ed) 1880 *Blain's History of Bute*. Rothesay: Harvey.

Roy, W 1747–55 *Roy Military Survey of Scotland*. http://maps.nls.uk/roy/index.html

Smellie, W 1792 'An historical account of the Society of Antiquaries of Scotland', *Archaeologia Scotica* 1, iii–xiii.

Smith, J 1798 *General view of the agriculture of the county of Argyle*. Edinburgh: Board of Agriculture.

Fig 11.1 The north end of the island of Bute reflected in a calm sea, looking south from Tighnabruaich (© Matthew Molony).

Chapter 11

The witches of Bute

Lizanne Henderson
University of Glasgow

FEW PARTS of Scotland, in the early modern period, remained totally unaffected by the belief in, and prosecution of, witchcraft and Bute was no exception. Although the island did not experience the full brunt of the witch-hunts it did, nevertheless, produce one of the most compelling episodes in Scottish witch trial history during the winter of 1662. The witches of Bute were, by the standards of the times, relatively few but their impact was large upon a close-knit island community and, when placed within the context of the so-called 'Great Scottish Witch-Hunt' of 1661–62 (a nationwide search for witches, charmers and other such profaners of the law, morality and faith), the Bute confessions have a significant part to play in widening our understanding of folk belief and the complexities of witch persecution.

All of the currently known legal proceedings concerning witchcraft in Bute occurred in the seventeenth century representing, between the 1630s to 1670s, around sixty-five cases though the actual figure may exceed seventy. Accuracy on the exact numbers of those accused is impossible due to the incompleteness of the sources and the occasional vague report of unnamed witch suspects.

Two of the Bute cases which resulted in execution furnish interesting information about the beliefs and assumptions of the period. The accusations against Margaret NcWilliam and Jonet Morrison take the form of clear narratives deriving from neighbourhood hostilities and long-held suspicions. What follows is not intended to be an investigation of the causes behind the 1662 witch-hunt, some exploration of which has been adventurously, if unconvincingly, undertaken by William Scott in *The Bute Witches* (2007). Rather, this discussion will sample a few key ideas and motifs that emerge from the narratives of NcWilliam and Morrison, such as to what extent do their stories compare with others? What can we glean about everyday life, mindset, and folk belief in seventeenth-century Bute from these confessions?

The first recorded evidence of witch prosecution was in 1630 when it was stated that 'several women' were locked in the Castle dungeon at Rothesay where, allegedly, they were left to starve to death. No names or details are given and it seems likely they died without trial (*Highland Papers* 1920: 14). There was a strong element of fairy belief in the majority of cases which occurred between 1649 and 1660. In 1649–50, Finwell Hyndman of Kilchattan Bay was under investigation for disappearing with the fairies, for a twenty-four hour period, around the Quarter Days. It was reported that when she returned she had upon her 'such a wyld smell that none could come neire her, and that she was all craised [crazed] and weary as if it were one after a farr journey'. As Hyndman could provide no satisfactory explanation for her irregular absences, she was 'bruted for a witch or (as the commone people calls it) being with the fayryes'. Jeane Campbell of Ambrismore farm, near Scalpsie, was apprehended for charming in 1660: the Rothesay Kirk Session reported that she 'gangs with the faryes' indicating that she was most likely believed to have acquired her charming skills from the fairies. In a similar later case of 1670, James McPhee of Kerrycresach complained that his good name was being wrongly tarnished following accusations that he had a mistress 'among the furies commonly called Fairfolks' (*Kingarth Kirk Session Records*: CH2/219/1, ff17; *Kingarth Parish Records*: 19–21, 57–8; Hewison 1895, ii: 261–9; Henderson & Cowan 2001: 213).

A particularly large series of trials hit Bute in 1662, which coincided with the biggest witch-hunting episode in Scottish history with over six hundred formal accusations and approximately three hundred executions across the country (Levack 1980). On the orders of a privy council commission Bute's contribution to the tragedy of the 1662 witch-hunt was fifty-one accused, twenty-four of whom went to trial, and four were executed. A fifth suspect, Jonet McNicol, was found guilty and faced execution in 1662 but somehow managed to escape to the mainland. On her return to Rothesay in 1673 the sentence was carried out and she was executed (SSWD; Scott 2007: 246–52). At McNicol's side stood Mary NcThomas, executed for charming and incest (*Argyll J Rec*: 20–1). With the deaths of these two women the record of witch prosecutions in Bute comes to an end.

It would be fair to say that Bute's experience of witch-hunting was not extensive but it was certainly intense. The impact the events of 1662 had on the local inhabitants would have been something akin to a natural disaster, impacting not only upon those who were immediately accused of witchcraft, but on their families, friends and neighbours. Witch-hunts bred an atmosphere of poison and distrust among people by which few would have been unaffected, at least to some extent, while the trials were going on. Some may also have experienced ongoing prejudice and distrust well beyond the period of the trials, never truly free from the infection of suspicion. There is some evidence for this in case of Jonet McNicol's family. She had been tried in 1662 and executed in 1673, but in 1686 the Rothesay Kirk Session heard a complaint by Donald McNicol, Jonet's son, that he was being libelled by John Ochaltrie who 'sadly abused himself and his parents calling him the child of a witch and severall other uncharitable and scandalous names'. The Session found in favour of McNicol and charged Ochaltrie ten pounds Scots, ordering him to acknowledge his sin before the congregation (*Rothesay Parish Records*: 62; Scott 2007: 301). There are no easy answers as to why the small island community experienced such a comparatively large-scale witch-hunt but the timing of events is probably not accidental given what was taking place elsewhere in the country. Also, the location of Bute and its close proximity to the mainland counties of Renfew and Ayrshire may well have had a part to play.

In the seventeenth century, Bute lay comfortably within the Gaelic-speaking belt of Scotland, on the fringes of the predominantly Scots-speaking Lowlands. The islanders' main orientation may well have been more fixed northwards, towards Inveraray and Argyllshire, but its geographical position, situated at an interface between the two cultures, allowed for open access to Lowland exchange. In this regard, when assessing the potential cultural influences upon Bute witch beliefs, both Highland and Lowland custom and practice must be taken into consideration.

There is, of course, a fundamental question over whether witch beliefs, at folk or learned level, were substantively different in Highland and Lowland Scotland. Previous work undertaken on Gaelic witch beliefs, when compared with other parts of Scotland, revealed very little that was particularly unique or distinctive (Henderson 2008). Greater emphasis was, perhaps, given to dream interpretation, the possession of second sight, and the harmful power of the evil eye, although these phenomena also feature in non-Gaelic contexts. As elsewhere in Scotland, Gaelic witches were mostly blamed with interference in dairy production and agricultural problems, as well as causing disease, death and general misfortune. The Devil, demonic pacts and attendance at sabbat meetings were not particularly strong traits, though the relatively high demonic content found within the Bute witch confessions is most likely indicative of Lowland influences.

How typical was Bute? In terms of gender, of the fifty-six suspects during the 1662 trials, there were forty-seven female, seven male, and two gender unknown, a ratio which corresponds with national percentages of 80–85 per cent female and 15–20 per cent male accused (SSWD). Many of the same motifs and stereotypes that appear in confessions elsewhere in Scotland are similarly present in the Bute evidence. For instance, witches interfered with agricultural production, such as causing a cow to stop giving milk or producing blood instead of milk. They were credited with causing sickness and death in animals and humans, including the death of infants. The witches killed children and horses by 'shooting' them, a term that refers not to gunshot but to elf-shot, a type of magical projectile in the form of an arrow or dart. There are references to demonic shapeshifting and animal transformation, while cursing and charming feature prominently. Some of the accused could cure certain illnesses with rituals, charms and herbs, often involving transference of the disease onto an animal. Jonat McNeill cured Jonat Man's son with a charm which involved putting a string of beads around the child for forty-eight hours and then removing the string and binding it around a cat which, it was claimed, immediately died on contact with the beads (*Highland Papers* 1920: 4). Margaret McLevin had Gaelic charms to protect against the evil eye, as well as to heal children of the 'Glaick' (bewitchment), which she could do, she said, 'without suffering either a dog or catt' (*Highland Papers* 1920: 4, 9). The glaick may possibly refer to the belief in changelings, or human children stolen by fairies and replaced by a fairy child. Jonet Morrison could cure the fairy blast (*Highland Papers* 1920: 23–4; Henderson & Cowan 2001: 94–100). Gaelic was the preferred medium when charming cattle, or applying ointment to sprains and bruises in humans, and in protecting people from harm. Margaret McLevin confessed that she had a charm for the evil eye that she had frequently used on humans and animals. One such formula began *Obi er bhrachaadh* etc.; another was quoted as *er brid na bachil duin* etc (*Highland Papers* 1920: 5–6, 9). 'Obi' is *Obaidh*, meaning a 'charm' or 'incantation', but unfortunately the rest is obscure (MacKenzie 1892: 101).

On the other hand, no witch trial is typical, and each case brings its own special set of particular circumstances. Disruption to sailing and the harvest of the sea features quite prominently in these trials, especially as it affected the herring fishing. Margaret McLevin was able to calm rough seas and bring sailors home safely but she also created a storm by casting a pebble into the sea with the intention of sinking a boat. On another occasion the Devil lifted her up and carried her under his oxters to the rocky isle of Inchmarnock with a plan to sink a boat on its way to Arran but, McLevin revealed, this was prevented by God, who turned the boat onto another course and away from danger (*Highland Papers* 1920: 24). The interweaving of continental-style diabolism with traditional fairy belief is, as already indicated, quite marked in the Bute confessions, as are dreams and prognostications, the evil eye, and charming. One witch had the unusual ability of inflicting an illness on a man that simulated the pains of childbirth. Concerns about the Witches Sabbat (meetings held under cover of darkness with the Devil himself in attendance) and entering into a Demonic Pact with Satan, their master, while far from absent were not especially common in many parts of rural Scotland, yet these issues are paramount in the Bute interrogations. The Devil was a consummate shapeshifter who appeared to them in various guises such as a 'little brown dog', a cat, a 'wele favored young man', a 'black rough fierce man', and as a 'gross copperfaced man'. He baptised them and gave them a new name. Issobell McNicoll first met the Devil, in the likeness of a young man, in her own house while she was making whisky. He promised that 'she should not want' and she, in turn, promised to become his servant and thus entered into a covenant with him. To seal the deal he performed an unholy baptism and renamed her Caterine.

Many told of large gatherings with the Devil and other witches, often around Halloween, thus stressing the importance of calendar customs. At these covens, or sabbats, some of the witches spoke of a 'young lasse', the daughter of Alexander Mcillmartin of Kelspoge, who had black hair, a broad face, and a merry disposition, who was 'maiden' at the meetings. Annie Heyman was also their 'maiden' and she danced 'in the midst of them' (*Highland Papers* 1920: 8). This is highly reminiscent of the trial of Isobel Goudie in Auldearn, also in 1662, who spoke of 'the maiden' as the Devil's favourite. It is difficult to determine whether this is a coincidence, elite imposition, or evidence of widespread folkloric story and tradition (Pitcairn 1833, iii: 602–16).

Perhaps it is the sheer size of the Bute witch-hunt that truly sets it apart. Large-scale witch-hunting was not common throughout the *Gàidhealtachd*, or indeed anywhere in Scotland (Henderson 2008). Out of this time of local and national crisis arise two women's narratives that serve to shine a light on ordinary lives that in 1662 became extraordinary.

From all accounts, Margaret NcWilliam was a force to be reckoned with. She was singled out in the records as one who, 'since the memory of any alive' that knew her, 'went under the name of a witch'. Over a thirty-year period, she had been accused of witchcraft, and imprisoned, in 1631, 1645, 1649, and once again in 1662. On this occasion her luck ran out for she was executed (*Highland Papers* 1920: 14–20). NcWilliam, who may have been close to sixty at the time of her death, is among one of the more disturbing confessions containing lurid stories of infanticide and devil-worship.

In the process against her in 1662, we discover that her initial brush with the law was in 1631, when the confessing witches, who were left to languish and die in Rothesay Castle prison, named her, though details are unknown. On 16 January 1645 she was accused of witchcraft and investigated by the Rothesay Kirk Session on 'the evils quhilk she threatened to doe and came to pas', on the evidence gathered by former Session clerks, and on the 'ill report and brute she has amongst her nichbouris'. However, on 13 July of that same year the Session admitted that they could reach no conclusion regarding her case but would take it under advisement. In 1649 NcWilliam was again apprehended on charges of witchcraft, imprisoned and this time searched for the Devil's mark which was, apparently, found on several parts of her body. It was said that due to the 'confusion of the tymes she was lett out upon bands' (*Highland Papers* 1920: 14–20). Discovery of the Devil's mark should have proven her guilt beyond a shadow of a doubt but if the 'confusion of the times' in 1649 allowed her to escape punishment, this would not be the case in the panic that ensued in 1662.

As with many accounts of witchcraft, the case begins with a dispute between neighbours. In the initial presumption against Margaret NcWilliam, John McFie declared that when his father and brother were flitting out of Kerecresoch to Lochly (or Lochend) with three horse loads, they had to pass through NcWilliam's field. When they came to the slap, an opening in the boundary dyke, it had been blocked up and NcWilliam herself was lying on top of it. When McFie senior began opening up the gap so that they might continue their journey a physical fight began when NcWilliam attempted to prevent him from removing the stones. They struggled until they both fell down and on rising she came over to his brother and pulled the horse's halter out of his hand, turning the horse away from the direction of the slap. However, the father got hold of the horse and led it over the slap whereupon the animal collapsed. A short time after this incident McFie took a 'sudden sickness' which lasted for a quarter of the year and which he described as 'very unnaturall, lyk a weeman travelling [travailing] with sicknes' or, in other words, simulated the pains of childbirth. Furthermore, another of his children died suddenly in the space of a few hours after contracting an illness. These calamities he suspected NcWilliam to have laid on him.

According to NcWilliam she embarked on the path of witchcraft during a troubled period in her life. She recalled that in the year before 'the great Snaw', about twenty-eight years earlier, while living in Corsmoir (Crossmore), she first met the Devil. At Candlemas, around twelve noon, she went out to the field, named Faldtombuie, beside her house. In the middle of the field there appeared a 'spreit' in the 'lyknes of a litle browne dog' that 'desired her to goe with it'. Initially she refused but it followed her down to the foot of the enclosure where it 'appeared in the lyknes of a wele favored yong man'. Again he asked if she would go with him and in return she should want for nothing. He 'griped her about the left hench [thigh]', causing her much pain, and went away 'as if it were a green smoak [smoke]'.

In May, in the same field as before, 'the devill apeired to her first in the lyknes of a catt and speared at her [asked] How do ye? Will ye not now goe with me and serve me?' This time the offer was too good to refuse and she entered into a 'covenant', or demonic pact, with him and promised to be his servant. He put his mouth upon the sore area on her thigh and it was healed. She renounced her baptism, the Devil re-baptised her, and she 'gave him a gift of a hen or cock'.

NcWilliam saw the Devil again, some ten years later, while then living at Chapeltoune (across Loch Fad from Crossmore), when he appeared to her in the kailyard. She had recently lost her horse and cows and was in great poverty when the Devil assured her 'be not affrayd for yow shall get ringes [wealth] eneugh'. However, what he wanted in return was NcWilliam's seven-year old son William. He supplied an elf arrow which he ordered her to shoot at the boy who died instantly which, not surprisingly, 'grieved her most of anything that ever she did' (*Highland Papers* 1920: 14–20).

These three initial encounters with the Devil, recorded as NcWilliam's own testimony, are a curious blend of folk tradition and learned demonological theory. Reading between the lines, it would appear that as a result of the pressures she was inevitably put through during questioning, NcWilliam was drawing upon fairy beliefs, which would have been more familiar to her; her words were then warped and reinterpreted by her interrogators and coated in a diabolical smear. There are several motifs here that are common to narratives of encounters with the fairies. For instance, fairies were more likely to be encountered around significant calendar customs, such as Candlemas or Beltane, and at particular times of the day, the hour of noon being one of them. The name of the field where she first saw the 'spreit' or spirit, Faldtombuie, has been interpreted by William Scott as the 'field of the tombs' perhaps referring to standing stones or gravestones (Scott 2007: 267). The association between fairies and the realm of the dead was well established and so may be significant in this context. The ability to appear and disappear was also attributed to the fairies. The promise of gifts from fairies usually came with a penalty attached. In this instance, the penalty may have been NcWilliam's own son whom she allegedly killed using a fairy arrow. It is therefore possible that NcWilliam believed her son had been taken by the fairies, and might still live among them, but the demonic interpretation saw it rather as child sacrifice. It may even be significant that the initial encounters happened at a time when NcWilliam was at a low point, struggling to survive. Ayrshire witch Bessie Dunlop, for example, confessed that her relationship with the fairies was first forged during a time of economic hardship and following the death of a newborn child. Her story is not wholly incompatible with Margaret NcWilliam's (Henderson 2009).

There are also some outstanding examples of textbook-style encounters with the Devil. He changes his shape from animal to human, to ephemeral green smoke. He lures his victims into service with promises of wealth and security, though frequently reneges on these promises. He physically marks his conscripts, or has sexual relations with them, which may have happened here in NcWilliam's account. Then follows a formal ritual during which the new recruit renounces their baptism and enters into a Demonic Pact. He then performs an inversion of holy Christian ritual by re-baptising and re-naming the witch. He demands sacrifice from the witch: at first the offering of an animal sacrifice was sufficient in NcWilliam's case, but later on the stakes were raised and she had to offer up her son if she wished to avoid the Devil's wrath.

We will never know if NcWilliam actually murdered her own child or, in her grief, simply blamed herself for his untimely death. She may have created the story as a cover for infanticide, or she may have come to believe, after several years of community pressure, that she was indeed evil and the Devil took her child. It is possible that she believed the fairies had stolen the child, the discovery of an elf arrow connecting these events.

The confession of Margaret NcWilliam is particularly rich in detail. She was to be accused of murdering at least one other child using the fatal elf-shot. She met the Devil in the shape of a cat who, quite matter-of-fact, asked her how she was. She renounced her baptism and promised to be the Devil's servant. In 1649 and 1662 she was searched for the Devil's mark. Three such marks were found: one on the shinbone of her left leg, another between her shoulders and a third mark upon her thigh. Her daughter Katherine was also searched for the mark and a small, white spot, insensitive to pain, was discovered on her right shoulder. And she was seen dancing on Halloween with other witches on Kilmory Hill. Specific locations were frequently associated with witches and fairies, in Scotland and beyond, a supernatural landscape coinciding with the natural landscape. For instance, John Stewart, tried for witchcraft in Irvine in 1618 regularly met with fairies on Lanark Hill and Kilmaurs Hill (*Trial . . . Irvine* 1855: 9). Further afield, sixteenth-century author Olaus Magnus remarked that Nordic witches gathered on the hill of Blåkulla, or Blue Hill, while older traditions associated the legendary spot as the home of trolls. In Germany witches assembled atop the hill of Brocken. Kilmory Hill may have been Bute's equivalent of Blåkulla and Brocken (Henderson forthcoming; Henderson & Cowan 2001: 39–45).

NcWilliam's reputation in the community was seriously tarnished. When Major David Ramsay of Roseland's cows stopped producing milk, giving blood instead, his suspicions automatically fell on NcWilliam, his neighbour. The trouble originated when, according to Ramsay, a stirk belonging to NcWilliam came onto his property, devouring corn. He tied up the beast to prevent further damage but NcWilliam freed it. It was then that his cows ceased producing milk. He went to see NcWilliam threatening that if she did not restore his cows' milk, 'I'll burn thee myselfe' which seems to have done the trick. By the time he returned home the cows had resumed milking.

It would seem that witchcraft was a family tradition for NcWilliam's daughters, Katherine and Elspeth Moore, were also under investigation. According to fellow witch, Margaret McLevin, they sometimes operated as a team as in the attacks against Donald McGilchrist for whom 'nothing did thrive'. A quarrel erupted between McGilchrist and Katherine Moore when he accused her of stealing a child's coat. Katherine and her mother put a 'pock [poke] of witchcraft' and a cat, presumably dead, under his bed. They had enacted the same spell upon the minister, John Stewart of Kingarth, the previous Halloween, which resulted in the sickness and death of his wife. He too was made ill but 'God gave them not the liberty' to take his life as well. Similarly they placed a poke, or small parcel, of witchcraft in Provost John Glasse's stable.

Jonet Stewart complained that NcWilliam and her two daughters had inflicted her with a particularly difficult labour following a disagreement over the cutting down of rushes at the bog of Ambrisbeg. The curse upon Stewart ensured that when the time came for the delivery of her baby she was 'sorely handled being 20 dayes in labour'. She further reported that all her cows died suddenly as a result of the curse (*Highland Papers* 1920: 14–20).

Difficulties in childbirth were commonly attributed to witches, but what was not so common was afflicting men with such problems. The witching of Alexander McNeiven, following a quarrel over malt silver Katherine owed him, is a case in point. NcWilliam stepped in to defend her daughter and said that she would 'gar him repent it', or regret it. When he returned home he was struck down with a 'very unnaturall disease lyk a weeman travelling' in which agony he endured for three days. McNeiven's wife Agnes, sure of the cause behind her husband's pain, begged NcWilliam to visit her husband and thus remove the spell. NcWilliam admitted that his suffering was because he had threatened her daughter Katherine but said that by the time she returned home she would find her husband healthy once again, which she did. However, the ill feeling between the two families did not dissipate and two years later another quarrel broke out while McNeiven was at their house. NcWilliam and her daughter somehow managed to tie him to a post using a sack, to be later released from his tethers by John Moore, Katherine's son and NcWilliam's grandson. When he got home he once again fell sick and was 'pitifully tormented most unnaturally till he dyed'. Again his wife Agnes, who was sure that NcWilliam was behind her husband's illness, implored her to come to her husband's sick bed and reverse the curse. This time there would be no pity from NcWilliam who allegedly said, while 'lifting up her curcheffe', 'devill let him never be seene till I see him and the devill let him never ryse'.

Katherine Moore was accused by Jonet Boyd of stopping her breast-milk. Boyd claimed that she had a dream in which Katherine 'came violently upon her' and took a great nip, or bite, out her breast; when she awoke her milk was gone and her breast was blue where she had been bitten. Boyd, convinced by the authority of the dream, went to see Katherine to beg for her milk to be restored which it duly was a few days later (*Highland Papers* 1920: 19–20).

Furthering the family's reputation for witchcraft, NcWilliam's grandson John occasionally took part in his mother and grandmother's evil activities. All three went to Birgidale Broch where NcWilliam 'shot' James Andrews' son. They instructed another witch, Marie More McCuill, to take away the body and leave the stock of a tree in its place. This is a clear instance of a conflation between fairy and witch lore and the demonisation of folk belief (*Highland Papers* 1920: 14–20; Henderson & Cowan 2001: 80, 106–41).

The story of Jonet Morrison is, perhaps, not as formulaic as that of NcWilliam but it is equally rich in detail. Morrison was a practicing charmer before the suspicion of witchcraft landed at her door. In the eyes of the Kirk, charming and healing were not condoned being considered morally questionable activities, even when the results were positive. Only God could provide true healing. The problem was the potential source of the charmer's power and from where it derived. If it did not come directly from God then it must come from the Devil. Previously, Morrison's skills as a healer had been accepted, or at least tolerated, but during the heightened tensions of the 1662 trials her knowledge of charms and fairylore would ensure she was strangled and burnt for witchcraft.

She first met the Devil in the twilight hours, describing him as a 'black rough fierce man' who desired her to go with him. He coaxed her with promises of a better life for she was a poor woman 'begging amongst harlots and uncharitable people'. The Devil said, 'I will make thee a Lady'. She agreed to meet with him again on the hill of Knockanrioch where he furthered his promise to make her rich and 'put thee in a brave castall quhair thou shalt want nothing and I will free thee of all the poverties and troubles thou art in'. Morrison asked the Devil what his name was and he told her it is 'Klareanough' probably meaning 'clear enough', in other words it should be obvious who he is.

Following her tryst with the Devil, she was visited in the night, while she lay sleeping with her husband, by Adam Kerr who came to her window and asked her to rise up out of her bed and let him in. However, as Kerr was actually dead, his death blamed on the witchcraft of Margaret NcWilliam and her daughter Katherine, she was understandably nervous about letting him through the door. She asked, if you be a good spirit I will let you in, but if you be an evil spirit God be between me and you. With that he went away from the window 'mourning and greeting [crying]'. The appearance of the dead was experienced by other convicted witches, such as Bessie Dunlop (1576) and Alison Peirson (1588) (Henderson 2009).

Morrison provided a great deal of detail about the witches' sabbats where she saw 'a great number of people' and the Devil who appeared to her dressed in white or as a man 'naked with a great black head'. She spoke of a sabbat meeting on the mainland near Kilwinning, potentially reinforcing the fear among the authorities that witches were highly organised cells that kept in touch with one another. This would have been furthered when she likened one sabbat meeting to a 'great army' of whom she only recognised one other local witch, Jonet McNicoll. She included a rather interesting detail about Katherine Moore who was asked by the Devil why her husband was not present. She replied that 'there was a young bairne at home and they could not both come'. This revelation challenges our assumptions about fatherhood and parenting in the seventeenth century for it is the father who is left at home looking after the baby. It is also an example of the inversion principle often connected to the witch stereotype. Women who are witches do the opposite of expected social behaviour and fail to conform (Larner 1984: 84). In this instance, the mother has neglected her stay at home duties leaving the father to care for and nurture the child.

Jonet Morrison was a skilled healer, particularly where attacks from the fairies were concerned. She claimed that she healed three people who had been blasted by the fairies using herbs:

> And being questioned anent her heiling of Mcfersone in Keretoule his dochter who lay sick of a very unnaturall disease without power of hand or foot both speichles and kenured [meaning is obscure]. She answered the disease quhilk ailed her was blasting with the faryes and that she healed her with herbes. Item being questioned about her heileing of Alester Bannatyne who was sick of the lyk disease answred that he was blasted with the fairyes also and that she heiled him thereof with herbs and being questioned anent her heileing of Patrick Glas dochter Barbra Glas answred that she was blasted with the faryes also.

Morrison made a clear distinction between elf-shot and the blast:

> quhen they are shott ther is no recoverie for it and if the shott be in the heart they died presently bot if it be not at the heart they will die in a while with it yet will at last die with it and that blasting is a whirlwinde that the fayries raises about that persone quhich they intend to wrong and that tho ther were tuentie present yet it will harme none bot him quhom they were set for.

A victim of the blast, according to Morrison, could be healed using herbs or by charming: 'all that whirlwind gathers in the body till one place; if it be taken in time it is the easier healed and if they gett not means they will shirpe [shrivel] away'. Elf-shot, on the other hand, was beyond her skills to heal. A woman declared that about two years previously she had a dream about Jonet Morrison which frightened her and within half an hour of waking her young son started to tremble with 'a very unnaturall disease' which eventually killed him. Presumably as a result of the dream, the woman claimed that she asked Morrison to heal the child but Morrison diagnosed that 'it was twice shot and could not be healed' (*Highland Papers* 1920: 3, 23–4, 27). What remains unclear from this woman's premonition is whether she was anticipating the need to call upon the assistance of Morrison as a known healer or if she was, in retrospect, attributing the dream and subsequent death of her child to Morrison's witchcraft. It is also unclear if the mother believed the child had been elf-shot by fairies or by a witch.

Morrison was occasionally under orders by the Devil to 'shoot' specific targets, such as the horse of Provost John Glass but she refused to comply. She was also told to take the life of the Bailie Walter Stewart by shooting him, and again she refused. Such alleged rebellion against the Devil tells us something about Morrison's strength of character; she was not prepared to admit to murder. She was rather keener to impress upon her interrogators that she was not the cause of recent misfortunes and deaths but that the fairies were responsible. The Devil told her that it was the fairies who took away the life of John Glass's child, adding that they were minded to take his life also. Indeed Morrison reminded them that she had attempted to cure his child of the fairy blast with herbs. She was not, however, above accusing others of such crimes, notably Margaret NcWilliam and her daughters Katherine and Elspeth for shooting to death William Stephen and paralysing Adam Kerr who later died. The nature of these men's deaths bears all the hallmarks of what was once traditionally attributed to fairy attack but in the context of a witch trial took on a demonic edge and motivation.

It was fairly common, with witchcraft accusations, for the accused and their accusers, to operate around the concept of 'deep time', referring to events that took place over a long duration, while making connections between these happenings. For instance, a man by the name of Glen, who testified against Morrison, recalled a dispute between her and his wife some two years previously. Morrison was apparently displeased with the amount of goods she received from the wife and angrily told her 'I will garr yow rue it', in other words live to regret it. Within three months, as Glen's wife was going into the byre, she felt something strike her and the whole house grew dark; 'she still compleins that it was Jonet Morison that did it' (*Highland Papers* 1920: 23–7).

The imposition of 'learned', and possibly Lowland, ideas upon local folkloric beliefs about witchcraft, specifically the way fairy traditions were demonised, is evident in the trials. The proximity of Bute to the mainland allowed easier access to Lowland conceptualisations. Some of the evidence from Bute could just as easily have been recorded in East Lothian, such as the high demonic content, the pact made with the Devil, witches meeting in covens, the Devil assuming the shape of a dog, and so on. A Gaelic element can perhaps be detected in relation to the stress on charming, for notably many of the charms and spells were specifically stated to have been in Gaelic, and also fairy lore, the importance of dreams, and the evil eye, though again such material can be found in the Lowlands as well. Margaret NcWilliam's life was one of conflict and strife with her neighbours. For whatever reason, she was not accepted by her community who, on more than one occasion, turned against her and thus she had built up a reputation for witchcraft over the duration of her life. Jonet Morrison had most likely operated relatively successfully as a charmer, a perceived useful member of the community, before the scourge of witchcraft and devilry cast a shadow over her activities. Her superior healing skills, in combination with advanced knowledge of the fairy world, were sufficient to warrant suspicion during a time of crisis. The sheer scale of the 1662 trials is remarkable and, beyond the obvious details the confessions and witness statements provide regarding attitudes and beliefs about witchcraft, demonism and fairies, it is also an illuminating insight into sixteenth-century human relationships, rivalries and feuds. The stories that emerge from the surviving records serve to remind us that every person who ever stood accused of witchcraft had their own unique tale to tell.

References

Argyll J Rec Cameron, J (ed) 1949 *Justiciary Records Argyll and the Isles*. vol. 1. 1664–1705. Edinburgh: Stair Society.

Henderson, L 2009 'Witch, Fairy and Folktale Narratives in the Trial of Bessie Dunlop', in Henderson, L (ed) *Fantastical Imaginations: The Supernatural in Scottish History and Culture*, 141–66. Edinburgh: John Donald.

Henderson, L 2008 'Witch-Hunting and Witch Belief in the *Gàidhealtachd*', in Goodare, J, Martin, L & Miller, J (eds) *Witchcraft and Belief in Early Modern Scotland*, 95–118. Basingstoke: Palgrave Macmillan.

Henderson, L forthcoming 'Witchcraft and Shamanism in Northern Communities'.

Henderson, L & Cowan, E J 2001 *Scottish Fairy Belief: A History*. East Linton: Tuckwell Press (reprinted 2011, Edinburgh: John Donald).

Hewison, J K 1895 *The Isle of Bute in the Olden Time*. 2 vols. Edinburgh & London: Blackwood.

Highland Papers MacPhail, J R N (ed) 1920 *Highland Papers*, vol 3, 1662–1677. Scottish History Society.

Kingarth Parish Records Paton, H (ed) 1932 *Kingarth Parish Records: The Session Book of Kingarth, 1641-1703*. n.p.

Larner, C 1984 *Witchcraft and Religion: The Politics of Popular Belief*. Oxford: Basil Blackwell.

Levack, B P 1980 'The Great Scottish Witch-Hunt of 1661–1662', *Jour British Studies* 20: 90–108.

MacKenzie, W 1892 'Gaelic Incantations, Charms, and Blessings of the Hebrides'. *Trans Gaelic Soc Inverness* 18 (1891–2): 97–182.

Pitcairn, R 1833 *Ancient Criminal Trials in Scotland*. 4 vols. Edinburgh.

Register of the Privy Council. 1908 3rd ser. 16 vols. Edinburgh: HMSO.

Rothesay Parish Records Paton, H (ed) 1931 *Rothesay Parish Records. The Session Book of Rothesay, 1658-1750*. Edinburgh: Bute Scottish Record Series.

Scott, W 2007 *The Bute Witches*. Rothesay: Elenkus.

SSWD Goodare, J, Martin, L, Miller, J & Yeoman, L 'The Survey of Scottish Witchcraft'. http://www.arts.ed.ac.uk/witches/(archived January 2003).

Trial, Confession, and Execution of Isobel Inch, John Stewart, Margaret Barclay & Isobel Crawford, for Witchcraft, at Irvine, anno 1618. 1855 Ardrossan & Saltcoats: A Guthrie.

SCOTTISH SOCIETY FOR NORTHERN STUDIES

Previous Titles

1. *Scandinavian Shetland: An Ongoing Tradition?* 1978
   [ISBN: 0950599409] (out of print)

2. *Caithness: A Cultural Crossroads.* 1982
   [ISBN: 0950599417] (out of print)

3. *The Scandinavians in Cumbria.* 1985
   [ISBN: 0950599425] (out of print)

4. *Firthlands of Ross and Sutherland.* 1986
   [ISBN: 0950599441] (out of print)

5. *Galloway: Land and Lordship.* 1991
   [ISBN: 0950599468] £7.50

6. *Moray: Province and People.* 1993
   [ISBN: 0950599476] £10.00

7. *Peoples and Settlement in North-West Ross.* 1994
   [ISBN: 0950599484] (out of print)

8. *Shetland's Northern Links: Language and History.* 1996
   [ISBN: 0950599492] £12.99

9. *The Province of Strathnaver.* 2000
   [ISBN: 0953522601] £12.00

10. *Mannin Revisited: Twelve Essays on Manx Culture and Environment.* 2002
    [ISBN: 0953522628] £13.00

11. *The Faces of Orkney: Stones, Skalds and Saints.* 2003
    [ISBN 095352261X] £14.00

12. *Barra and Skye: Two Hebridean Perspectives.* 2006
    [ISBN: 0953522636] £12.50

All prices exclude P&P